Bridging the Gap, Breaching Barriers

American Society of Missiology Monograph Series

Series Editor, James R. Krabill

The ASM Monograph Series provides a forum for publishing quality dissertations and studies in the field of missiology. Collaborating with Pickwick Publications—a division of Wipf and Stock Publishers of Eugene, Oregon—the American Society of Missiology selects high quality dissertations and other monographic studies that offer research materials in mission studies for scholars, mission and church leaders, and the academic community at large. The ASM seeks scholarly work for publication in the series that throws light on issues confronting Christian world mission in its cultural, social, historical, biblical, and theological dimensions.

Missiology is an academic field that brings together scholars whose professional training ranges from doctoral-level preparation in areas such as Scripture, history and sociology of religions, anthropology, theology, international relations, interreligious interchange, mission history, inculturation, and church law. The American Society of Missiology, which sponsors this series, is an ecumenical body drawing members from Independent and Ecumenical Protestant, Catholic, Orthodox, and other traditions. Members of the ASM are united by their commitment to reflect on and do scholarly work relating to both mission history and the present-day mission of the church. The ASM Monograph Series aims to publish works of exceptional merit on specialized topics, with particular attention given to work by younger scholars, the dissemination and publication of which is difficult under the economic pressures of standard publishing models.

Persons seeking information about the ASM or the guidelines for having their dissertations considered for publication in the ASM Monograph Series should consult the Society's website—www.asmweb.org.

Members of the ASM Monograph Committee who approved this book are:

Michael A. Rynkiewich, Professor of Anthropology (retired), Asbury Theological Seminary

Robert Gallagher, Chair of the Intercultural Studies department and Director of M.A. (Intercultural Studies), Wheaton College Graduate School

RECENTLY PUBLISHED IN THE ASM MONOGRAPH SERIES

Emily Ralph Servant, *Experiments in Love: An Anabaptist Theology of Risk-Taking in Missione*

Vinod John, *Believing Without Belonging?: Religious Beliefs and Social Belonging of Hindu Devotees of Christ*

Taylor Walters Denyer, *Decolonizing Mission Partnerships: Evolving Collaboration between United Methodists in North Katanga and the United States of America*

Bridging the Gap, Breaching Barriers

The Presence and Contribution of (Foreign) Persons of African Descent to the Gaboon and Corisco Mission in Nineteenth-Century Equatorial Africa

MARY CAROL CLOUTIER

American Society of Missiology Monograph
Series vol. 50

PICKWICK *Publications* • Eugene, Oregon

BRIDGING THE GAP, BREACHING BARRIERS
The Presence and Contribution of (Foreign) Persons of African Descent to
the Gaboon and Corisco Mission in Nineteenth-Century Equatorial Africa

American Society of Missiology Monograph Series 50

Pickwick Publications
An Imprint of Wipf and Stock Publishers
199 W. 8th Ave., Suite 3
Eugene, OR 97401

www.wipfandstock.com

PAPERBACK ISBN: 978-1-5326-9749-4
HARDCOVER ISBN: 978-1-5326-9750-0
EBOOK ISBN: 978-1-5326-9751-7

Cataloguing-in-Publication data:

Names: Cloutier, Mary Carol, author.

Title: Bridging the gap, breaching barriers : the presence and contribution of
(foreign) persons of African descent to the Gaboon and Corisco mission in
nineteenth-century equatorial Africa / by Mary Carol Cloutier.

Description: Eugene, OR: Pickwick Publications, 2021 | American Society of
Missiology Monograph Series 50 | Includes bibliographical references and index.

Identifiers: ISBN 978-1-5326-9749-4 (paperback) | ISBN 978-1-5326-9750-0 (hard-
cover) | ISBN 978-1-5326-9751-7 (ebook)

Subjects: LCSH: Missions—Africa, West—History. | Africa, West–Church history.

Classification: BR1460 C56 2021 (print) | BR1460 (ebook)

Manufactured in the U.S.A.   03/02/21

Contents

Contents

Illustrations

Illustrations

Acknowledgments

I'D LIKE TO EXPRESS my sincere gratitude and honor to my committee, Dr. Robert Priest, Dr. Tite Tiénou, and Dr. Alice Ott, for their wisdom and encouragement in this work. Thanks, also, to Dr. Harold Netland, Dr. Craig Ott, Dr. Douglas Sweeney, Dr. Richard Cook, Dr. Darrell Whiteman, and my dear friend, Dr. Erskine Clarke, for their input in this project.

Many thanks to L'Eglise Evangélique du Gabon: Pasteur Rostan for giving me my initial tour of Baraka Mission in 2005, and lamenting that the church had forgotten its missionaries and history; thanks to Pasteur Akita, for his collaboration in exploring Baraka, Nengenenge and Angom missions to retrace the steps of the missionaries. Thank you to Dr. Khonde Tona, Director, and my many students at L'Institut Biblique de Bethel, for your enthusiasm and grace as I developed the class on Mission History in Gabon. I'm so proud that our Gabonese churches have sent missionaries to the nations!

Thanks to Vincent Menkel, Holly Lemons, Pam Ploeger, Amy Perry, Laura O'Brien and the Gault family, descendants of the missionaries, for sharing their family archives. Thanks to fellow Gabon scholars, Henry Bucher, John Cinnamon, David Gardinier, and Jeremy Rich, for our conversations. Numerous friends have been supportive in so many ways: Roberta Ziegler, Marian Shroads, Dale and Audrey Craig, John and Sue Schmucker, Allegheny Center Church (Pittsburgh), the Cranberry CMA Alliance Women, the Women at Work group (Lake Forest), and Trinity African Fellowship.

Acknowledgments

Much love and appreciation to members of my extended Cloutier-Swanson-Smith family, who share with me a love of both education and history.

A Dieu soit la gloire, for the privilege of studying His redemptive history in Gabon, Africa, and for allowing me to tell it to a new generation.

Abbreviations

ABCFM	American Board of Commissioners for Foreign Missions
ACS	American Colonization Society
BFM	Board of Foreign Missions (Presbyterian)
GAPC	General Assembly of the Presbyterian Church
MSMEC	Missionary Society of the Methodist Episcopal Church
PCUSA	Presbyterian Church in the United States of America
SCA-UM	Students' Christian Association of the University of Michigan (Ann Arbor)
USCDL	University of Southern California Digital Library
UMAA	University of Michigan-Ann Arbor
WFMSPC	Women's Foreign Missionary Society of the Presbyterian Church
WPBMN	Women's Presbyterian Board of Missions of the Northwest

1

Introduction

FROM ITS VERY BEGINNING, God's mission work in Gabon, Africa, was carried out by a diverse group of people, American-born and African-born, white and black, male and female, whose work focused primarily on evangelization, education, and Bible translation. They had transferred from their original mission at Cape Palmas, Liberia, having fled the increasing opposition of Liberian colonial rule, and seeking a new and unevangelized field. Their coming to Gabon was in answer to a request for missionaries by the people of Glass, a community situated on the estuary then called Gaboon. The various kings and their people welcomed the multi-ethnic missionary team, providing space and structures for mission schools and their foreign teachers.

Foreign-born persons of African descent—African Americans, Americo-Liberians and West Africans—contributed to the pioneer mission work in Gabon through teaching, evangelism, translating, and printing materials into the indigenous languages. The earliest served as *assistants* to the appointed missionaries, though they participated fully in all aspects of the ministry. All came freely and voluntarily, to serve in the Lord's work. While many eventually returned to their homeland, others remained, becoming an integral part of the local community. Many proved to be invaluable members of the mission, quietly serving where needed and stepping up to *bridge the gap* when their white co-laborers were removed by illness or death. Others served (perhaps unintentionally) to *breach the barriers* of race and gender, so prevalent in the American culture of that time.

Due to the high death toll among white missionaries in Africa, American churches proposed the training and sending of *colored brethren*, African American clergymen, to the mission fields in Africa. While the churches and Mission Board put the idea forth, and consistently promoted it, various missionaries on the field seemed to resist the idea, giving their reasons in private letters to the board, in an ongoing conversation dating from the 1850s through the mid-1890s. The result was an impasse in the sending of *colored brethren*,[1] and overwhelming losses, in terms of human life and ministry progress. The mission's internal controversies over race and gender, and its ongoing tensions with the indigenous African pastors, led to the 1895 decision not to receive willing and qualified African American missionary candidates, causing missionary Robert Hamill Nassau to reveal publicly what he termed the hidden "color line" in the mission.

The last African American mission assistant, Mrs. Lavinia Sneed, departed Gabon in 1891. That same year, the American missionaries began withdrawing from their stations in Gabon and Corisco, due to the overwhelming opposition of French colonial powers, who prohibited preaching and instruction in any other language than French, and the missionaries of cultivating the habits and sympathy of the indigenous people, and educating them "away from a true loyalty to France."[2]

Private correspondence from the 1830s through the 1890s reveals how American missionaries serving in Africa grappled with perceptions of the identity, nationality and status of persons of color within the mission context, as well as the question of equality and integration between whites and blacks (foreign and indigenous) who served with the mission. These documents also reveal the quiet but powerful impact of women in Gabon's mission history—the relationships of missionary women and their co-laborers of African descent, as well as the women's mission organizations who cultivated, promoted and supported women of color, and indigenous ministry workers.

One of the most prominent missionaries of this time period was Dr. Robert Hamill Nassau (1835–1921), who was both an ordained minister and medical doctor. Nassau carefully recorded and maintained personal and mission records, authored a collection of mission historical books, and

1. One African American female missionary was appointed, but through the dedicated and generous support of the *Women's Presbyterian Board of Missions of the Northwest*.

2. Good, "Gaboon and Corisco Mission," 554. The mission stations were turned over to French-speaking European missionaries in 1892, and the American missionaries moved north to coastal Cameroon.

served on the field from 1861 until just after the turn of the century. Nassau's work offers a rare glimpse into the interconnected lives of the persons serving with the mission and in the local church, including individual names, roles and personalities in this community. A proponent of African American missionaries and indigenous leadership, Nassau openly expressed his objections to restrictive mission policies and practices which limited the opportunities for advancement, authority and autonomy of Blacks (foreign or indigenous) working with the mission and church.

While the presence and *voices* of persons of African descent are largely absent from official records and historical documents, their stories are gleaned from private journals and confidential letters exchanged between missionaries and their mission boards. Juxtaposed with the material on these mission workers are communications by the earliest indigenous church leaders, whose insights and experiences shed light on the dynamics of the multi-ethnic church and mission community of that period. Also juxtaposed with the American mission effort is the parallel presence and increasing power of the foreign colonial structures, whose interaction with the missions indicate animosity, rather than collusion, between them. This period in Gabon's history, and particularly its church history, supports Lamin Sanneh's 1991 deconstruction of the view that missionaries were agents of Western imperialism, and that Africans were its victims.[3] Evidence shows that the Africans involved in this history were independent of thought; they capitulated to, or resisted, foreign control at will. Likewise, this history embodies Dana Robert's concept of mission history as "the story of those who spread the gospel message and those who responded to it. The missionaries and the converts are like the two sides of a bridge, the anchors for the span across which the faith travels."[4]

3. Sanneh, "Yogi and the Commissar," 2.
4. Robert, *Christian Mission*, 177.

2

Prologue: Cape Palmas Mission 1834–1842

INTRODUCTION

THE CAPE PALMAS MISSION of the ABCFM was inaugurated a decade after the establishment of the African American colony of Liberia, and amid heated debates in the US and Great Britain as to the best way to end the slave trade, emancipate existing slaves and ameliorate the condition of free people of color residing in the United States.

In the early 1830s, the American Colonization Society enlisted the support of the press and the Christian churches to both elevate and uplift free persons of color by returning them to their *native land*, where they would have freedom, liberty, property rights, education and control of their own government, a republic based on that of the United States. The ACS was formed by slaveholders, who sought to repatriate free people of color (by their free will) to Western Africa. Alarmed at the growing percentage of free blacks in the US, the ACS sought to neutralize this growth by sending large numbers of freedmen each year to the colony in Africa. The ACS was convinced that the person of color would never have full rights in America, would always be a subject of derision, contempt and prejudice, and would never be amalgamated into the white community.[1]

William Lloyd Garrison and other abolitionists denounced the ACS for their views that Blacks in the US were native to Africa, and, while the ACS readily admitted the problems of prejudice and injustice shown to Blacks in America, they were unwilling to address and ameliorate these conditions,

---

1. Civis, "Communication," 47.

4

preferring, instead, to export them to Africa.[2] The ACS often described the colonists as guides, teachers and missionaries to native Africans, though they were not equipped or trained in Christian leadership.[3]

The Colonizationists believed they were situated between slave-holders (or those against emancipation) and abolitionists (those seeking immediate emancipation), both of whom were bitter enemies and opponents. All three groups believed that their position was honoring to God; all three used scripture to reinforce their position on the subject of slavery, and what was best for the free persons of color in America. One belief common to all was that blacks and whites were distinct peoples, and could not unite, through marriage or other alliance; at best, the two races could attain "separate but equal" status.[4]

BIRTH OF THE ABCFM CAPE PALMAS MISSION

The Cape Palmas Mission began in 1834, with the arrival of Rev. and Mrs. Wilson and their *colored associate*, Mrs. Margaret Strobel. Cape Palmas was located some 230 miles southeast of Monrovia, Liberia,[5] and situated on an elevated area, fronting the sea, on six acres of land granted to the ABCFM by the Maryland Colonization Society.[6]

The Rev. John Leighton Wilson, and his wife, Jane Bayard Wilson, had come from slaveholding families in the South. Wilson had desired to go to the "Dark Continent" since his childhood, when he would visit the slaves in their cabins, and hear their stories about Africa, handed down through the generations.[7] Years later, while preaching to a crowd of slaves, Wilson told them of his calling to bring the gospel to the people in Africa. An elderly man came to him, and told Leighton that he had been praying for the spread of the gospel in Africa for many years; he believed that this was an answer to his prayers.[8]

---

2. Garrison, *Thoughts on African Colonization.*

3. Gurley, *Address of the Managers of the American Colonization Society*, 5.

4. Anonymous, "Amalgamation of the Races, Part One," 70.

5. Smith, "Work of the American Board in Africa," 451.

6. DuBose, *Memoirs*, 67.

7. DuBose, *Memoirs*, 39.

8. DuBose, *Memoirs*, 56.

Recruiting Teachers of African Descent

From the very beginning of his African missionary career, John Leighton Wilson purposed to hire *colored teachers* from America to staff the mission schools in Cape Palmas. He negotiated with a number of persons whose slaves were skilled in various crafts, and at least one young girl had been trained and educated by her mistress to become a teacher in Africa.[9] Wilson seemed to be negotiating the freedom of these persons, while cautiously awaiting the approval of the Prudential Committee. Despite his best efforts, Wilson was only able to employ one woman as an educator during the first year of the mission,[10] who manifested a very good state mind about going to Africa and whom they expected would be "useful in every way."[11]

Doubts about Sending "Colored Teachers"

Within a month of his arrival in Liberia, Wilson wrote to the Board Secretary, Rufus Anderson, expressing doubt about sending out *colored teachers* from America. He believed that those who were educated had only received a basic education and that the Americo-Liberians, now free from any restraints, were developing a "self-important spirit."[12] Furthermore, Wilson doubted that any native man would accept an American Negro as a teacher. Wilson attributed this to the authority and influence white men have on the native population, and their derision of the Americo-Liberians for having been slaves. Wilson proposed that the mission educate native Africans on site, rather than preparing and sending *emigrant* teachers to Liberia.[13]

Wilson's objection to *colored teachers* from America was that they were "liable to be jealous of their white brethren, and not condescending enough to be useful to the natives."[14] While Wilson saw the two groups at different levels of civilization, he was surprised that African American colonists in Liberia were "as averse to be equalized with the natives as would a Southern planter to be [compared] to his slaves."[15]

9. John Leighton Wilson to Rufus Anderson, May 13, 1834.
10. John Leighton Wilson to Wisner, September 2, 1834.
11. John Leighton Wilson to Rufus Anderson, November 5, 1834.
12. John Leighton Wilson to Rufus Anderson, January 10, 1835.
13. John Leighton Wilson to Rufus Anderson, January 10, 1835.
14. John Leighton Wilson to Rufus Anderson, August 4–31, 1835.
15. John Leighton Wilson to Rufus Anderson, August 4–31, 1835.

EQUALITY THROUGH EDUCATION AND RELIGIOUS TRAINING

Despite these suspected animosities between American colonists and native Africans, the mission hoped to nurture a "free amalgamation" of the two groups through means of education and religious training. Wilson believed that colonists harbored great prejudice against the native Africans in that area, and that their aversion would be gone if native Africans were "raised to an equality with" the colonists through religion and education;[16] Wilson felt that their educational work with American children and African children would help to build a bridge between them. One solution was to teach native African children English, while teaching Americo-Liberian children the native languages of Bassa and Grebo.[17] The education of native African girls would prepare them as suitable spouses for young educated men, and as domestic assistants for the mission.[18]

MISSION TEACHERS

Margaret Strobel

Margaret Strobel was the first African American to serve with the ABCFM mission at Cape Palmas, having accompanied the newly-wedded Wilsons on their initial voyage as missionaries.[19] Both Margaret and her eight-year-old daughter, Catherine, could read and write well. Mrs. Strobel was expected to serve as a teacher at Cape Palmas, and her daughter would continue her education, with the hope that she would also eventually teach.[20] Mrs. Wilson and Margaret Strobel started a small day school, composed of native children and some children of colonists, totaling about fifteen pupils.[21]

The Wilsons soon felt a strong *disappointment* with Mrs. Strobel. They had perceived a change in her demeanor, just prior to their voyage, which they attributed to her being "elated at her promotion and the attention that was being paid her . . . or from fears that she might be regarded as a menial."[22] Mrs. Strobel had shown no concern for their domestic needs, was frequently

16. John Leighton Wilson to Rufus Anderson, November 3, 1836.

17. John Leighton Wilson to Rufus Anderson, April 1, 1836.

18. John Leighton Wilson to Rufus Anderson, October 7, 1834.

19. ABCFM, "Statistical View," 18. Margaret was born in Savannah, Georgia on January 10, 1804.

20. John Leighton Wilson to Rufus Anderson, May 13, 1834.

21. John Leighton Wilson to Rufus Anderson, August 4–13, 1835.

22. John Leighton Wilson to Rufus Anderson, September 30, 1835.

absent from church and school, and was both spirited and unhappy. Wilson gave Mrs. Strobel an ultimatum, and three choices: to go back to Savannah, to live with colonist friends, or to live in her own home and have authority over her own small school. She chose the last.

Mrs. Strobel was assigned as teacher for the *colonist* children, at Cape Mesurado, in the only school for American children. The school rapidly grew to more than forty-five pupils.[23] Rev. Wilson observed that Mrs. Strobel performed well when given independence and had her own school; her pupils were doing quite well, despite their disadvantages. Given Mrs. Strobel's improvement, and promising future, Wilson suggested that she be put on a fixed salary, as would be necessary for future Negro teachers. Mrs. Strobel then transferred to continue the "American" schools. She negotiated her own salary with a women's group in Philadelphia, who were seeking to support a teacher. With these developments, Mrs. Strobel would be independent, in both support and direction, from the ABCFM mission.[24]

Margaret Strobel's career as an independent teacher soon ended, however, when the Methodist Mission replaced her with a male teacher. Anticipating that she would no longer be eligible to receive her teacher's salary through the women's groups, Rev. Wilson arranged for Mrs. Strobel and her daughter to return to Cape Palmas, where they would teach in the native schools, under the inspection of the Wilsons.[25]

Other Assistants

While a boarding school required many more workers and resources than a day school, Wilson believed that the pupils—both "native" and "emigrant"—were best trained if they were separated from their parents and home environment and could benefit from the extra supervision. Wilson believed that three of the American colonist boys could be trained to become respectable teachers within eighteen months to two years.[26]

By the end of 1836, the mission had several Americo-Liberian teachers for their schools, some of whom were among the earliest members of the Presbyterian Church at Cape Palmas.[27] Local communities evidently desired

23. John Leighton Wilson to Rufus Anderson, April 1, 1836.
24. John Leighton Wilson to Rufus Anderson, June 28, 1836.
25. John Leighton Wilson to Rufus Anderson, July 10, 1836.
26. John Leighton Wilson to Rufus Anderson, March 7, 1836.
27. John Leighton Wilson to Rufus Anderson, August 30, 1836.

schools, and welcomed these colonist teachers. When Americo-Liberian John Banks was assigned to Graway station, more than one hundred African men and boys from that community worked together to erect a small house for him, complete with a fenced-in garden. Another young colonist, Mr. Polk, taught at the Rocktown station schools.[28] He also formed a Sabbath School and gave religious instruction at that location.[29]

After eighteen months on the field, with no missionary reinforcements from America, the Wilsons were thrilled that a white couple and a "coloured brother from Andover"[30] would be arriving before the end of the year.

Benjamin Van Rensselaer James

Mr. Benjamin Van Rensselaer James arrived in Cape Palmas on December 25, 1836, along with Rev. and Mrs. White. These three were among the sixty-three appointed missionaries sent out by the American Board that year.[31]

Mr. James was an educated young man of color, and had come to Liberia, not as a colonist, but as regular missionary. Official Board reports, generated from America, categorized him as a missionary,[32] though Mr. James was not listed as a missionary in mission reports, likely because only ordained men were given that designation, at the time. His stated ministry assignment, initially, was that of "printer."[33]

Both Rev. and Mrs. White fell sick and died within a few weeks of their arrival, and Mr. James was, thereafter, the sole missionary colleague of Rev. and Mrs. Wilson until the arrival, three years later, of Dr. Alexander E. Wilson and his wife, Mary. This afforded Mr. James a more closely-knit and interdependent relationship with Rev. Wilson, as well as a greater opportunity to develop and demonstrate his competency in ministry and to give credibility to the hiring of American blacks in missionary work. Though he suffered frequent bouts of ill health, B. V. R. James excelled in teaching and other ministry roles, proving to be a great asset to the mission, as well as a comfort to the Wilsons, who felt alone in their work.

28. John Leighton Wilson to Rufus Anderson, January 28, 1837.
29. John Leighton Wilson to Rufus Anderson, February 7, 1837.
30. John Leighton Wilson to Rufus Anderson, April 10, 1837.
31. ABCFM, *Annual Report [1937]*, 34.
32. ABCFM, *Annual Report [1937]*, 34; ABCFM, *Annual Report [1845]*, 46.
33. ABCFM, "West Africa [1837]," 4; *Report of the ABCFM [1837]*, 41.

Mr. James apparently lived with the Wilsons for almost two years, and they considered him to be "exemplary in a very remarkable degree for piety, industry and devotion to the missionary work,"[34] and highly esteemed by those who knew him. Though Mr. James was an experienced printer, and much needed in that ministry role, Rev. J. L. Wilson also remarked on his giftedness in teaching. In April 1837, Wilson was hoping to hire a young printer from Cape Mesurado, as Mr. James was "so valuable as a teacher and so much needed in that capacity that I . . . hesitated about getting someone to take the principal part of the labour of printing from his hands."[35] That year, Mr. James taught the advanced native pupils as well as American colonist children.

Teacher Salaries

Rev. Wilson asked the Board whether every teacher should get equal pay or if their salaries ought to be based on the circumstances of the particular individuals. For example, Mr. Polk has a family, and would get $200, while John Banks has no family or dependent friends, and his salary would be $100.[36] In early 1837, Rev. Wilson hired three *colored men*, and one *colored woman*, all of whom were "of good moral and religious character and members of our church."[37] Catherine Strobel also began teaching in the Grebo schools by early 1837,[38] at which time she would still have been a young girl, in her early teens. By late 1837, after more than three years of teaching in the Cape Palmas mission schools, Margaret Strobel was deprived of her teacher role and salary, largely due to her repeated failures to maintain the schools assigned to her, and her lack of interest or support of the mission; she was then restricted to the work of seamstress, which afforded her a modest private income.[39]

Teacher Preparation and Qualification

The apparent success of several of the mission teachers seemed counter J. L. Wilson's doubts about the efficacy and expediency of sending *colored*

---

34. John Leighton Wilson to Rufus Anderson, January 14, 1839.
35. John Leighton Wilson to Rufus Anderson, April 10, 1837.
36. John Leighton Wilson to Rufus Anderson, August 30, 1836.
37. John Leighton Wilson to Rufus Anderson, November, 3, 1836.
38. John Leighton Wilson to Rufus Anderson, April 10, 1837.
39. John Leighton Wilson to the Prudential Committee, October 20, 1837.

men from America, to serve with the ABCFM mission. Those teachers who showed the most promise and competence in teaching received their training and experience through the mission. The one exception is B. V. R. James, who had been trained in a formal education program, at Andover Teachers' Seminary, and had benefitted from the special interest and mentoring of Samuel Read Hall, who founded that institution in 1830. Samuel Read Hall was both clergyman and educator; he founded the first teacher training school in America,[40] and later headed up the teachers' seminary at Andover; Hall compiled the first formal teacher training manual, and was known for his unique and effective teaching methods. He is credited for having invented the blackboard and eraser.[41]

Rev. Wilson praised Mr. Hall for having done much good for the mission and for Africa for having *received Mr. James into his family*, believing that Mr. James's excellent preparation for the mission work was due, in large part, to his having been connected with a pious, white family; Wilson saw this as an ideal model for training *colored men* for mission labour in Africa, adding that Mr. James concurred with his views.[42] Mr. James, in fact, had grown up in several small, almost exclusively white communities in rural New York and Vermont. Census records indicate that his parents were mulatto, and were engaged in farming in Essex County, New York.[43] James's 1846 passport application papers include a signed letter by nine individual white neighbors who vouched for his identity, and knew him as an infant, and knew his parents. All were Caucasian, and were long-term members of the community.[44] This indicates that Mr. James was already familiar with what was considered *white* culture, and an integral part of it, from childhood. Census records from the mid-1800s reveal interracial marriages and households in the areas where Mr. James had lived, as well as *mulatto* and *black* families living in predominantly white towns.[45]

---

40. Tyler, *Freedom's Ferment*, 237.

41. Currier, "Dr. Currier's Letter on the History of the Blackboard."

42. John Leighton Wilson to Rufus Anderson, April 10, 1837.

43. 1810 and 1820 United States Census, Essex County, New York. Ancestry website.

44. Benjamin V. K. James [*sic*], Passport Application, dated June 17, 1846. Ancestry website.

45. Racial designations seemed to be fluid. Joseph James, his brother, was married to a white woman, and raised a large family in Essex County, New York. Joseph was listed as *black* in the 1880 census, but *white* in the 1870 census, and *mulatto* in the 1860 census. Westport, New York was less than 1 percent black, in 1860.

Mr. James was highly skilled in both printing and teaching, but Rev. Wilson didn't want to overburden him with responsibility in both domains. While Mr. James was occupied with the mission's printing activities between 1837 and 1839, he gave equal time to teaching. Though the mission halted printing during much of 1838, it eventually hired two young apprentices who did much of the printing, under Mr. James's supervision, which freed him to teach in the schools.[46]

Mr. Polk's background and education are unknown, but Wilson praised his commitment to spiritual as well as educational concerns for the people at the Rock Town mission station. When Polk died, in 1837, after a long and painful illness, Wilson lamented his loss: "I know not where we shall find a man of equal worth to take his place. Mr. P. really loved the souls of the Heathen and labored faithfully in various ways to secure their salvation."[47]

After Mr. Polk's death, J. L. Wilson placed another Americo-Liberian teacher, Josiah Dorsey, at Rock Town. Mr. Dorsey had arrived on the same ship as Rev. and Mrs. White and Mr. James, in December 1836.[48] Wilson noted that Mr. Dorsey had already been teaching in the schools for some time, and was, thus, qualified for the role.[49]

OBSTACLES AND DISAPPOINTMENTS

A "Regrettable Choice"

In July 1838, the Wilsons were shocked and greatly disappointed when B. V. R. James announced his intention to marry Margaret Strobel, who was ten years his senior. Mr. James had originally considered marrying her daughter, but the Wilsons had dissuaded him, due to her lack of health and piety. The Wilsons felt that Mr. James had made a regrettable choice, which would likely compromise his status and esteem among influential people in the community.[50] Mr. James had been living and working closely with the Wilsons, and they had admired his high level of industry, piety and commitment to the mission work. They did not have the same high opinion of Margaret. The couple married in Fair Hope on November 28,

---

46. John Leighton Wilson to Rufus Anderson, February 1, 1839.
47. John Leighton Wilson to Rufus Anderson, May 30, 1837.
48. Maryland, "Report of the Colonization Society," 19.
49. John Leighton Wilson to Rufus Anderson, August 16–December 5, 1837.
50. John Leighton Wilson to Rufus Anderson, January 14, 1839.

1838.[51] Miss Catherine Strobel remained in their household. She did not receive a separate salary, though she served as a teacher in the Grebo-speaking school.[52]

Financial Strain

The Cape Palmas Mission welcomed Dr. and Mrs. Alexander E. Wilson, in October 1839, with great hope of further developing the educational ministry, as well as providing medical care.[53]

In 1840, the Mission Board found itself strained for lack of funding, which compromised both the printing operations and the expected hiring of the advanced students, who were now prepared to serve as teachers.[54] Wilson worried that they would lose qualified personnel indefinitely if they either dismissed current employees or failed to hire those who had been essentially promised a teaching post. Parents of the advanced students, some of whom had been studying for *five years*, had placed their children in the mission schools fully expecting that they would tangibly benefit from this education.[55]

By March 1841, advanced students were teaching in four of the five night schools, which served about one hundred students.[56] The mission implemented the *Lancastrian System* of education, whereby one instructor could oversee multiple levels of education, by giving *advanced* students teaching or tutoring responsibilities for younger, or less advanced, students. This method was widely used in domestic and overseas education, especially when funding was limited, and was commonly practiced in Liberia.[57]

Despite the financial strain, the mission schools appeared to be thriving, and provided education and employment to both native Africans and Americo-Liberians. Developing tensions between the mission and the Liberian leadership, however, proved to be more disruptive than the financial constraints.

---

51. ABCFM, "Statistical View," 18.
52. Wilson et al., Schedule of funds for 1840, December 6, 1839.
53. John Leighton Wilson to Rufus Anderson, October 11, 1839.
54. John Leighton Wilson to Rufus Anderson, May 20, 1840.
55. John Leighton Wilson to Rufus Anderson, December 27, 1841.
56. John Leighton Wilson to Rufus Anderson, March 13, 1841.
57. Beyan, *African American Settlements*, 113.

Mission-Colony Discord

Growing tension between ABCFM mission leadership and the Americo-Liberian government eventually erupted in an open controversy. Initially, the dispute centered on whether Americo-Liberian mission teachers should be required to perform military duty. The underlying discord, however, appears to have been caused by deep racial tensions, revealed in detailed written records of both the mission and the colony.

MILITARY DUTY CONTROVERSY

The greatest disagreement between the mission and the colony was the issue of compulsory military duty of colony subjects. The mission argued that any mission worker, white or black, ought to be considered a "foreigner" (non-resident) within the colony, and exempt from military duty.[58] An American teacher should not be required to bear arms against the very community of people among whom he was living and serving as a teacher as this would be oppressive to the native population.[59]

RACIAL PREJUDICE

The relationship between Rev. J. L. Wilson and the Governor John Russwurm grew controversial and bitter over the next few years. Each side would give their perspective on the tensions, based largely on issues of race and power.

Wilson felt that American colonists harbored hatred toward all white men, and took pleasure in annoying them. Second, he suspected that the colonists wanted missionaries out of way so that they might begin their work of oppression against the native African population, even to the point of exterminating them.[60] Rev. Wilson deplored the deception and duplicity of the Liberian colonists, many of whom were actively involved in the slave trade. The tensions between the mission and the colony escalated up to the respective heads of the ABCFM and the Maryland Colonization Society. The Board Secretary sent a swift reprimand to Rev. Wilson, who subsequently apologized to Governor Russwurm and assured that there would

---

58. Rufus Anderson to J. H. B. Latrobe, July 11, 1835.

59. John Leighton Wilson et al. to Rufus Anderson, August 24, 1841.

60. John Leighton Wilson to Rufus Anderson, March 28, 1838. See also Mwakikagile, *Relations between Africans and African Americans*, 30.

be no more disagreements between them. Wilson felt humiliated, having allowed his feelings to get the better of his judgment.[61]

Governor John Russwurm sent a letter to the mission Corresponding Secretary, Rufus Anderson, outlining his complaints against the ABCFM missionaries, whose lack of due respect for the colonial government he attributed to "bitter prejudice, which, as Christian missionaries, should be laid aside for the time being, at least, while they continue in the black man's country."[62] Samuel F. McGill, a Liberian colonist and physician, also refuted the mission's charges against the colony, stating that the cause was "the extreme aversion on the part of the white missionary to be subject to the authority of a coloured man."[63] This is evident in a private letter Wilson wrote in 1836, when Russwurm first became governor, "I am disposed to think that the appointment is judicious, though we feel that it is quite a revolution in affairs that brings us under a black government."[64]

By late 1841, tensions escalated to the point of a colonist rebellion. Rev. Wilson felt that the mission should "get out of this place and jurisdiction of the colony as soon as we can."[65]

SEEKING A NEW LOCATION

When missionary physician, A. E. Wilson, died of dysentery in October 1841, at Fishtown, the James family relocated to that mission station.[66] Mr. James took over as head of the schools and conducted Sabbath religious exercises.[67] Because he was the only experienced printer, the mission would do no printing until more help arrived from America.[68] By early 1842, the Cape Palmas mission had lost several Americo-Liberian mission teachers who were no longer exempted from military duty. Three new missionaries arrived in early February, including Rev. and Mrs. William Walker and Rev. Benjamin Griswold, just as Rev. J. L. Wilson, with the permission of the

61. John Leighton Wilson to Rufus Anderson, January 14, 1839.

62. J. B. Russwurm to Rufus Anderson, September 26, 1842. Underlining in the original.

63. S. F. McGill to the Editors, October 1, 1842, 261. Italics in the original.

64. John Leighton Wilson to Rufus Anderson, August 30, 1836. Underlining in the original.

65. John Leighton Wilson to Rufus Anderson, September 30, 1841.

66. John Leighton Wilson to Rufus Anderson, October 20, 1841.

67. Wilson and James, "Annual Report of the Cape Palmas Mission [1841]."

68. John Leighton Wilson to Rufus Anderson, October 20, 1841.

ABCFM Board, began preparations to search for another location, not under colonial control.[69] Captain Lawlin, a friend of the mission, had an extensive network of trade relations along the coast, and was willing to take them to at least two locations, Cape Lahon and Gaboon River. Rev. J. L. Wilson chose to make the journey with one missionary and several of the advanced students of the mission school. The Walkers and Mr. James were ill at the time, so Rev. Benjamin Griswold would make the exploratory trip with Wilson. Liberian colonist teacher Josiah Dorsey also went with them.[70]

The "Final Straw"

Just prior to their departure from Liberia, Rev. J. L. Wilson and Rev. Benjamin Griswold offended Governor Russwurm in handling a robbery as a private matter, and not involving the colonial authorities. Governor Russwurm felt they had treated him with great contempt based on race prejudice. The controversy continued to brew after their departure, leaving Mr. James to report the developing situation to the Mission Board.[71]

Mr. James's own response to these problems was to call the indigenous people of Fishtown together, and tell them about the difficulties between the mission and colony. He asked their sympathy towards those at Cape Palmas, and the people of Fishtown responded that they did not sympathize with the colonists at Cape Palmas, and hoped that justice would overtake them. They hoped that Mr. James and his family would remain with them until God should take them, and if the colony didn't want them, the people of Fishtown did. Mr. James assured them that he had no will to leave their country and that his "heart was with them until God should cause it to cease to beat."[72] Though the James family hoped to remain quietly at Fishtown station, away from the tensions, they were suddenly transferred back to Cape Palmas mission in December of 1842. Mr. James's correspondence with the Board Secretary reveals his neutral stance in the colony-mission controversy, but also communicates clearly Governor Russwurm's accusation that it was an issue of power and race.[73] The imminent departure of the mission seemed to resolve the problem for both mission and colony.

69. John Leighton Wilson to Rufus Anderson, February 1, 1842.
70. John Leighton Wilson to Rufus Anderson, April 7, 1842.
71. B. V. R. James to Rufus Anderson, October 3, 1842.
72. B. V. R. James to Rufus Anderson, October 3, 1842.
73. B. V. R. James to Rufus Anderson, February 13, 1843.

Cape Palmas Students

A number of advanced students at Cape Palmas, Liberia, willingly transferred with the ABCFM mission, beginning with the initial voyage in mid-1842, to serve in the first schools at Gaboon River, near the equator. Among these early Gaboon Mission teachers were: Robert Cross, Francis Allison, Packard Wilson, and Sarah Holt.[74] Others transferring later were Mary Clealand, John Edwards, James Bayard and Wâsâ Baker, who had been the first native convert at Cape Palmas.[75] Three of the Cape Palmas advanced students would eventually contribute a great deal to the fledgling mission in Gaboon, and merit a more thorough introduction:

Mary Clealand

Mary Clealand was the niece of King Freeman, at Cape Palmas.[76] She was received into the Wilson household, and became the first female pupil of the mission school, and an example to encourage other families to send their daughters to school. Mary Clealand accompanied Mrs. Jane Wilson to America in 1842,[77] and later transferred to the Gaboon Mission in 1843. Mary Clealand would eventually marry Americo-Liberian colonist teacher, Josiah Dorsey.

Francis Allison

Francis Allison was among the first Grebo pupils of the Cape Palmas mission; his studies were supported through the First Presbyterian Church of Savannah, Georgia.[78] In 1841, the Mission sent Francis to America to learn the printing and bookbinding trade, with specific instructions to the Board Secretary from the boy's father that he be well-cared for and treated tenderly should he become sick.[79]

Francis spent three years in America for his printer training. He then asked that his return to Africa be delayed by six months. He was willing to go home, but thought that he could learn more things which can make

---

74. ABCFM, "General Letter," 221.

75. John Leighton Wilson to Rufus Anderson, April 10, 1837.

76. John Leighton Wilson to Rufus Anderson, August 4–31, 1835.

77. ABCFM, *Annual Report* [1843], 191.

78. ABCFM, "Catalogue of Pupils," 135.

79. John Leighton Wilson to Rufus Anderson, June 23, 1841.

him more useful to his country.[80] After visiting his family in Cape Palmas, Francis also joined the ABCFM mission work in Gaboon, though his parents were not in favor of it. He told them that he wanted to go and to do whatever good he could.[81] Francis would eventually marry Sarah Holt, who had been one of first Cape Palmas students at Gaboon. Francis served for many years, intermittently, with both the ABCFM Gaboon Mission and the Episcopal Mission in Cape Palmas.

JOHN EDWARDS

John Edwards, also a native West African, went to the Gaboon Mission in 1842 and remained a teacher there until his death in 1854. Mr. Edwards married Lorena Brent (also from Cape Palmas) and the two raised their family in Gaboon.

THE ENDURING LEGACY OF MR. B. V. R. JAMES

Benjamin Van Rensselaer James was the only person of color appointed by the ABCFM to serve at the Gaboon Mission, *and* was the last missionary to transfer to Gaboon from Cape Palmas.[82] He was also the first to leave, for health reasons, after just one year of service at Gaboon. The James family eventually returned to Liberia under another mission board, and served for the duration of their lives. For this reason, his (and their) continuing story appears in this Cape Palmas section, and not that of the Gaboon Mission.

Early Life

Benjamin V. R. James was born in Elizabethtown, NY, on April 21, 1814.[83] His parents were both mulatto, and were farmers in upstate New York. Mr. James also passed some of his childhood at Weybridge and Wells, Vermont. In his eighteenth year, B. V. R. James went to Andover, Massachusetts. He enrolled at the Teacher's Seminary, then run by Rev. Samuel Read Hall, who

---

80. Francis Allison to Rufus Anderson, March 26, 1843

81. Francis Allison to Dr. Armstrong, July 11, 1843.

82. B.V.R. and Margaret James are both in the ABCFM Missionary Index. He for 1836–1846 (Cape Palmas/Gaboon), and Margaret for 1838–1848 (Cape Palmas/Gaboon). Margaret was considered a missionary only after her marriage, and never in mission documents.

83. MCS, "Massachusetts Colonization Society Annual Meeting," 233.

"received him into his family, and gave him instruction for three years."[84] Mr. James sailed for Africa shortly thereafter.

Missionary Life

Mr. James was appointed as a missionary to Cape Palmas in the mid-1830s, though there are no specific details on his sense of calling to mission work. His private correspondence to the Board Secretary offers insights into his private experiences and profound soul-searching as he navigated that calling in a difficult mission field.

REFLECTIONS ON BEING A MISSIONARY

Mr. James identified himself as a missionary in a poignant letter written to the Board Secretary, during his last year at Cape Palmas mission. An ocean voyage for his health afforded him the opportunity to visit Presbyterian missionary colleagues, a couple named Sawyer, at Setta Kroo.[85]

> They have their own peculiar trials but they put their confidence in God and bear up under it with proper Christian fortitude. I trust I have gained some valuable lessons from this providential meeting and pray God to sanctify it in deep[en]ing the work of grace in my own soul. If I ever regret any thing [in] my life it is that I had not obtained more solid experience moral and Christian before I had been placed in this *awfully responsible place of a missionary* in this peculiar trying field . . . O had I for my own past been wise as a serpent and as harmless as a dove, what bitter regrets I might have been saved, and when I take a retrospective view of our last eight year labour now to become dashed to the ground like water that . . . cannot be gathered up.[86]

ON SENDING COLORED MISSIONARIES

Less than a year after his visit to Setta Kroo, Mr. James received the news of the death of his white friend, Mr. Sawyer, and reflected on the issue of white and *colored* missionaries: "I would not for my life discourage anyone, white or col'd, from entering on the missionary work in Africa, but I do candidly

---

84. American Colonization Society, "Colored Men in Liberia," 342.

85. Robert W. Sawyer arrived with his wife in Monrovia in December 1841.

86. B. V. R. James to Rufus Anderson, February 13, 1843.

think that past experience goes to show that if Africa is to be civilized and Christianized it is to be effected by its own race."[87]

Mr. James felt that the work would not go forward until *colored* men and women of the right qualification were sent, though even blacks were susceptible to the African climate.[88]

MISSIONARY FAMILY STRUGGLES

The one personal complaint Mr. James expressed to the Board Secretary was that his step-daughter, Catherine Strobel, was teaching full-time at the mission school, but did not have a separate salary. Mrs. James was fully occupied with the household, and was unable to hire help, due to their limited finances.[89]

The James family welcomed a baby daughter in 1843, just as the last of their colleagues transferred to Gaboon. They delayed their own move so that Mrs. James could sufficiently recuperate her health. The baby soon was fell victim to the "fiery ordeal that awaits all newcomers into this land of sickness and death."[90] Her frequent illnesses took much of their time, which they could not give. Mr. James was also suffering with long-term stomach problems, and needed a health furlough. Now alone at Cape Palmas, the James family also endured the rising tensions between the colony and the indigenous people, which prevented their departure for Gaboon. The Liberian colonist government imposed laws on the native population, and threatened to use cannons against them. An American squadron arrived, and the situation was quickly diffused, with no bloodshed.[91]

MISSION TRANSFER

There seemed to be an imperceptible change in Mr. James's role and standing among the ABCFM missionaries after his transition to Gaboon, and his poor health also seemed to keep him from active ministry for much of the time. With the increase of ordained male missionaries, Mr. James appeared to become a minor figure in mission reports, as compared to the Cape Palmas era.

---

87. B. V. R. James to Rufus Anderson, January 9, 1844.

88. B. V. R. James to Rufus Anderson, January 9, 1844.

89. B. V. R. James to Rufus Anderson, February 13, 1843.

90. B. V. R. James to Rufus Anderson, October 2, 1843.

91. B. V. R. James to Rufus Anderson, January 9, 1844.

The James family remained in Gaboon only one year, leaving in mid-1845 for a health furlough in the United States.[92]

When the family returned to Africa, their ministry was funded through a ladies' society in New York,[93] and their place of ministry was once again in Liberia.[94] Mr. James continued his long and fruitful career in education; he also served as elder in the Monrovia Presbyterian Church, giving oversight and biblical instruction in the local Sabbath School,[95] though his feeble health hindered him throughout his life.

HOSPITALITY AND EDUCATION

Over the years, Mr. and Mrs. James maintained close ties with missionaries of both the Gaboon and Corisco missions, offering hospitality and warm fellowship during their brief port visits in Monrovia. The Jameses were mentioned in the journal of Mrs. Nancy Porter, a new missionary and bride, en route to Gaboon in 1851. Mr. James came their ship to welcome the Porters and to invite them to his home, to breakfast and pass the day; he devoted his whole day to them.[96] Mrs. Porter described the James home in great detail, including a newly-built room for an anticipated missionary couple, and a small room reserved for Captain Lawlin. She described Mr. James as slightly colored and sickly in appearance, very intelligent and agreeable; she also noted that he was "proud to be called a Yankee."[97]

Rev. James L. Mackey, of the Corisco Mission, visited the Presbyterian Mission in Liberia, in August 1861, much of the time with B. V. R. James, whom he described as "long an excellent teacher employed by the Board in Monrovia."[98]

In August 1864, Mrs. Mary Latta Nassau, returning to the Corisco Mission with her infant son, received a warm welcome from the James family,

92. ABCFM, *Annual Report* [1845], 80.

93. BFM, *Annual Report [1850]*, 17; Ellis, "Presbyterian Board," 280.

94. BFM, *Annual Report [1850]*, 17; Ellis, "Presbyterian Board," 280. Lowrie, *Manual* (1854], 161. This education ministry would eventually be transferred to the Board of Foreign Missions and both Catherine Strobel and B. V. R. James were considered "missionaries" with the Presbyterian Board. Catherine served 1850 to 1866, and Mr. James 1849 to 1868. Catherine Strobel died March 20, 1866 (BFM, "Recent Intelligence, Notices [1867]," 81).

95. BFM, *Annual Report [1850]*, 17; *Annual Report* [1851], 14.

96. Nancy Porter, *Diary*, April 25, 1851.

97. Nancy Porter, *Diary*, May 5, 1851.

98. ACS, "Intelligence," 24.

and they spent considerable time together.[99] Mrs. Nassau mentioned Anna, a colonist girl who lost both her parents shortly after their arrival to Liberia, and whom the Jameses were raising as an adoptive daughter.[100]

Edward Wilmot Blyden also expressed his appreciation for the hospitality of the James family. He arrived alone in Liberia on January 26, 1851, "an entire stranger, without a single letter of introduction, I was received with great kindness by the people. Especially do I remember the cordial welcome and hospitable treatment extended to me by Mr. B. V. R. James and his family.[101] The young Blyden apparently boarded with the James family for at least his first year in Liberia.[102] The two men, both affiliated with the Presbyterian Board, would maintain a relationship through the 1860s. Mr. Blyden recalled meeting Rev. and Mrs. John Leighton Wilson, who were staying as guests of the James family, in 1852.[103]

B. V. R. James rose to prominence in the Liberian government, serving as treasurer in his later years.[104] Yet, he maintained his identity as *missionary* throughout his time there, even as late as 1866.[105]

Rev. Edward Boeklen, a German missionary sent to Liberia to help with the Alexander High School, was brought to James's house with a fatal case of fever, and Mr. James "did everything possible for his comfort."[106] B. V. R. James, himself, died months later, in January 1869. *The African Repository* printed a brief notice, stating: "The death, on the night of the 8th of January, at his residence at Monrovia, of Hon. B. V. R. James, is a calamity greatly to be deplored."[107] Mr. James was remembered for his educational contribution in Liberia, as well as his "integrity and ability."[108] Mr. James was about fifty-four years of age at his death.

99. Nassau, *Crowned*, 154.

100. Nassau, *Crowned*, 155.

101. Blyden, *Liberia's Offering, ii.*

102. Holden, *Blyden of Liberia*, 29.

103. Holden, *Blyden of Liberia*, 36.

104. ACS, "Colored Men in Liberia," 342. James and others served in government roles in Liberia, believing that their education and leadership skills were helpful in promoting and building a Christian republic. See McArver, "Salvation of Souls," 150.

105. Ancestry, Port of New York. Passenger list for the Thomas Pope. New York Passenger Lists, 1820–1957.

106. ACS, "Death of Rev. Edward Boeklen," 31.

107. ACS, "Late from Liberia," 96. See also Shavit, David, "James, Benjamin Van Rensselaer James," 119. The author gives an incorrect death date of 1849, however.

108. WFMSPC, *Historical Sketches [1891]*, 10.

The Presbyterian Board of Foreign Missions published this obituary:

> Mr. James, though long in infirm health, was able to engage in most of his usual duties until nearly the close of his well-spent life. He was born and educated in [America], and he was a missionary in Liberia for the long period of thirty-two years. He had been called to fill high stations of trust in the government, and was held in great respect by all classes of people, his highest honour was that of being an exemplary follower of Christ and a devoted labourer of his service.[109]

The Presbyterian Board of Foreign Mission records indicate that B. V. R. James was a missionary from 1849 through 1868.[110] His step-daughter, Catherine Strobel, was listed as a missionary from 1850 to1866,[111] the year she died. Mrs. Margaret Strobel James was not named on this list, and it is unclear whether she was still living at that time.

THE ABCFM HISTORICAL RECORD

Nearly sixty years after the birth of the ABCFM Cape Palmas mission, a published history described the first missionaries in this way:

> Mr. and Mrs. Wilson arrived on the field in December of 1834, and were joyfully welcomed by the entire population. They immediately set about the task of reducing the language to written form, opening schools for the natives, and preparing textbooks for school work and translating the Bible into the native language. In 1836 they were reinforced by Rev. and Mrs. David White and Mr. Benjamin V. James, a printer, and the work of teaching and of translation and of preaching was pressed forward with increased energy. In 1839 the mission, which had suffered the loss of Mr. and Mrs. White had been reinforced by the coming of Dr. and Mrs. Wilson.[112]

---

109. BFM, *Annual Report* [1869], 16.

110. Mr. James was with the ABCFM until 1843, then supported by a Women's Society for several years, until his appointment with the Board of Foreign Mission (PCUSA).

111. WFMSPC, *Historical Sketches [1886]*, 118.

112. Smith, "Work of the American Board in Africa," 451. The paragraph gives a superficial and inaccurate description of the Cape Palmas Mission. Mr. James served as a full missionary, teacher and printer, while Rev. and Mrs. White lived only four weeks in Africa, and died without having contributed any of the work mentioned. Margaret Strobel James and her daughter Catherine were overlooked entirely, despite their roles in the early mission.

Benjamin V. R. James and his vital role in the early ABCFM mission have been largely overlooked and forgotten, yet ABCFM archives reveal his whole-hearted presence, and selfless commitment, to the people of Liberia, through publishing, education and compassionate public leadership. He stands as one of the earliest, and longest-serving, African American missionaries to Africa.

TIMELINE FOR THE GABOON AND CORISCO MISSION(S)

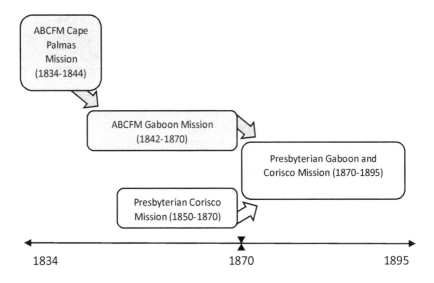

The ABCFM Cape Palmas Mission transferred to Gaboon in 1842. The Presbyterian Corisco Mission began in 1850, and merged with the Gaboon Mission in 1870, forming the Gaboon and Corisco Mission, under the Presbyterian Board of Foreign Missions.

3

Gaboon Mission (Baraka) 1842–1870

OVERVIEW

MISSIONARIES FROM THE ABCFM Cape Palmas Mission first arrived in the Gaboon estuary in June 1842, the guests of the village of King Glass, located near the mouth of the river.[1] While the people of Glass traded primarily with English and American commercial agents, many other villages in the estuary traded with agents from France, Germany, Portugal and Spain.[2] The coastal people, the Mpongwe, had long since adopted various aspects of European culture and had acquired a working knowledge of several languages as they forged socio-political as well as economic alliances with European commercial agents.[3] When the missionaries arrived, they were astonished to find a robust economy and a community of people who were far more advanced than any that they had seen along the western coast of Africa.[4] Rev. Benjamin Griswold was impressed with the well-constructed

---

1. Wilson and Griswold, "New Mission," 498.

2. Bucher, "Village of Glass," 377; ; Barnes, *Gabon*, 17.

3. Dubose, *Memoirs*, 131; Bowdich, *Mission to Ashantee*, 425. Prior to 1819, T. E. Bowdich met two Mpongwe princes who had received a substantial education during eight years in England in France. Bowdich also met a local headman who spoke English well, was well-travelled and had large troop of slaves from many nations and languages.

4. Wilson and Griswold, "New Mission," 498. Griswold noted the superior construction of their dwellings and boats, their orderly streets, and the manner of their dress. The people had *independence* and work ethic (Griswold, "Western Africa," 499).

buildings, boats and roads, and the superiority of the Gaboon people, though no schools yet existed among them.[5]

The village of Glass welcomed the missionaries, and discussed with them plans for a primary school; the missionaries also hoped to establish a seminary within two years. The community was so eager to have education that they had previously sent a request to the Wesleyan missionaries on the Cape Coast, and had been willing to leave their land and relocate elsewhere, if they couldn't get the missionary teacher they were seeking.[6]

Ntâkâ Truman, a prominent trader and local headman, led the missionaries to a portion of land overlooking the estuary, and offered it to them for their mission station.[7] Following their visit, Wilson remained at Gaboon as a guest of the village of Glass, while Griswold returned to Cape Palmas, to gather up the rest of the mission personnel there,[8] comprised of white American missionaries and their wives, several Americo-Liberian assistants and teachers, and many of their most promising advanced students from the Cape Palmas mission schools. They were considered promising teachers because of their "acclimation, experience, and knowledge of African manners, character and climate,"[9] developed at Cape Palmas.

The missionaries listed a number of reasons why the Gaboon Estuary was selected as their new site: the invitation and welcome of the local people, their interest in the establishment of a Christian church and school, access to the interior tribes, no missionary presence within two hundred miles, a safe location for ship landings, and a potentially healthier climate than Cape Palmas.[10] Missionaries grimly noted the lucrative slave trafficking in the estuary, clandestinely carried out by local traders.[11] The land given to the mission had been, up until their arrival, the site of a Portuguese slave barracoon. The local people called the hillside "Baraka," a local adaptation of the Portuguese word *barracaon*.[12]

---

5. Wilson and Griswold, "New Mission," 498.

6. Wilson and Griswold, "New Mission," 498.

7. Gardinier, "American Presbyterian Mission," 63.

8. Wilson and Griswold, "New Mission," 498.

9. ABCFM, "Annual Survey [1844]," 2–3. The Cape Palmas mission schools in Rocktown and Fishtown were turned over to the American Episcopal Mission.

10. Wilson and Griswold, "New Mission," 498–500.

11. Griswold, "Recent Intelligence," 404. British warships were patrolling the coast and intercepting slave-ships, however.

12. Parsons, *Life for Africa*, 31; Ratanga-Atoz, *Histoire du Gabon*, 18.

The visiting missionaries witnessed first-hand, the torture and murder of the captives during their visit to the site. As they assessed the work before them, they lamented that the centuries of European trade had brought only the worst vices of Europe—slave trafficking, debauchery, drunkenness and material greed—and none of the good.[13] *Christian* nations had brought immorality and death, and had neglected to communicate the Gospel of Jesus Christ.

With the transfer of the Cape Palmas Mission to Gaboon, the AB-CFM missionaries felt the freedom to evangelize and build relations with the various people groups in the region, as well as explore the interior for future development, without the interference of a colonial government or the competition of other denominations or mission organizations.

The mission faced immediate challenges of a largely unchecked slave trade, the increasing presence of European and American traders (and with them a corresponding increase in debauchery, materialism, alcohol abuse and greed), and the growing threat of French political control.[14] As they explored the interior regions, and met diverse people groups, the missionaries also witnessed the devastation of intertribal conflicts, as well as the crippling fear of witchcraft and the unseen spirit world. Leading families sought mission education for their children, mostly to *prepare them for lucrative secular careers in trade*. The mission established schools and churches for the purpose of *raising up an educated and pious generation*.

In the early years, Americo-Liberian teachers and advanced students from Cape Palmas served as teachers and (in some cases) preachers at various mission stations and villages. Aside from those who transferred to Gaboon *from the Cape Palmas Mission*, there was only one African American, Miss Jane Cowper, who served with the ABCFM in Gaboon, during its twenty-eight year history there, from 1842 to 1870.

The subject of appointing *colored brethren* came up from time to time, as the white missionary force fell to illness, exhaustion and death. At the time, many believed that persons of African descent were more likely to survive the tropical illnesses than white persons. The missionaries preferred to

13. ABCFM, "Annual Survey [1870]," 8. See Nesbit, "Four Months," 104. Nesbit observed that Liberian colonists brought to Africa all the vices of civilization, but none of its virtues.

14. See Barnes, *Beyond the Colonial Legacy*, 15–16; see also Ratanga-Atoz, *Histoire du Gabon*, 26–28. Local kings established economic and political agreements with France, beginning in 1839. King Louis was the first to sign a treaty of French sovereignty in 1842, months before the American missionaries arrived.

raise up a *native agency*, training indigenous church leaders on the ground.[15] Their hopes and best efforts were continuously disappointed, however, as educated young men were lured into trade and educated girls into liaisons with wealthy and powerful international traders.

Mission correspondence and official reports provide many details of this time period, but leave significant gaps in the record of the persons of color who lived and served in the mission community, their names, roles, placement and interpersonal relationships. It is difficult to discern the Cape Palmas personnel (Americo-Liberian and West African) from the indigenous (Gabonese) teachers or catechists, in published mission reports, as all were categorized anonymously as *native workers*. Though numerous young men and women arrived in Gaboon from Cape Palmas in the early 1840s, the highest number of *native workers* in any given annual report was five, and those individuals were not identified by name.

In this chapter, all details and names of persons of color who served with the mission have been gleaned from handwritten missionary reports and letters found in mission archives, as well as missionary journals or private papers. Such documents give evidence of a hierarchy of roles, with persons of color invariably serving in subordinate roles to the white missionaries, and no indication of a plan for further training or promotion to higher levels of responsibility and authority. This hierarchy further subordinated young women of color, many of whom made the transfer from Cape Palmas to Gaboon. The mission clearly placed its hopes and best efforts on the training and placement of indigenous male teachers and catechists in the Gaboon Mission stations. Ironically, the most devoted and effective teachers and *preachers* raised up during the ABCFM era of the Gaboon Mission (prior to 1870) were *women*. One unanticipated group of mission trainees came to them as *recaptive* orphan children, who had been rescued from slave ships and given to the mission to be raised. Several of these recaptive children, through careful nurturing, became faithful church members, schoolteachers and evangelists.

This chapter gives a broader portrait of the appointed missionaries, while including what few details are available of the persons of color serving alongside them in the mission. More importantly, it reveals the private and public discussions on the subject of sending "colored brethren" and the repercussions of their policies, as white missionaries struggled to maintain the work, with little relief or reinforcement.

15. ABCFM, "Annual Survey [1848]," 3.

Two persons' stories are separated and given in biographical form at the end of the chapter, as they were present, but unnamed in official reports, throughout the time period of the Gaboon Mission. Both women served well into the period of the (merged) Gaboon and Corisco Mission, and details about them and their ministries were revealed only in the later years.[16]

ARRIVAL AND INSTALLATION: BARAKA STATION

Missionaries John Leighton Wilson and Benjamin Griswold, Americo-Liberian teacher, Josiah Dorsey, and several Cape Palmas students, arrived in Gaboon on June 22, 1842.[17] Three days later, Wilson wrote to Board Secretary, Rufus Anderson, to relate the details. Captain Lawlin had provided free passage for the group, and had also rendered valuable service in the negotiations between the missionaries and the prominent men of the Gaboon River.[18] The ABCFM mission received a portion of land on rising ground a half-mile from the river's edge, and in the immediate vicinity of King Glass's Town. Rev. Wilson and the Cape Palmas teachers remained, as guests of King Glass and his community, while Griswold returned to Cape Palmas to arrange for the transfer of the remaining mission personnel from Liberia to the Gaboon.[19]

In early November, 1842, nearly five months after the Gaboon Mission was established, the second wave of mission personnel arrived from Cape Palmas. These included Rev. William Walker, whose wife had died at Cape Palmas, the widowed Mary (Mrs. A. E.) Wilson, and five Cape Palmas advanced students, B. B. Wisner and four unnamed girls.[20]

Josiah Dorsey, who had been in Gaboon since the previous June, was now serving as superintendent of the Sabbath School, which had already

---

16. See Bowie et al., *Women*, 8. Nineteenth-century mission women were less likely to be recognized for their work, or to be given responsibility, resulting in the waste of time, talent and energy. This may be true of women of color serving at the mission, though one could argue that this ambivalence also gave them greater freedom and autonomy than their male counterparts.

17. Ratanga-Atoz, *Histoire du Gabon*, 18, recognizes that both black and white American missionaries served in Liberia, and that there were racial tensions between the colony and ABCFM mission in Liberia. He does *not*, however, mention that persons of African descent arrived in Gaboon with the ABCFM missionaries in 1842.

18. Wilson, "New Station Selected," 498.

19. John Leighton Wilson to Rufus Anderson, June 25, 1842.

20. William Walker, *Diary*, November 3–7, 1842.

grown to thirty participants.[21] Mr. Dorsey's day school had about thirty pupils, though attendance was irregular. Soon, Mrs. Wilson organized the first girls' school, which numbered thirteen girls, all from the principal families in the nearby towns.[22]

Impact of Slave Trafficking

Exploring the area immediately surrounding the mission, J. L. Wilson and William Walker were shocked to discover, a short distance from the house, the bones of captives who had died in the Portuguese barracoon, left unburied. The missionaries observed that the powerful coastal Mpongwe people showed great contempt for those enslaved, most of whom came from "inferior" tribes in the interior regions. Slaves were numerous in Gaboon, and treated with no more regard than cattle, valued only in their useful labor.[23]

Despite British ships patrolling the African coast to prevent further trans-Atlantic slave trafficking, Spanish and Portuguese traders were still carrying on a very lucrative trade with the Mpongwe in the estuary, slipping clandestinely in and out of port. Rev. Walker saw one Portuguese schooner leave the estuary with as many as three hundred slaves on board.[24]

Rev. Walker spoke with Will Glass (a local headman) about his involvement in this trade, and warned him that "slave palaver would surely shut him out of heaven if he did not abandon it." Will Glass replied that he understood it was wrong, but it brought him plenty of money.[25] Walker visited several prominent towns in the region, observing that they were actively engaged in the slave trade, which resulted in drunkenness and the most shocking licentiousness.[26] He found one town hopelessly drunk, after exchanging six slaves for six barrels of rum.[27]

Loss of a Valuable Teacher

In late December 1842, Rev. Benjamin Griswold accompanied the third group of teachers from Cape Palmas, en route to Gaboon. Among them

21. William Walker, *Diary*, December 10, 1842.
22. William Walker, *Diary*, December 13, 1842.
23. William Walker, *Diary*, December 27, 1842.
24. William Walker, *Diary*, February 13, 1843.
25. William Walker, *Diary*, February 11, 1842.
26. William Walker, *Diary*, March 21, 1843.
27. William Walker to Rufus Anderson, May 29, 1843.

was a native couple, Mr. Thomas Brent and his wife, Lorena. Mr. Brent had been a teacher and secular agent for the mission for many years. He died during the voyage, when a canoe transferring passengers to shore over-turned in the rough surf. His unexpected death deprived the mission of a godly man, earnest and trustworthy in all things.[28] His grieving widow, Mrs. Lorena Brent, continued on to Gaboon.

Establishing Mission Schools

In February 1843, Rev. William Walker traveled throughout the Gaboon estuary, negotiating with local kings regarding the placement of mission schools in their towns. King Qua Ben was anxious to have a school and mis-sionary in his town.[29] King Lewis preferred to send a boy to the (Baraka) mission school, rather than have a school in his town. Walker also met with King Duka, who agreed to have a school in his town.[30] In late March, 1843, Walker visited King George's town, on the opposite side of the estuary. King George also desired to have a school and missionaries, and promised to build a school and house according to the mission's desires.[31] Prince Glass was so eager to have a school in his town that he turned his own son out of one of the best houses in town, and gave it to the teacher, until a school-house could be erected at the Prince's expense.[32]

While Rev. Walker was setting up schools in each town, under the authority of community leaders, Rev. J. L. Wilson was working to establish boarding schools, run by mission personnel, which would give them more influence over the pupils, and enable them raise up native agency (indig-enous leaders) as quickly and efficiently as possible.[33] Boarding schools were much more costly to the mission than community-based schools, which were built, furnished and funded by the townspeople. By May 1843 the Baraka Mission had several schools in operation, with around forty boys and nearly twenty girls.[34] Mrs. Mary Wilson was in charge of the

28. Benjamin Griswold to Rufus Anderson, December 28, 1842.
29. William Walker, *Diary*, February 10, 1843.
30. William Walker, *Diary*, February 22, 1843.
31. William Walker, *Diary*, March 21, 1843.
32. Benjamin Griswold to Rufus Anderson, May 8, 1843. The teacher was a Cape Palmas native.
33. John Leighton Wilson to Rufus Anderson, March 1, 1843.
34. Benjamin Griswold, "Recent Intelligence," 404.

girls' school, with the aid of the Cape Palmas girls now employed at the Gaboon Mission.

Map from the ABCFM Annual Report for 1843, 85

    Life at the new mission was challenging, particularly the endless drumming each night in the village of Glass. This ritual was meant to ward off illnesses of the townspeople, but it was also depriving their teacher, Mr. Josiah Dorsey, of his health and needed rest. Nighttime thieves also robbed him of sleep and peace of mind. These many stresses caused him to fall ill, and nearly cost him his life.[35] Days later, Rev. Walker was ill, and asked Mr. Dorsey to preach at Prince Glass's town in his stead. He was pleased to hear from the interpreter that Mr. Dorsey had preached a very good message.[36]

35. William Walker, *Diary*, March 5–6, 1843.

36. William Walker, *Diary*, March 10–12, 1843.

Cape Palmas Teachers in Gaboon

In July 1843, another group transitioned from Cape Palmas to Gaboon, including Mrs. Jane Bayard Wilson, who had just returned from America with Cape Palmas students, Mary Clealand and Francis Allison. Mrs. Wilson brought with her a young African American assistant named Jane Cowper, who was also from Savannah, Georgia.[37] Six additional advanced scholars from the Cape Palmas mission schools included John Edwards and Wâsâ Baker. These many Cape Palmas natives would play a vital role in the early education of the Gabonese people.[38]

All of the passages (on multiple voyages) were free of charge by Captain Lawlin, and the savings to the mission was invested in the establishment of the new schools at Gaboon. With the successful transfer of their Cape Palmas personnel, the mission was now able to formally establish the Gaboon church, and to plan their ministry assignments for the year.

The Gaboon Church

On July 21, 1843, the members of the Cape Palmas church, with a few others present, met together and formed the church in Gaboon, adopting articles of faith and a covenant, and electing Rev. John Leighton Wilson pastor.[39]

The mission community celebrated two weddings on July 23rd, 1843, following the Sabbath service. The first couple married were Cape Palmas natives, the widowed Mrs. Lorena Brent and Mr. John Edwards. Immediately following was the marriage of two missionaries, the widowed Mary (Mrs. A. E.) Wilson and the Rev. Benjamin Griswold.[40]

On July 30, 1843, the newly-formed Gaboon church celebrated its first communion service. One of the West African teachers, Mr. B. B. Wisner, was admitted to membership. The church now consisted of fifteen members, seven of whom were native Africans.[41] As yet, they had no converts or serious inquirers among the Gaboon people.[42] The mission provided preaching at three locations near Baraka Mission and Glass Town, with a combined attendance of thirty to one hundred persons on a given Sabbath.

37. John Leighton Wilson to Rufus Anderson, November 25, 1843.
38. John Leighton Wilson to Rufus Anderson, June 23, 1843.
39. ABCFM, "West Africa [1844]," 184.
40. William Walker, *Diary*, July 23, 1843.
41. ABCFM, "West Africa [1844]," 184.
42. William Walker to Rufus Anderson, August 18, 1843.

Mission personnel were also traveling to ten or more towns, ranging from three to forty miles' distance from Baraka station, all with good attendance. Their goal was to offer preaching at all ten locations each month.[43] As there were only three ordained missionary men, it is likely that the Cape Palmas teachers took part in this important ministry.

BROADENING SCOPE OF MINISTRY IN THE ESTUARY

Rev. William Walker continued to pursue relationships with the local kings and headmen of the various towns, seeking permission to preach and to establish mission schools. However, these leaders were increasingly wooed away by the French, who were gaining both favor and power in the estuary. After a visit to King Qua Ben's town, Walker lamented that there was "little hope of doing anything there. The French are now their Gods, and they feel no want of any other."[44] King Lewis frankly told Walker that they expected the French to bring them plenty of teachers. King George, however, was anxious for a missionary in his town, and agreed to erect a building to be used as a school and teacher's house.[45]

The mission assigned the newly-wedded John Edwards to begin the new school at King George's town.[46] In early December, Rev. Walker and Mr. and Mrs. Edwards arrived at the town, only to find the townspeople drunk, and the house left unfinished. The next day, Walker and Edwards hung the doors and windows of the house, while the local leaders, in a continual drunken state, disrupted them and asked for gifts.[47]

Rev. Walker's diary traces his preaching engagements in various towns and tribal groups, including the "Bakali" and "Shikana" people. Josiah Dorsey, still serving as teacher with the mission schools, was preaching regularly in the communities, with great response. On the Sabbath of October 29th, 1843, he spoke to a gathering of around forty persons in the local king's house.[48]

As the mission personnel increased in their preaching and teaching ministries, they were encouraged to see positive changes in the region. One English captain in the estuary told Walker that they had freed a thousand

43. ABCFM, "West Africa [1844]," 184.
44. William Walker, *Diary*, July 23, 1843.
45. William Walker, *Diary*, July 25, 1843.
46. William Walker, *Diary*, September 13, 1843.
47. William Walker, *Diary*, December 6, 1843.
48. William Walker, *Diary*, October 29, 1843.

slaves the past year.[49] Local interest in both preaching and teaching varied, however, as the French gained power, and as international traders increasingly demanded natural resources, rather than slaves.

By December 1843, King Duka's Town was preparing a house to welcome Mr. Josiah Dorsey as their assigned teacher. Mr. Francis Allison had been installed as a teacher at Tom Lâson's Town, situated on a creek in King William's territory.[50] Mr. B. B. Wisner was teaching at Prince Glass's town, and Mr. George W. Coe was at Case's town.[51] Rev. William Walker visited each one, to check on their progress, either in building the schools, or in their teaching. Walker estimated that the schools each averaged from ten to twenty-five students, and that many locations offered night school for adults, who were learning to read and write. Francis Allison's role as teacher was temporary, until he was needed as a bookbinder. Rev. Walker anticipated that the first educated boys would soon serve as interpreters and language tutors for future missionaries.[52]

First Year's Progress

OZYUNGA MISSION

By the end of 1843, Rev. Griswold and his wife were overseeing a second mission station at Ozyunga, two miles from Baraka Mission, with at least two assistants from Cape Palmas. Griswold remarked, in his handwritten report to the Board, that they were *too dependent on their Cape Palmas assistants*, yet he expressed the need for someone who could superintend the school and household affairs should his wife become sick. Griswold felt that the Cape Palmas assistants did well when someone was there to oversee their work, but did not work well when left to themselves.[53] The published report for the Gaboon Mission did not contain these details, nor did it mention any assistants at Ozyunga, though "five native assistants" were reported at Baraka.[54]

---

49. William Walker, *Diary*, October 8, 1843.

50. William Walker, *Diary*, December 7, 1843.

51. William Walker to the Prudential Committee, December 28, 1843. See ABCFM, "General Letter," 221. George Coe, Robert Cross, Francis Allison, Packard Wilson, and B. B. Wisner had been Cape Palmas scholars, supported by donors in America, in the late 1830s and early 1840s.

52. William Walker to the Prudential Committee, December 28, 1843.

53. Benjamin Griswold to Rufus Anderson, December 26, 1843.

54. ABCFM, *Annual Report* [1844], 85.

Bridging the Gap, Breaching Barriers

PERSONNEL AND SALARIES

In their request for appropriations for the year 1845, the mission anticipated a total of "nine colored teachers"—six of whom had already come from Cape Palmas, and were already teaching in Gaboon, two were expected to arrive with Mr. James, and one more would be needed. The proposed salaries show that married couples (Wilson, Griswold, James) would receive $500, unmarried missionaries William Walker and Mrs. Stocker would have $300 and $200, respectively, and $1280 would be divided among the nine "colored teachers."[55] To date, none of the Cape Palmas girls were named in any documents, with the exception of Lorena Brent Edwards and Mary Clealand, and there is no indication what roles they assumed in the Gaboon Mission.[56] Missionary correspondence does not identify these girls, though there were no less than seven who had transitioned from Cape Palmas. It is possible that they were brought to Gaboon as potential brides for the young male teachers, though this is not stated.[57] The last of the Cape Palmas personnel, including the James family, arrived in Gaboon on February 19, 1844, courtesy of Captain Lawlin.[58]

MISSION ROLES AND CATEGORIES

As the mission personnel adjusted to their new environment and roles, there emerged distinct categories within the mission community. Rev. John Leighton Wilson was associated with the first mission station [Baraka] in King Glass's town, Rev. Griswold with the second [Ozyunga] in Prince Glass's town, and Rev. Walker hoped to establish a third in the near future.[59] These three ordained men were the "missionaries" of the Gaboon Mission, while the married or single missionary women were considered "assistant missionaries."[60] Though B. V. R. James was an *appointed missionary* of the ABCFM, he was categorized a *printer and catechist* in the 1844 mission report, yet he shared in the preaching and religious teaching work

55. John Leighton Wilson to Rufus Anderson, December 1843.

56. DuBose, *Memoirs,* 132. Wilson would later mention "Helen" who had arrived in June 1842 with the first group from Cape Palmas

57. Robert, *American Women in Mission,* 121. The three–self policy offered education to women to prepare them as pastors' wives, though many became teachers.

58. William Walker to David Green, February 18, 1844; Walker, *Diary,* February 19, 1844.

59. ABCFM, "West Africa [1844]," 184.

60. ABCFM, *Annual Report* [1844], 84.

of the mission. Mrs. James apparently had a teaching role at the Baraka Mission, and was categorized among the *female assistant missionaries*. The Americo-Liberian teacher, Josiah Dorsey, and the West African teachers who had transferred from Cape Palmas, were not considered missionaries (though they were foreigners and mission employees), and were categorized anonymously as *natives* or *native assistants* in mission reports.[61] Jane Cowper also assisted in the mission schools, but was likewise unnamed in the mission reports. Her few personal details are included in DuBose's biography of John Leighton Wilson:

> When Mrs. Wilson returned to Africa she took as an assistant teacher a colored girl whom her mistress had educated. This girl was a great help to her, and also very companionable, and in the evenings, when Dr. Wilson was busy or absent, they would talk about Savannah, and the people they knew there, and both felt happier for their conversations.[62]

This short passage indicates that Jane Cowper had been enslaved at one time, but was now emancipated. She was educated, and had a role in the Baraka mission school, assisting Mrs. Wilson. It is evident that the two women had a warm and mutually comforting relationship, and that Jane was a *companion*, and not simply an assistant, to Mrs. Wilson.[63]

FLOURISHING SCHOOLS

Mission reports indicate that the ABCFM Gaboon Mission work was fruitful: there was a boarding school for boys at Baraka, with about twenty pupils; the girls' boarding school at the Ozyunga had six pupils, and five additional schools were under the care of teachers from Cape Palmas.[64]

With these many schools, the mission put into operation their printing press to produce needed books. The printing types were set up by Mr. Packard Wilson, one of the Cape Palmas students who had come to Gaboon to serve with the mission.[65]

---

61. ABCFM, *Annual Report* [1844], 85.

62. DuBose, *Memoirs*, 146.

63. See Jacobs, "Three African American Women," 334. Race differences were often overlooked when Americans living overseas, as they shared common nationality.

64. ABCFM, *Annual Report* [1844], 86.

65. William Walker, *Diary*, December 31, 1843.

LOCAL CULTURE AND GOVERNMENT

Mission personnel observed and recorded their impressions of Mpongwe society and government. Generally, a King had limited authority, and his decisions and actions were subject to approval by the principal men, or all of the old men. The missionaries did not seek to interfere in this local government. They lamented, however, the widespread and terrible effects of slavery, polygamy and intemperance in the local communities, and estimated that nine out of ten crimes committed arose from either slavery or polygamy.[66]

The mission personnel were saddened and horrified at the cruelty and neglect shown to domestic slaves, who were not only treated as chattel, but also frequently accused of witchcraft, and put to death for it.[67] Walker saw four slaves drag the corpse of a female slave by a rope around its neck, and abandon it in the bush. Mission workers took tools to the site, dug a grave and buried her. In another instance, as Walker was walking to Prince Glass's town, he saw smoke and smelled a powerful stench. He came upon a scene where a human corpse—a woman of about twenty—was being roasted over a "slow, wasting fire."[68] Walker inquired as to the cause for this and was told that the child of one of the principal men of the town had gotten sick, and the slavewoman was accused of "poisoning" the child.

Challenges

In the earliest years, the mission schoolteachers faced a variety of challenges to their health and safety, due to inter-ethnic conflicts, French colonial aggression, and natural circumstances which endangered their health. Though they were never direct targets of aggression, the mission teachers experienced much trauma in their host communities.

FEAR, FIGHTING AND FAMINE

Terror gripped the people of the Gaboon, Rev. William Walker noted in his diary: "They fear witches, and poison and tigers and each other. O blessed day when they shall be delivered from this bondage. Satan now rules them

66. ABCFM, "West Africa [1844]," 185–86.
67. John Leighton Wilson to Rufus Anderson, December, 1843.
68. William Walker, *Diary*, November 20, 1843.

with a rod of iron."[69] Such paralyzing fear caused much fighting, destruction and death in the towns.

Rev. Walker visited King George's Town, in February 1844, and found the mission house closed, though the townspeople were present. "Bush men" had recently come and burned the house of King George's head-women and children. They carried off some slaves, and killed others. The townspeople were in a state of semi-starvation, too terrified to walk the long distance to their gardens to get food, of which there was an abundance. This had also traumatized their mission-appointed teacher, Mr. Edwards, to the point that he was recalled to Baraka station. Rev. Walker regretted removing Mr. Edwards, as it only increased the townspeople's sadness and terror.[70] Months later, Mr. Robert Cross was sent to King George's Town, as a replacement.[71]

French "Outrage"

In mid-March 1844, the mission was outraged when a local French officer tricked King Glass and two others into signing a document which ceded their rights and power to the French. This covert meeting was done hastily, and in the middle of the night, without the knowledge and permission of the community.[72] The result was a long stand-off between the people of Glass and the French military.[73] Though the missionaries didn't interfere, they ensured that Mpongwes' rights were restored and that all signed petitions were heard and read correctly to the people.[74] Walker hoped France and England would leave the Gaboon people free and unmolested.[75]

---

69. William Walker, *Diary*, March 4, 1844. See Rich, *Workman.* Europeans living in Gabon were likewise afraid of "poisoning" by their employees, lovers, and enemies, a subject which blurred the boundary between "science" and superstition. "Poison rumors" abounded where educated local Africans challenged white hierarchies of gender and race.

70. William Walker, *Diary*, March 14, 1844.

71. William Walker, *Diary*, July 2, 1844.

72. William Walker to David Green, April 3, 1844.

73. William Walker, *Diary*, April 3, 1844.

74. William Walker to David Green, April 3, 1844. See M'Bokolo, *Noirs et Blancs*, 52. The French believed the Mpongwe were compliant and cowardly; they suspected that conniving English and Americans encouraged their strong collective resistance to the French, and that American missionaries had "fanaticized" the people of Glass.

75. William Walker to Rev. David Green, April 3, 1844.

ADJUSTING EXPECTATIONS OF COLORED PERSONNEL

In its annual report for 1845, the ABCFM Mission reflected on its three years' progress and experience in Gaboon. Wilson shared his sense of urgency for preaching the gospel and raising up indigenous leadership, and expressed doubt that *colored brethren* from either America or Liberia would be prepared to help them in this work. Regardless, Wilson felt that they would need the constant labors of white missionaries for many years to come.[76] Mr. Josiah Dorsey was, in fact, an Americo-Liberian colonist, though he was not distinguished as such in the Gaboon mission records. Those who prepared the mission reports referred to all Cape Palmas teachers and workers as "natives" in their reports.[77]

Despite the political, spiritual and economic tensions which weighed upon the mission community, several of the Cape Palmas teachers remained in Gaboon, fully committed to the work and community.

MISSION PERSONNEL LOSSES

The Annual Report for 1844–45 included the July 1844 death of missionary Benjamin Griswold, the absence of Rev. Walker for most of the year, the departure of Mr. James, in early 1845, and that of Mrs. Mary Griswold in May 1845, all due to their failing health. The two remaining missionary couples, the Wilsons and the Bushnells,[78] were likely suffering in health at least part of the time. Yet, the 1845 report notes that preaching had been maintained on a regular basis at the two stations, and periodically at six other locations. The average attendance at Baraka was around one hundred and twenty, at Ozyunga about seventy-five, with forty to fifty at the outstations. There were two sermons preached every Sabbath at the mission stations, and regular weekly meetings in some of the villages.[79]

Rev. Walker's diary gives evidence of Josiah Dorsey's preaching activity. It is possible that other non-ordained mission personnel also shared in the task of preaching, though none of these are named in the report. Despite the loss of at least three of the Cape Palmas workers in 1845, the mission reported that "six schools were kept in operation during the year, and recently three night schools have been established. The number of pupils

76. ABCFM, *Annual Report [1845]*, 80.

77. ABCFM, *Annual Report [1845]*, 80.

78. Rev. Albert Bushnell arrived and had married Mrs. Lydia Stocker that year.

79. ABCFM, *Annual Report [1845]*, 82.

exceeds one hundred and twenty."[80] In addition to this, the mission produced 185,000 pages of printed works in the Mpongwe language, including textbooks, catechisms, hymnbooks and other works.

Given the shortage of missionaries, and the breadth of the ministry, it is reasonable to expect that much of this work was accomplished by those who had come to Gaboon from Cape Palmas, male and female, West African and Americo-Liberian.

Mission Crises

Though there was only one missionary death in first five years at Gaboon, the missionaries were frequently ill, and found it necessary to take extended health furloughs in America. Albert and Lydia Bushnell left in August 1845, and William Walker was absent from May 1845 to December 1846. This left the Rev. John Leighton Wilson and his wife alone, with the assistance of "five native helpers."[81]

French Colonial Power

The year of 1845–46 was fraught with great danger and violence, as armed French forces invaded the resistant towns near the mission, bombarding them from ships and endangering the lives of all who lived and worked there. The mission was not a direct target, but did receive some damage. The schools and church services eventually resumed and the area became quiet again, though the Gaboon had become a "French province."[82]

Wilson argued that the mission ought to remain in Gaboon, and be reinforced with more missionaries, unless they were expelled by the French.[83] He called for an additional "six missionaries and two white teachers, if men of suitable character can be found."[84] The mission was well-established in education, translation and printing, they were respected among the people and the climate was reasonably healthy. Wilson argued for pressing forward with the work.

80. ABCFM, *Annual Report [1845]*, 82.

81. ABCFM, *Annual Report* [1846], 89.

82. ABCFM, *Annual Report* [1846], 91.

83. Zomo, *Le Travail des Missions,* 52. French colonial government placed many limitations and difficulties on the American missions, beginning in 1845.

84. ABCFM, *Annual Report* [1846], 91–92.

Bridging the Gap, Breaching Barriers

Rev. William Walker returned to Gaboon in late December 1846, accompanied by his new bride, Zeviah. They overlapped with the Wilsons for four months. For that time, the mission had two missionary couples and an unknown number of assistants.

FIVE-YEAR MARK

After five years of ministry, the mission could report only two converts though Rev. Wilson asserted that many were adhering to their teachings, resulting in outward behavioral change, such as "observance of the Sabbath, abstinence from intoxicating drinks and greater punctuality and honesty in their commercial transactions."[85] Both Rev. Wilson and Rev. Walker argued that mission work continue in Gaboon. They were preaching regularly in the villages near Baraka station, and occasionally in fifteen to twenty settlements in more remote regions.[86]

Mission School Progress and Challenges

In the late 1840s, mission teachers faced many obstacles in maintaining regular school attendance in communities that were always unstable, and often dangerous. Rev. Walker's diary of his quarterly school visits traces the movement and impact of the mission teachers, and the environments in which they lived and taught.

INADEQUATE TEACHER SALARIES

By the fifth year of the Gaboon Mission, many of the Cape Palmas teachers seemed to have returned to their homeland, and those remaining were experiencing significant challenges in daily living and ministry roles. John Edwards, whose wife had just given birth, wrote a note to Rev. Walker:

> Rev'd Sir I hope this may not offend you as I do not mean to ask you to do me such unreasonably but reasonable, to solicit in favor of my salary to raise. If you could affort [sic] to furnish me such it will support me fully all my wants that shall be needed. But my condition of state at this time is in much reflections of this very thing. Yet I am happy in this style still to do the will of God as one

85. ABCFM, *Annual Report* [1847], 82.
86. ABCFM, *Annual Report* [1847], 82.

self-denial if is consistent to his will to help on Missionaries to do good. I am dear Sir Yours truly, etc John Edwards."[87]

This rare document indicates the West African mission teacher's willingness to endure deprivation in his ministry role, with clear indication that his salary was inadequate for the needs of his family.

TEACHER ATTRITION

The significant loss of mission teachers necessitated the closure of two of the six schools and the merger of two others, leaving three schools in operation in 1847. Mr. Robert Cross was still teaching at King George's Town,[88] Mr. John Edwards was at Baraka and Mr. Josiah Dorsey, at Ozyunga. Mr. Edwards's letter, coupled with the unexplained teacher attrition, may indicate broader dissatisfaction with salary and working conditions.

FAMINE

In late 1847, King George's town experienced a critical food shortage and widespread hunger, due to a combination of elephants raiding their gardens, chronic trade deficits and other injustices, which prevented the people from purchasing food from the interior tribes. When Rev. Walker examined the school, he found no improvement since their last examination. Robert Cross, the teacher, suggested that it was the result of hunger.[89] The acute food shortage necessitated the temporary closure of the school, and Robert Cross was recalled to the Baraka mission station, though he returned to King George's Town several weeks later.[90]

Mission Crises 1847–1848

After the departure of the Wilsons in late April 1847, Josiah Dorsey continued in the preaching ministry, and his house became one of the places where the people of Prince Glass's Town gathered for Sabbath services. Rev. Walker's frequent bouts of ill health kept him from preaching on

---

87. William Walker, *Diary*, January 1, 1847. John Edwards likely taught in Mpongwe; he used English much less often.

88. William Walker, *Diary*, May 17, 1847.

89. William Walker, *Diary*, November 9–10, 1847.

90. William Walker, *Diary*, December 24, 1847.

the Sabbath.[91] Both Josiah Dorsey and John Edwards served as substitute preachers for Rev. Walker on those occasions.[92]

MRS. WALKER'S DEATH

Zeviah Walker became pregnant shortly after the Wilsons' departure, in mid-1847. On February 26, 1848, after a week of physical suffering, she gave birth to a son, who died moments later. For the next few days, they feared for Zeviah's life. While French physicians gave occasional assistance, Rev. Walker and Miss Jane Cowper were her full-time caregivers. Mrs. Walker deteriorated over the next two months, and died in late April 1848. Rev. Walker noted the great mourning among the mission family and community, observing that Jane Cowper felt the loss more keenly than the others, as she "had long had much care of Zeviah."[93] During this time of crisis, Mr. Edwards conducted the Sunday services in Rev. Walker's stead.[94]

Periodic mentions of the Edwards and Dorsey families in Walker's diary indicate that the Walkers lived and worked closely with both couples. William Walker visited the Dorseys during a difficult time when Mrs. Dorsey miscarried.[95] He noted the subsequent birth of their son, in June 1848, just months after the loss of his own infant son and wife. He also baptized their baby, William Leighton Dorsey, in early July.[96] On one occasion, Walker preached at King William's Town, accompanied by Mr. and Mrs. Edwards and their 15-month-old daughter, Jane.[97]

These brief glimpses of missionary life in 1847–48 indicate that both Josiah Dorsey and John Edwards were fully participating in the preaching ministry of the mission, though this is not evident in the published Annual Report of the Board. They also reveal the shared joys and sorrows among this small mission community, and that the Walker, Dorsey and Edwards couples ministered to one another, as they worked together in ministry in the Gaboon.

91. William Walker, *Diary*, July 4, 1847.

92. William Walker, *Diary*, February 27, 1848.

93. William Walker, *Diary*, April 23, 1848.

94. William Walker, *Diary*, February 27, 1848.

95. William Walker, *Diary*, July 15, 1847. Josiah Dorsey and Mary Clealand may have married during Walker's absence in America, as he does not record this significant event in his diary.

96. William Walker, *Diary*, July 2, 1848.

97. William Walker, *Diary*, March 15, 1848.

Jane Cowper's Mental Crisis

Following Zeviah Walker's death, Jane Cowper showed signs of either exhaustion or spiritual crisis, which Rev. Walker described as fits of hysteria followed by faintness, and ending in violent crying or laughing. He treated her with an anti-spasmodic, and consulted the local French doctor about Jane's unusual case.[98] Multiple diary entries indicate Walker's concern for Jane's physical and mental health. In a letter to the Board Secretary, Walker determined that her hysteria could only be relieved by a change of air and recuperation on the open ocean. This was a remedy often used by ill and exhausted missionaries, and Walker arranged for Jane to take a short voyage along the coast on Captain Lawlin's ship.[99]

Teacher Misconduct

Despite the shortage of teaching personnel, Walker was willing to dismiss a teacher who proved morally unfit, necessitating the closure of a viable school, in July 1848: "the school at King George's was discontinued a few days since and cannot be resumed until another teacher can be procured. I am sorry to say that the last teacher, Robert Cross, has proved himself unfit for such a place, but more from moral than mental delinquency . . . His scholars have made very good proficiency in reading and writing, and are familiar with all our Mpongwe books, and have gained much religious instruction. But it is half lost by the immoral example of the teacher."[100]

Missionary Reinforcement

After more than three years of minimal missionary presence, an American ship arrived in Gaboon, in August 1848, carrying returning missionaries, Rev. J. L. Wilson and wife, Jane, Rev. Albert Bushnell and wife, Lydia, and Mrs. Mary Griswold. In addition to these were three new recruits: Rev. Ira and Jane Preston, and Mr. William Wheeler. Financial shortages in the US, however, resulted in a shocking reduction of mission appropriations to one-third their previous budget.[101]

98. William Walker, *Diary*, July 14–17, 1848.
99. William Walker, *Diary*, October 26, 1848.
100. William Walker to Rufus Anderson, July 21, 1848.
101. William Walker, *Diary*, January 6, 1848.

Missionary Death and Attrition

Mary Griswold died very suddenly of fever, in January 1849, just five months after returning to the field.[102] Mr. Wheeler's constitution proved to be incompatible with the African climate; he lasted only nine months on the field before departing again.[103] Mrs. Lydia Bushnell was diagnosed with tuberculosis just prior to her return to Gaboon, in August 1848; she was an invalid from that time until her death at Baraka, in March 1850.[104]

Decline of Mission Schools

The Gaboon Mission schools declined further in 1849, due to 1) colonial authorities driving the populations deeper into the bush, impeding school attendance, 2) polygamy, which thwarted girls' education, and 3) some parents' fear that their children would adopt Christian sacraments, which they viewed as sorcery, and abandon the customs of their forefathers."[105]

Rev. Walker noted the shortage of teachers, but so many had failed on their own, and he felt they needed to work with a missionary.[106] In May 1849, the Mission voted to reopen the schools at King George's and King Duka's towns, both of which had been closed for one to four years. Mpongwe scholars were appointed as teachers at these sites.[107]

RETURN OF FRANCIS ALLISON

In late 1849, Francis Allison, one of the Cape Palmas teachers, returned to Gaboon after several years' absence. He had been serving as teacher and catechist with the Protestant Episcopal mission in Liberia for the previous five years.[108] He arrived in Gaboon with his wife, and would both print and bind books for the mission. Rev. J. L. Wilson wrote to the Board Secretary that Francis had done well and was a source of comfort to the mission.[109] Wilson, however, credited Francis's work ethic to *careful oversight*, rather than intrinsic motivation: "He has done as well as one out of a hundred would

102. ABCFM, *Annual Report* [1849], 99.
103. Walker, William, Annual Report [1849].
104. William Walker, *Diary*, Sept 30, 1848.
105. Walker, William, Annual Report [1849].
106. William Walker, *Diary*, May 18, 1849.
107. William Walker, *Diary*, May 22, 1849.
108. Payne, "Journal of Rev. John Payne," 59.
109. John Leighton Wilson to Rufus Anderson, December 30, 1849.

be likely to do who had been placed in similar circumstances and this I attribute, apart from the grace of God, to the fact that he was kept steadily at work in New York, and was not made a show of as most heathen youths, who are taken to America are apt to be by injudicious friends."[110]

JANE COWPER

Though Jane Cowper's role was not clearly stated in mission correspondence, nor was she named in any report, her salary seems to have come through mission appropriations. In 1848, she was earning an estimated $40 per annum,[111] which was equal to what a native interpreter was paid, and two-thirds what a single male teacher earned. Jane was a regular communicant of the Gaboon Church, whose membership roll was usually very small, and consisted of missionaries and assistants. She was part of a committee (comprised of missionaries, West Africans and at least one Gabonese member) which met in December 1849, to plan for the reorganization of the Gaboon Church.[112]

When missionary Mary Griswold died, suddenly, in late January 1849, Jane Cowper took over her responsibilities at the Baraka Girls' school, supervising the girls and living in the house with them,[113] though it is unclear whether she had any teaching responsibilities. Around the same time that Jane took on her new role with the girls' school, she became the subject of "slanderous reports" circulating in the community. Though Rev. Walker did not clarify the nature of the reports, he noted in his diary that both Mr. Dorsey and Mr. Edwards had taken part in their circulation.[114]

In late 1850, Jane Cowper transitioned to the United States. Rev. Wilson arranged for her passage, and alerted the Board Secretary: "We send home Jane Cowper, a colored girl whom Mrs. Wilson brought to Africa from Savannah seven years ago. She has been serviceable to the mission in various ways ever since she has been here, but her health for a year past has been very poor."[115] Wilson added that an employment situation would be provided for

---

110. John Leighton Wilson to Rufus Anderson, December 30, 1849.

111. William Walker to the Prudential Committee, March 8, 1848.

112. William Walker, *Diary*, December 11, 1842.

113. John Leighton Wilson to Rufus Anderson, October 14, 1850.

114. William Walker, *Diary*, January 4, 1849.

115. John Leighton Wilson to Rufus Anderson, September 17, 1850.

Jane by a Mr. Eckard, in Washington, so that she would be capable of supporting herself "without taxing anyone."[116]

The mission now needed a caregiver for the boarding school girls. Mr. Dorsey recommended his sister, who lived in Baltimore, and Rev. Wilson suggested that his friend, Mr. Eckard, interview her. There is no further reference to Mr. Dorsey's sister. Neither is there any indication that the mission was seeking to hire *colored* Americans for roles in the Gaboon Mission. Wilson stated, in the same letter, that they would prefer a white woman of education and piety, though he doubted that they could find such a person for the Gaboon mission.[117]

Silence on Mission Assistants

The mission did not seem to be recruiting persons of African descent from Liberia or America. Their lack of financial resources prevented them from hiring qualified teachers, even those trained at the Gaboon mission schools. Walker lamented that the Fernando Po missionaries were able to pay their teachers a more competitive salary, "so much more than we do that we can scarcely keep ours in decent subordination."[118] One native teacher had just left, due to his insufficient salary.

The Annual Reports for 1849 through 1851 list appointed missionaries, and make *no reference* to "assistants," though several were still serving with the mission and contributing much to that work. Francis Allison, John Edwards, Josiah Dorsey and Jane Cowper all filled *significant gaps* due to personnel shortages and health crises, relocating when needed and taking on tasks ordinarily reserved for those with more formal training.

Despite the health crises and multiple departures of mission personnel, the Baraka schools were apparently flourishing in 1851. The French Commodore made an official visit, and "expressed no little surprise and pleasure to find that we could produce sixty or seventy pupils who could read fluently both in English and Mpongwe and translate from one to the other."[119]

116. John Leighton Wilson to Rufus Anderson, September 17, 1850.
117. John Leighton Wilson to Rufus Anderson, September 17, 1850.
118. William Walker to Rufus Anderson, April 1, 1850.
119. John Leighton Wilson to Rufus Anderson, October 4–November 14, 1841.

1850s—MORTALITY AND IMMORALITY

The decade of the 1850s showed a further decline in the number of West African and African-American workers in the Gaboon Mission, as the Cape Palmas pioneer teachers either died, returned to West Africa, or assimilated into the local Gabonese culture. Mission schools were often suspended, due to the lack of teachers. Many young men educated at the mission were capable of teaching, but those of good character were in demand among the traders, and were lured by higher wages than the mission could afford to pay.[120] That same decade, many new missionaries came from the United States, but none were persons of color. Most new missionaries suffered chronic health issues, and either died or returned to the United States after a short duration on the mission field. Those that remained were often sick, or were caring for their sick colleagues.[121] John Leighton Wilson, on hearing of the deaths of Rev. and Mrs. Porter and their newborn, remarked on God's judgments, and pondered whether it inferred that the mission was "going contrary to his holy will."[122]

Church and Schools

The year-end report for 1852 tells of school closures at Nomba (Ozyunga) and King George's Town, Konig Island and Olandebenk.[123] The report also notes that there was little printing and binding being done, and that the church at Baraka had twenty communicants, out of an attendance of sixty.

Lowering Mission Standards

The mission board continued to consider applicants for service in Africa. John Leighton Wilson suggested that candidates be men appropriate character, principles and temperament. The candidates with collegiate and/or seminary training would better understand their co-laborers, but someone with the right disposition and principles could also be useful in Africa, *even without such an education.*[124] While missionary men, to this point, were seminary graduates and ordained ministers, there is little indication that they were identifying or preparing indigenous church

---

120. William Walker to Rufus Anderson, May 6, 1853.

121. James L. Mackey to the Corresponding Secretary, April 13, 1857.

122. John Leighton Wilson to Rufus Anderson, December 9, 1852.

123. Walker, Annual Report, May 2, 1853.

124. John Leighton Wilson to Rufus Anderson, February 22, 1853.

leaders. Mission schools were offering a basic education to both boys and girls, but the shortage of mission personnel limited the amount and type of education available to them.

Mission Assistants

Despite their lack of specialized training or ministerial studies, several native Cape Palmas "assistants" remained fully engaged in the evangelization and teaching ministries of the local church, as well as serving in the mission schools.

FRANCIS ALLISON

In February 1852, Francis Allison wrote to an unspecified recipient at the ABCFM headquarters, whom he had met a decade earlier, during his printing/bookbinding training in America. Francis assured his friend that his faith was strong and he hoped that nothing would separate him from the Lord, not even "silver or gold, if I should posses[s] any at all."[125] Francis reported that he was enjoying good health in Gaboon; he had visited his tribe at Cape Palmas and married his betrothed girl whose mission name was Sarah Holt, though her Grebo name was Nedah. The couple now had a three-year-old daughter. Francis expressed a fervent desire, through the Spirit of the Lord within him, "for the salvation of *my own perishing people*."[126] Though Francis was Grebo, and from West Africa, he seemed to broaden this meaning to include the people of Gaboon and Corisco, as he was then working in Gaboon, and had just returned from a seven-month assignment at the Presbyterian mission at Corisco island.

    Francis Allison continued to teach when and where needed, as well as printing and binding books for the various works of the mission.[127] He was still there in 1854, when the Gaboon Mission reported six American missionaries, one missionary physician, and six female missionaries, divided among the three mission stations at Baraka, Ikoi and Nengenenge, with two couples at each location. That year, missionary couples were receiving $450–500, and one single man received $300. The "native agency" and their estimated salaries were: John Edwards $200, Francis Allison $92,

125. Francis Allison to Unknown Recipient, February 23, 1852, from Gaboon.

126. Francis Allison to Unknown Recipient, February 23, 1852, from Gaboon. Italics added.

127. William Walker to Rufus Anderson, May 6, 1853.

Rosagiza \$72, and Commananda \$84;[128] only the latter two were Gabonese men. The same report shows that there were no "native preachers" at these locations, and only one "native assistant" at Baraka. Each of these mission stations had boarding schools, with a reported total twenty-eight pupils at Baraka, sixteen at Ikoi and twenty-six at Nengenenge. The same report locates Francis Allison at Nomba (Ozyunga), and includes him in the category of "native preachers and helpers."[129] Francis had seventeen students at his school at Nomba.

Mr. James Bayard, a Grebo man, and the brother of Francis Allison, was also in Gaboon in 1854. He accompanied Rev. Albert Bushnell to the interior station at Nengenenge, two weeks after having been "admitted to the fellowship of the church on profession of [his] faith."[130]

JOHN EDWARDS

The 1854 Annual Report does not name the one "native assistant" working at Baraka, though it is likely John Edwards, whose death was announced in the same report. It is the only instance, in the twelve years that Mr. Edwards served in full-time mission work, that he was *named* in an annual report. The brief notice, gleaned from a letter written by Rev. Walker to the Board Secretary, reads "One native helper, Mr. Edwards, a member of the church, who had been long a teacher in the schools, and whose example was always good, has been removed by death. This is regarded as a serious loss to the mission."[131] Walker described Mr. Edwards's funeral at Baraka Mission, which was "attended by a great concourse of the people and especially by great numbers of the youth who had been under his instruction."[132] Walker described Mr. Edwards as the mission's "oldest and most reliable teacher."[133] Later, the Baraka school was placed under the supervision of missionary Dr. Henry Ford, with the assistance of a former pupil.[134] This suggests that Mr. Edwards had been serving as both *teacher and superintendent* at the school, prior to his death.

128. Ford, Henry, Copy of the Estimate Prospective, June 27, 1853.
129. ABCFM, Gaboon Missions 1854 Statistics.
130. Walker, William, "Letter," July 22, 1854, 29.
131. ABCFM, *Annual Report* [1854], 59.
132. William Walker to Rufus Anderson, April 10, 1854.
133. William Walker to Rufus Anderson, July 19, 1855.
134. Bushnell, "Journal of Mr. Bushnell," 36.

DEATH AND ATTRITION OF MISSION ASSISTANTS

The 1855 annual report for the Gaboon Mission described the "unusual amount of sickness and debility in the mission,"[135] the death of one missionary wife (Mrs. Pierce, in childbirth) and the loss, due to medical furloughs, of five other missionaries. The roster for the year named seven missionaries, one physician, six "female assistant missionaries" (missionary wives), and two unnamed "native helpers." However, in the body of the report, two assistants are named: Rosagiza, an esteemed Mpongwe teacher at Baraka, who died in May 1855, and Francis Allison, who relocated from Nomba (Ozyunga) to Baraka to fill this vacant position. The Nomba school was then closed, for lack of a teacher. Rev. Walker lamented the mission's loss, in the space of a year, of *two valuable men of faith and integrity*,[136] who had served as teachers in the Baraka school. In a letter to the Board Secretary, Walker mentioned a third potential loss for that year: Francis Allison was disappointed with his wages of $200 per annum, and Walker didn't believe that an increase in salary would induce him to remain at Gaboon. With his departure, the mission would have no more assistants of his kind. There were now plenty of educated boys in the towns who could teach, though most were not interested. Wilson added, "We need more faith, and we ask your prayers that God will pour out his spirit here and bring these young men into his service."[137]

That same year, Rev. Walker felt it necessary to bring both Josiah Dorsey and his wife, Mary Clealand Dorsey, under church discipline. Mr. Dorsey had, at some earlier point, left mission employment and went into secular trade. Walker expressed his disgust that "some white men settled down here like an abiding pestilence, utterly corrupt themselves and corrupting all they can."[138] The Dorseys were now involved in that community, and its worldly lifestyle. Mary Clealand Dorsey had left on an English vessel, the *guest* of the Captain, and with her husband's consent. The same captain left Mr. Dorsey in charge of a small trading factory a few miles from the mission. Walker felt that their actions merited excommunication from the church.

---

135. Walker, Annual Report [1855].
136. John Edwards, of Cape Palmas, and Rosagiza, a "native" of Gaboon.
137. William Walker to Rufus Anderson, July 19, 1855.
138. William Walker to Rufus Anderson, August 17, 1855.

Unnamed Assistants

The Gaboon Church, in late 1855, was reduced to ten members in good standing, which included four missionary men, two missionary wives, two local Mpongwe men and two unnamed "native women *belonging to different tribes on the upper coast.*"[139] Mission personnel rosters for 1855 and 1856 exclude the names and roles of mission assistants of African descent, with the exception of Francis Allison, who was listed as a "native helper" in Walker's handwritten report,[140] though eliminated in the published report.[141] While Francis is the only *noted* assistant in the handwritten report, there were one or two other "Kroomen" from Cape Palmas teaching or assisting missionaries.[142] Likewise in the 1856 annual report, when the mission was reduced to one "native assistant," it is likely Francis Allison, who was at Baraka.[143]

Lack of Reinforcements

Walker hoped for reinforcements for Baraka station and for the interior stations. He specified the need for a female teacher,[144] but also looked for a man to serve at Baraka.[145] He felt that the mission needed four more male teachers, admitting that he did not expect the Board to send any from America, and that the young men educated by the Gaboon mission would not likely be of service to them. Walker blamed the climate for the loss of missionaries. Walker's request for more became his mantra: "We want men. We pray for men and we look for men."[146]

Missionaries Overwhelmed

In the mid-1850s, many of the pupils were housed within the missionary families, and schools were maintained by the missionaries. Though this was costly and laborious for the mission, many felt it was necessary, as

139. Epaminondas J. Pierce to Rufus Anderson, October 3, 1855. Italics added.

140. Walker, Annual Report [1855].

141. ABCFM, *Annual Report [1855]*, 46.

142. Epaminondas Pierce to Rufus Anderson, October 30, 1855.

143. Ford, Fifteenth Annual Report for the Gaboon Mission [1856], dated January 1857.

144. William Walker to Mr. Pomroy, February, 25, 1855.

145. William Walker to Rufus Anderson, October, 11, 1855.

146. Walker, Annual Report [1855].

parents cared little for education, and did not press their children to attend. Missionaries were doing virtually all care and teaching of pupils in 1856,[147] for lack of native teachers and assistants. Dr. Henry Ford asked for prayer that the young men educated by the mission would be "prepared to exert a wide influence."[148]

"Dry Bones"

By late 1857, after fifteen years' concentrated investment in education, the mission had few or no native teachers for the many schools they had established. More than one hundred young men had received an education at Baraka, yet most of them sought employment at secular establishments, or were "lounging away their time idly in the towns."[149] Rev. William Walker viewed the Gaboon field as one of "dry bones."[150]

Walker insisted that education was necessary for raising up a *native agency* to carry the gospel into the interior. The mission most needed an outpouring of the Holy Spirit to change the hearts of young educated Gabonese men, and those presently studying. They needed the sort of piety that would make a young man content with the common labors of teaching and preaching, when he could gain so much more in honest trade.[151]

With the continued depletion of mission personnel, the lack of *native agency*, and little hope for additional white missionary recruits, at least one missionary advocated for the training and recruitment of *colored missionaries*.

ON SENDING COLORED BRETHREN—1858

Rev. Epaminondas J. Pierce, on several occasions, raised the question of whether the Board could attract *colored brethren* to reinforce the mission at Gaboon. His friends in the US often asked whether *colored* persons from America, having the necessary intellectual and moral qualifications, would be of great assistance in their work at Gaboon. Rev. Pierce agreed wholeheartedly, but insisted that they be proven men and have at minimum a common education. He added that the mission's experience with *colored*

---

147. Epaminondas Pierce to Rufus Anderson, September, 30, 1857.

148. Ford, Fifteenth Annual Report for the Gaboon Mission [1856].

149. Pierce, Epaminondas, Annual Report of the Gaboon Mission [1857].

150. William Walker to Rufus Anderson, August 12, 1857.

151. William Walker to Rufus Anderson, September 14, 1858.

persons from America had been similar to that of native helpers, as they were unable to resist temptation.[152]

Pierce's view supports the theory that the ABCFM mission was trending toward a *lower standard* of educational preparation for missionary recruits, coinciding with their *lowered expectation* of both the character and the leadership potential for those indigenous believers targeted for training as "native agency."[153] Subsequent letters reveal that Rev. Pierce was hoping for mission assistants with practical skills, and not ordained men of color.

"Wont of Proper Workmen"

Rev. E. J. Pierce was frustrated at how much time the Gaboon missionaries took away from their ministry, to complete necessary *secular affairs*. Dr. Ford had been building his house over three months, *for lack of proper workmen*, and hoped they might employ carpenters from Liberia.[154] Pierce suggested to Rev. Wood (of the Mission Board) that it would relieve the missionaries if they could find suitable *colored* help from America for this secular work. Furthermore, he had been corresponding with the Colonization Society and friends in America, suggesting they buy a tract of land and establish a school "to educate colored people—taking quite young boys and educating them until they are qualified to be useful at home or abroad and then looking to this establishment for yearly recruits to the African field."[155] Rev. Pierce felt that this was the best solution, though he clarified that he didn't wish to supplant white missionaries, but to provide *co-laborers* for them. Like many others, Pierce felt that America owed Africa a debt; he believed white missionaries were needed to assist Africans to take possession of their own land, and to govern themselves, based on a solid education. Pierce cited Mr. B. V. R. James and Mr. Edward Blyden, both now in Liberia, as an exemplary type of *colored* person for the work, but felt that blacks could not be placed alone at a mission station. He suggested to Rev.

152. Pierce, Annual Report [1857]. Likely referring to Mr. Dorsey, and possibly Jane Cowper; Mr. B. V. R. James was known for his piety, integrity and sound moral character.

153. That same year, Edward Blyden argued for *higher standards and a more thorough education for clergy and instructors* in Liberia, to elevate the country and to preserve the influence of Presbyterianism (Holden 1966, 51). Blyden lamented the weak white leadership at the high school, and asked for "colored men of integrity, liberally educated" (51), to maintain a permanent and efficient institution of learning. Blyden had requested seminary training, prior to his ordination, but the Presbyterian Church refused this (50).

154. Epaminondas Pierce to Rev. Thompson, January 15, 1858.

155. Epaminondas Pierce to Rev. Wood, February 12, 1858.

Wood that he read Blyden's 1857 address before the Legislature [Liberia as She Is], which he considered to be the *plain truth*.[156]

"A Dark Cloud"

In February 1858, a mere month after his arrival in Gaboon, the Rev. Andrew Donnell Jack wrote to the Corresponding Secretary that he and his wife had arrived immediately after the death of Rev. Hubert Herrick, and they witnessed the sudden illness and death of Dr. Henry Ford only weeks later: "Our hearts are burdened with grief—a dark cloud seems to be passing over this mission. Yet we can only turn to God and cling to his promises. We need the prayers of Christian friends at home."[157]

MISSIONARY SELF-EXAMINATION

In June 1858, Rev. Jacob Best was leaving the field for his second health furlough in eight years, after almost losing his life to fever. The missionaries, overwhelmed with loss and grief, had just observed a day of special prayer and fasting, where they humbled themselves before God and spent much time in somber self-examination. Rev. Best wrote to the Board Secretary of their prayer and hope, that "as God has visited us with affliction, so now he may [visit] us with an outpouring of his Spirit.[158]

Need for Pious and Educated Colored Men

Rev. Epaminondas Pierce also mentioned the prayer and fasting, and lamented that an important interior station had been unmanned for eighteen months. He asked the Board Secretary about sending a physician or missionary; the sudden deaths of Herrick and Ford had given him an even greater desire to have friends in America "establish schools and colleges to train colored men—that we may in time give them the work."[159] Until then, he felt that white missionaries were still needed.

Though Pierce doubted the efficacy and suitability of Americo-Liberian colonists, he continued to hope that candidates could be prepared and sent from America; that the churches would select and educate promising

156. Epaminondas Pierce to Rev. Wood, February 12, 1858.
157. Andrew Jack to Dr. Anderson, February 18, 1858.
158. Jacob Best to Rufus Anderson, June 9, 1858.
159. Epaminondas Pierce to Rufus Anderson, June 16, 1858.

black children, with the aim that they would be useful for the Lord's work.[160] It is likely that Pierce shared his views with missionary colleagues, but their correspondence of that time did not reflect his desires or thinking. Rev. Walker asked for men, or for a female teacher, or a doctor, but did not suggest, as Pierce did, the sending of "colored brethren" from America, even for the secular work. Rev. Walker preferred to educate and prepare indigenous Gabonese leadership, or *native agency*.

Mission Reassessment

In January 1859, missionaries William Walker, Ira Preston, and Epaminondas Pierce were all in the United States, and took the opportunity to meet with the executive officers of the Board of Foreign Missions, in order to assess the past and current accomplishments of the mission, and to determine whether it was expedient to continue the mission work in Gaboon. The resulting condensed report was included in the 1859 Annual Report. They noted that in its sixteen years, the Baraka church had had only forty persons who were communicants, ten of whom had *returned to Cape Palmas*, a similar number had been excommunicated and five had died. The mission had educated some two hundred young men, but was unable to obtain or keep native assistants due to the influence of trade.[161] Missionaries yet hoped to educate "native preachers and teachers, especially the former, taught by a lay teacher from this country"[162] and to secure suitable wives for the young men.

One significant discussion focused on the missions located in Sierra Leone, Mendi, Liberia, Cape Palmas and Yoruba, all of which were "less favorable to the life of the white man, than the field we occupy" and all of which employed great numbers of *native laborers* who were engaged in preaching and teaching. The report ended with the question, "Could we take young liberated slaves from [Sierra Leone], and educate them at the Gaboon for ourselves?"[163]

The period of the 1850s reflected the devastating toll on white missionary lives, and the cost of not sending suitable reinforcements, or raising up a strong native agency. Of the twenty-four missionaries who served during the decade of the 1850s, seven died and nine had left by 1860, almost

160. Epaminondas Pierce to Rufus Anderson, September 13, 1858.
161. ABCFM, Report of the Board [1859], 41.
162. ABCFM, Report of the Board [1859], 42.
163. ABCFM, Report of the Board [1859], 43.

invariably to preserve their lives. Of the eighteen missionaries *appointed* during the decade of the 1850s, only two—Mrs. Catherine Walker and Mrs. Lucina Bushnell—would serve for a significant amount of time. Four of these would serve on the field for 3.5 to 6.5 years, and the remaining twelve would serve for 2.5 years or less.[164]

1860S—MINIMAL MISSIONARY PRESENCE

Only two new missionaries were appointed to Gaboon in the decade of the 1860s: Rev. Walter Clark arrived in 1860 and transferred a year later, to the Corisco Mission, when he married Miss Jackson. A teacher, Miss Helen Green, arrived in 1863, but left after only seven months' service. Only three couples (Preston, Bushnell, and Walker) would serve on the Gaboon field in the 1860s. During that decade, the published Annual Reports would finally reveal the presence, activity, and promise of "native agency" after many years of overlooking such workers.

Recognition of Native Ability

In the 1860 Annual Report, Albert Bushnell noted that several persons attending his Bible class *showed interest in leading in times of prayer and exhortation.* Bushnell seemed surprised and pleased at their "unexpected powers of speaking."[165] Several in the class showed "talents for doing good, should they become preachers."[166] The report made a curious comment that the female members of the Baraka church were "all from other places,"[167] giving the barest hint of the presence of some of the Cape Palmas (West African) women who had come with the mission years before. The Annual Reports of the 1860s revealed the presence of "native assistants," and *further clarified* them as "native catechist" or "native teacher" in the mid-sixties, though they were still anonymous. For this reason, it is difficult to determine whether these individuals were male or female, local or foreign-born, how they were trained and prepared, and how long they served in these roles.

---

164. These figures are based on the arrivals and departures noted in the annual reports, and reflect only time *on the field*, as several missionaries were absent on health furloughs.

165. ABCFM, Report of the Board of Commissioners [1860], 40.

166. ABCFM, Report of the Board of Commissioners [1860], 40.

167. ABCFM, Report of the Board of Commissioners [1860], 40.

Increased Roles of Native Workers

By 1863–64, there was a "native catechist" serving as an *informal preacher* at Nengenenge station, preaching to *hundreds*.[168] Church members were evangelizing within a few miles' radius of Baraka, particularly to slave populations.

Limited Education Ministry

No schools were in operation, except those at Baraka mission station. A "feeble" Mrs. Walker superintended the girls' school at Baraka, with the assistance of an "inefficient pupil assistant."[169] The enrollment of girls grew from eighteen to twenty-four when the school was transferred to the care of the Mrs. Bushnell and Miss Green. One boys' school was taught by Mr. Preston and a *female assistant teacher*, and the other by Rev. Walker. The pupils first learned in their Mpongwe language until they mastered all books in that language, then they switched to English material.[170]

During the course of the year, Preston's illness prevented him from preaching and teaching, so he took on the task of printing the desperately needed books.

The annual report for the following year, 1864, showed the departure of Miss Green, due to illness. Baraka schools were still the only ones in operation, but for a school opened briefly at Cama, whose Mpongwe teacher contracted smallpox. The Baraka boys' school had twenty-two pupils, and the *unnamed female teacher,* who had been in the school for many years, was still teaching there.[171]

Hope for Freedmen Successors

Rev. Walker lamented the lack of missionary recruits, when those on the field had already been serving twenty-two, twenty, and sixteen years, "more than the average life of a foreigner in Africa."[172] He wondered, in his 1863 report, whether they'd even receive new missionary candidates, though there had been no deaths in the previous four years. Walker now expressed

---

168. ABCFM, Annual Report [1854], 51.

169. Walker, Annual Report [1863].

170. Walker, Annual Report [1863].

171. Walker, Annual Report [1864].

172. Walker, Annual Report [1863].

hope that Americans of African descent could be sent to the field: "You may sympathize with us in the hope that out of the millions of freedmen of African descent in the United States, there may be found those who will come and take our places, and carry on our work at less expense of life as has been suffered here in the past."[173] Walker knew that such candidates would not be immediately available, but he was confident that the Lord of the harvest would raise up them up.

Evidently, Walker believed that such persons would *replace* white missionaries, rather than *reinforce* them, in their mission work. It is unclear whether the Board was unable or unwilling to recruit missionaries or assistants of African descent in the US. Roughly one-eighth of the black population was free in 1860, and a small percentage of those (even in the north) had received an education which would qualify them to teach and to serve on the mission field. Persons of African descent living in the southern states were largely deprived of any education, with an estimated 5 percent having had received even "the simplest tools of learning."[174] In any case, none were sent to the Gaboon field, despite suggestions by missionaries on the field.

Ministry by Native Women

While the mission expressed disappointment in the lack of "native agency," there is evidence that the ministry activity of *women* was overlooked and unreported by the mission. Throughout the 1860s, the three remaining missionary couples were desperately hoping for reinforcements to assist or replace them, as needed. Despite the minimal missionary force, and the loss of educated men to the secular businesses in the area, Walker reported that the schools at Baraka continued to educate an average of twenty-four pupils. Remarkably, the combined day- and boarding-schools for boys had been taught by "a *native female teacher* under the influence of Mr. Walker."[175] This person remained unnamed in the reports, and was likely the same person mentioned in the reports in the decade of the 1850s. Walker described this female teacher as the "oldest native member of our church."[176]

173. Walker, Annual Report [1863].

174. Bond, *Education of the Negro*, 21.

175. Walker, Annual Report [1868]. Italics added. In all likelihood, this is *Bessie Makae*, whose is mentioned in her ministry/teaching roles as early as 1849 in Rev. Walker's diaries. This is confirmed in Jane Preston's letter to Mrs. Herrick, dated November 12, 1859.

176. Walker, Annual Report [1868].

In his 1869 Annual Report, Rev. Walker stated that the missionary women were teaching the older girls of the Baraka Mission School, while two of the older pupils were teaching the younger girls, indicating that the Mission was still using the Lancastrian Method of Teaching. Both of these *pupil teachers* had joined the church earlier that year, and were having a perceptible influence on everyone.[177] Walker noted that the two had been holding regular weekly prayer meetings, which had had a "happy influence on the minds and conduct of all."[178]

The 1869 report of the Gaboon Mission showed that only Rev. and Mrs. Walker were on the field, with no native helpers listed. Walker blamed the allurement of trade, which enticed the young men away from Christian service.[179]

THE INVISIBLE MISSION FORCE

Hidden in the history of the Gaboon mission are a number of foreign persons of African birth, who were raised to adulthood at the Gaboon Mission, and served in various capacities and roles for the mission. It would be difficult to "weave" their stories into the fabric of the mission history, as they were unnamed in mission reports, and appeared only sporadically (if at all) in missionary diaries and correspondence. Their stories have been compiled from a few published resources written by missionaries who knew them, as well as incidental mentions of them gleaned from private papers and mission correspondence

Recaptive Children

At least seven African *recaptive* children were raised by the Gaboon (Baraka) mission. Five boys came to the mission at one time, and two girls, another time. Two missionaries, Jane Preston and Robert Hamill Nassau, had personal acquaintance with these individuals, either as children or adults, and both gave brief histories of them in published works. Mrs. Preston tells their story as part of a collection of mission vignettes written for a juvenile audience. Nassau's accounts come from former Baraka Mission schoolgirls who had grown up at the mission, and described the school, its teachers

177. Walker, Annual Report [1868].

178. Walker, Annual Report [1868].

179. ABCFM, *Annual Report [1869]*, 7.

and assistants, from their own recollections and perspectives, during a span of thirty years, from 1850 to 1880.[180]

Nassau's informants, elderly Mpongwe women at the time of his writing, explained in detail the complicated social strata in that region: the Mpongwe contempt for interior peoples, whom they called "Bushmen," the marital customs which allowed a man to marry a woman from a "lower" tribe, but forbade a woman from a "higher" tribe to marry a man deemed lower than herself in status,[181] and their contempt for slaves. Persons sold into slavery by their community were often those accused of a crime, were troublesome in their family, or had been accused of witchcraft; those who were considered *useless*, such as the idiotic and the deformed, were gotten rid of in this way. Such persons were not enslaved by their own tribe, but sold to the next, changing hands until they reached the sea. Those considered useful and docile might be retained at any given point of this exchange, and were reasonably well-treated. Those who were "refractory" were sold away to the next tribe.[182]

Later, as white men came and sought slaves, greedy *kings* and *strong tribes* raided weaker communities, seizing men, women and children prisoners, and sold them to the traders.[183] Children were often pawned as payment for debt, and sold into slavery; some children were simply kidnapped. Nassau described one method of capturing slaves: men would carry little packets of salt, and drop them along well-traveled paths and near springs. When a child found the packet and took it (salt was a valuable treasure in the interior), they would be ambushed and "carried away on charge of theft."[184] The Mpongwe people practiced a relatively mild form of slavery, which was more paternalistic than cruel. The slaves came mostly from the interior, and from what they considered to be *inferior tribes*. According to Dr. Nassau, these slaves had particular *low habits* and personality traits which betrayed them, and only augmented their social stigma.[185] The Baraka (Gaboon) Mission school children from the local Mpongwe families ridiculed the recaptive mission children, and socially ostracized them for

180. Nassau, *Tales Out of School*, 14.

181. Nassau, *Tales Out of School*, 20.

182. Nassau, *Tales Out of School*, 10.

183. Nassau, *Tales Out of School*, 11.

184. Nassau, *Tales Out of School*, 11.

185. Nassau, *Tales Out of School*, 74.

their *oshaka* status.[186] Being orphans, they had no home but the mission, and remained there during vacations. Because they also worked at the mission, the recaptives had semi-slave status in the eyes of the elite Mpongwe children, whose parents owned slaves. According to Dr. Nassau, this *oshaka* stigma remained embedded in their character, in spite of the equality they had been officially given in the mission community.[187]

Jane Preston identified the five recaptive boys by name, but did not know the circumstances of their capture or rescue. She was only able to coax one boy to tell her the story of his capture, as the shame of being *oshaka* caused them to remain silent on the subject.

A child of five, Retenlo, told Mrs. Preston that he had been invited by two unknown men to go fishing, to help feed his family. The child willingly went with them to their canoe, and was subsequently taken to a Spanish trading house, "and sold for a quantity of salt."[188] Captain Lawlin, a great friend of the mission, saw Retenlo and four other captive boys at the trading-house, and paid for them, and then brought them to the Gaboon mission to be raised there.[189]

At the Baraka school, the recaptive boys proved to be fast learners, and "full of fun and play."[190] Mrs. Preston's description of the boys gives the impression that they were well cared for at the mission, and treated with love, but also given chores and rules to follow, which led to their rapid advancement in "civilization and refinement."[191] At the time that Mrs. Preston wrote *Gaboon Stories*, four of the five boys were still in school. The fifth boy had run away, and she feared that he had probably been "caught and reduced to slavery,"[192] having left the protection of the mission.

Mrs. Preston also described the circumstances which brought two little recaptive girls, Mbute and Pâle, to the mission. The little girls had

186. M'Bokolo, *Noirs et Blancs*, 20–21. There were six "orders" in the Mpongwe social hierarchy, with *asaka* at the bottom, and pure Mpongwe or mulattoes born of Mpongwe and European parents at the top. Black foreigners allowed to live among the Mpongwe were above slave status, but below Mpongwe and white foreigner status. One's rank determined whether one was servile or free, whom one could court or marry, and what type of work one could do.

187. Nassau, *Tales Out of School*, 74.

188. Preston, *Gaboon Stories*, 35.

189. Nassau, *Tales Out of School*, 70.

190. Preston, *Gaboon Stories*, 38.

191. Preston, *Gaboon Stories*, 42.

192. Preston, *Gaboon Stories*, 45.

been sold to Portuguese slave-traders at the Island of St. Thomas. They were then taken, with other captives, into an open boat, which was driven off-course in a storm. The Portuguese captain did not have a compass and they remained lost at sea for many days, finally running out of food and water. Captain Lawlin discovered them in the open sea, and (pitying the captives) gave them a supply of food and water, stipulating that he should be given the two little girls. He couldn't rescue all of the captives, but was able to help the two. He then brought them to the Gaboon mission. Mrs. Preston noted that their names were adapted: Pâle became known as "Polly" and Mbute's name became "Julia." Mrs. Preston gave little information on the two, but summarized that they "were married to husbands of their choice in a Christian manner."[193]

Missionary Julia Herrick, in a brief memoir of her two years as a missionary at Nengenenge Island in the Gaboon interior, also mentioned the two girls, though not by name. When Mrs. Herrick opened her school, about the time that the girls were given to the mission, one of them was sent to live with her. The child was very bright, and quickly learned to read; she was also adept at memorizing passages of Scripture with astonishing rapidity. Mrs. Herrick found that the girl was equally prone to lying and stealing, but usually to obtain food. The Herricks concluded that she had been half-starved, and they assured her she could have all she wanted to eat. She eventually overcame these faults. Mrs. Herrick noted that both of the recaptive girls eventually became useful Christian women.[194] As Mrs. Herrick served only seventeen months on the field, one can pinpoint the arrival of the recaptive girls to the time period from early 1854 to mid-1855.

Dr. Nassau gave detailed information on the recaptive children, most of whom he knew as adults, who were still part of the mission community. While no year is given, Nassau indicated that the events occurred between 1845 and 1855, and that the five little boys had been taken into Captain Lawlin's custody at his residence at "Camma," one hundred miles to the south of the Baraka Mission. These are likely the boys mentioned by Rev. Walker in the 1848 Annual Report:

> Some boys came from Kama a few months ago, and attended school the last quarter, who now read much better than other boys who have been in the school three years. There was a good attendance of the parents at the last examination; and they were amazed

193. Preston, *Gaboon Stories*, 36.
194. Johnson, "Reminiscences of a Short Sojourn," 6.

to hear boys, of three months' standing, strangers, *from a people not very much respected here*, reading much better than their own children, who have been in the schools as many years.[195]

The information given in that report indicates that the boys arrived at the mission in mid-to-late 1847. Four of the boys remained at the mission, but the fifth was taken to a prominent Mpongwe man, Sonie Harrington. Missionary William Walker had earlier noticed a bright slave boy at Harrington's, and was unsuccessful in persuading Harrington to allow the boy to attend the mission school, as the Harrington daughters did.[196] Walker brought the fifth recaptive boy to Harrington and "traded" him for the slave boy, *Igui*. Nassau, who recounted this story, did not know what became of the boy who remained as Sonie Harrington's (replacement) slave.[197]

Igui became a teacher, evangelist and preacher in the local church congregation, and never married. Nassau speculated that he was unable to shed the stigma of having been a slave, and from an inferior tribe.[198] He was, therefore, ineligible to marry any Mpongwe woman.

Nassau also revealed the names of the recaptive boys: "Jack" served as cook at the mission; "Maruga" developed his skill at cowherding. When Nassau brought cows to the mainland Benita station,[199] it was Maruga who trained the local Kombe employees how to care for the animals, and to milk them. "Retenlo" was a *valet* with the mission,[200] and worked with Nassau as interpreter and general assistant in the pioneering work along the Ogowe River, in the 1870s. "Njambia" was the young man who eventually ran away, without a trace.

The two girls, Pâle (Polly) and Mbute (Julia), were also acquaintances of Dr. Nassau, from their young adulthood. Polly, according to Nassau, had been burned after falling into a fire, during an epileptic seizure. Her mouth and face were deformed, and her leg was permanently lamed. While her natural disposition was sweet and kind, Nassau felt that her fits of temper were the result of years of being teased by the other schoolgirls because of her deformities. Employed for a short time by the

195. ABCFM, *Annual Report [1848]*, 134.

196. Two of the Harrington daughters, Anyentyuwe and Njiwo, were likely Nassau's sources for this story of the "trade."

197. Nassau, *Tales Out of School*, 71.

198. Nassau noted that *purchased freedom* was not equal to free birth.

199. Benita was a station of the (Presbyterian) Corisco Mission.

200. Nassau, *Tales Out of School*, 76.

Nassaus, at Benita, Polly was "obedient and affectionate,"[201] but she would often fly into a rage if she felt that other (Africans) were "cursing" her—which Nassau felt were just insults. This caused innumerable complaints between the local people and her employers, the Nassaus. Polly married a Kombe man (from the area of Benita), but was poorly treated by him. She died a few years after her marriage.

Nassau was fairly certain that all of these recaptives had died in the hope of salvation, despite personality issues and some moral failures. Of the seven, Nassau remarked that only one "lived to become of extended usefulness"—the one girl whose English name was Julia.[202]

Julia Green

Mbute, or Julia, was listed among the older scholars of the Baraka Girls' School, in 1859.[203] Nassau described Julia as the *chief servant of Mrs. Bushnell*; she later was given the role of assistant teacher.[204] According to Nassau, these roles were given to her, not due to her fitness, but rather "because of her availability and her subserviency."[205] She had no family, nor tribal bonds, which made her perpetually available. She earned the trust of missionaries by spying on the other girls, though this created problems between her and them. Many of the girls considered Julia to be severe, even cruel. Though she married well, Julia was quarrelsome and retained many of her "low characteristics,"[206] and she was eventually deserted by her Mpongwe husband. Julia returned to Baraka mission with her daughter, and was employed as *matron* at the girls' school. After the departure of Mrs. Bushnell, Julia took on the Sunday morning women's prayer meetings, and the monthly foreign mission meetings, during which the women of the Baraka church would raise funds for mission work *overseas*.[207]

Despite Julia's earlier difficulties, Nassau noted that "divine grace gradually refined her nature so that . . . she was employed by the Mission

201. Nassau, *Tales Out of School*, 77.

202. Nassau, *Tales Out of School*, 77.

203. Jane Van Allen to Rufus Anderson, December 24, 1859.

204. Nassau, *Tales Out of School*, 77.

205. Nassau, *Tales Out of School*, 78. See also Park, 120, and Kalu, "Gathering Figs," 37. During the nineteenth century, hundreds of African recaptives were raised by Liberian colonists, and by missionaries, to be "civilized" and to provide domestic labor.

206. Nassau, *Tales Out of School*, 78.

207. MSMEC, "Notes," 280.

as a Bible-reader, and became quite useful in village itineration."[208] Julia began this work in early 1885, just after the death of Mrs. Bessie Makae.[209] In her first year as Bible Woman, Julia was reported to have visited one hundred twenty villages and plantations. Women who had never before attended her meetings would arrive with their stools, sit down and listen to her message of salvation.[210] Julia likely began this work in her forties, after having already served more than twenty-five years in three distinct roles: first, as Mrs. Bushnell's domestic assistant, secondly, as teaching assistant at the Baraka school, and thirdly, in women's ministry. Julia lived to see her grandchildren, and died in August 1894, "respected for her church evangelistic work."[211] She appears briefly in several published works by missionaries, including J. H. Reading's *Ogowe Band*[212] and Dr. Robert Hamill Nassau's *My Ogowe*.[213]

Bessie Makae

Bessie Makae came to the Gaboon Mission at or around its beginning, in the early 1840s, though her name is not mentioned in mission reports. Earliest descriptions of Bessie can be found in the private journals of missionary William Walker, who occasionally described her gathering up women for the purpose of teaching them. *Makae* was Bessie's married name, and she seems to have married a local (Mpongwe) young man, as he had extended family in the area, at the time of their marriage. Rev. Graham Campbell, who met Bessie when he arrived in the early 1880s, stated that she had been "connected with the mission since it was established."[214] Rev. A. C. Good, who also knew her in her later years, noted that Bessie was *Kroo*, and had come to the mission as a child.[215] If so, Bessie may have been one of the Cape Palmas advanced students who came to Gaboon between 1842 and 1844, though she was never identified among them. Bessie's travels as a teacher and Bible-woman were mentioned throughout

208. Nassau, *Tales Out of School*, 78.

209. Campbell, "Personal Review," 144.

210. Jones, "Report [1886]," 7.

211. Nassau, *Tales Out of School*, 78. See Isabella Nassau to Dr. Gillespie, September 5, 1894. Julia died on August 31, 1894.

212. Reading, Joseph, *Ogowe Band*, 197–98.

213. Nassau, *My Ogowe*, 337, 634.

214. Campbell, "Personal Review" 144.

215. Parsons, *Life for Africa*, 62. Kroo or Kroomen tribe from near Cape Palmas.

William Walker's personal papers, the earliest instance appearing in a February 1849 entry, when he saw her in "Jim's town" where she had "succeeded in finding three or four women for her school. There were a dozen in town, but not disposed to go and hear instruction."[216] A few months later, Walker mentioned in his diary that Bessie had brought four women [from Jim's town] with her to Sabbath School, and remarked on the resistance of local women to Christian instruction and to church attendance: "They fear God's word, and are sunk so deep in vileness that recovery seems almost beyond hope."[217] While Walker didn't use the term *Bible Woman* during the early years, Bessie's activity was clearly that of an itinerating evangelist and teacher, primarily among the women.

During the 1850s, Bessie was given responsibility at the Baraka boys' school, when the educated young men proved to be a disappointment, either by giving in to moral temptation or leaving their posts to gain greater wealth in trade.

Missionaries recognized the need for a dedicated women's worker, and often credited and honored Bessie by describing her work to their constituents at home. In 1871, Rev. Albert Bushnell appealed for a women's group to sponsor her. Mentioning that she had been a teacher for many years, he explained that Bessie would be serving as a Bible reader, particularly among the women in the towns near the Baraka mission. Bushnell noted that Bessie was well-qualified, and would enter upon her work as soon as she recovered from an illness. Bessie's salary was to be about $75 per annum, and Bushnell asked which boards of elect ladies would be willing to support her. "There is no work connected with our mission more important. Pray that she may be successful in it.[218]

Miss Lydia Jones wrote, in August 1872, that Mrs. Reutlinger and "Bessie, a native woman, went to town to talk and pray with the natives."[219] It is possible that Bessie was training Mrs. Reutlinger for this work, as the latter was yet a timid and fragile missionary widow in her mid-twenties.[220] Bessie would have been much older, more experienced and much more confident in the work. At that time, Bessie had been engaged in the ministry of the mission for nearly thirty years, and was probably in her mid-forties.

216. William Walker, *Diary*, February 18, 1849.
217. William Walker, *Diary*, April 22, 1849.
218. Bushnell, "Communication, [1871]," 142.
219. Jones, "Extracts from Miss Jones's Letters," 242.
220. Robert Hamill Nassau to Dr. Lowrie, April 6, 1870.

Lydia Jones, a single missionary, worked part-time in village visitation, and collaborated with Bessie and another *native elder assistant* in this work. Women's meetings were held on Thursdays, and they would go to different houses, reaching large numbers of women and children. Miss Jones added, "Bessie's class on Sabbath has often from twelve to seventeen women in it. The Sabbath morning service is well attended."[221]

By the early 1880s, Bessie was in her fourth decade of service with the mission. When Rev. William Walker returned to the Gaboon Mission after an eleven-year absence in America, Bessie was still actively evangelizing in the interior, often traveling thirty miles or more, "preaching in many towns to different tribes, with audiences varying from fifteen to forty."[222] Walker's year-end report for 1881 described Bessie as having made one particular five-week journey "with great privation and fatigue, occasioned partly from not finding sufficient help to travel and to paddle her canoe, and partly from the setting in of the rainy season, which [caused flooding] and brought in mosquitoes by millions."[223]

Missionary letters and journals give details of the vast distances and time commitments Bessie and her boat crew made, to bring the gospel message to the interior peoples.[224] In his diary, in 1883, Walker remarked, "Bessie got away this morning to Moondah. *She has marvelous patience and perseverance in her work. Few of us have begun to hold on as she does.* Egalo goes with her and two Kroomen to go and return."[225]

Bessie died in January 1885, from a "paralysis"—likely a stroke.[226] Missionary Lydia Jones recounted to Rev. Walker (now in America), the details of Bessie's final days. Bessie was in a remote interior location, and finding it difficult to travel from place to place. Adande (a licentiate) offered food and help to her, remaining with her for several weeks before

---

221. Jones, "Miss Jones, Gaboon, Africa," 122. See Campbell, "Presbyterian West African Mission," 26. By the late 1890s, the church at Baraka had eighty members, sixty of whom were women, and thirty were of slave origin. The church was *spiritually dead* but for the Women's Monthly Missionary Society. The many years of educating young girls in the mission schools had produced lasting fruit; they proved to be the most reliable members of the local church. Higher levels of girls' education would have been beneficial to the church.

222. Walker, Year-end Report [1881].

223. Walker, Year-end Report [1881].

224. Lydia Jones to William Walker, May 23, 1884.

225. William Walker, *Diary*, February 7, 1883, italics added.

226. Lydia Jones to Rev. Walker, January 18, 1885.

returning to Baraka. Miss Jones sent medicine to her, and she seemed to recover. In November 1884, word came from the interior that Bessie was very sick. The Mission sent men and a hammock to carry her back to her house near the Baraka mission station.

Bessie described vivid dreams of being near heaven, seeing angels and hearing beautiful singing: "when I awoke I got up. I sent and called the people . . . many came. I talked earnestly to them of God, of Jesus and of heaven."[227] Later that week, Bessie asked for a meeting to be held in her home. Miss Jones describes the scene: "she called the women . . . I never saw her so earnest and eager to talk to the people. I could [scarcely] finish reading the Mpongwe Gospels before she poured out words of explanation. We had so many times of reading, praying and singing together."[228] Bessie encouraged them to continue attending classes and Sunday School.

Bessie was buried next to Mary Wilson Griswold in the Baraka Mission cemetery.[229] She is one of just a few non-white persons mentioned in Dr. Nassau's work, *A History of the Presbytery of Corisco*, in his very brief section describing the women's work.[230]

Though Bessie came to Gaboon from the West African coast, she seemed to have assimilated fully into the Gabonese culture, through marriage and through her life's investment in the spiritual edification of Gabonese people. Readers and mission supporters in the United States knew her simply as "a native woman, a Bible-reader of great usefulness."[231]

227. Lydia Jones to Rev. Walker, January 18, 1885.
228. Lydia Jones to Rev. Walker, January 18, 1885.
229. Lydia B. Good to William Walker, January 23, 1885.
230. Nassau, *History of the Presbytery of Corisco*, 23.
231. Jones, "Gaboon and Corisco Mission," 7.

Etching of the early Baraka (Gaboon) Mission (Samuel Wilson 1872, 218)

Drawing of Ntâkâ Truman, Mpongwe headman who negotiated the establishment ABCFM Gaboon Mission, Baraka, in June 1842. (J. L. Wilson 1856, frontispiece)

Rev. J. L. Wilson, Mrs. Jane Wilson, and Mrs. Mary
Wilson Griswold (WFMSPC 1906, 55)

Mrs. Zeviah Walker and Rev. William Walker (WFMSPC 1906, 55)

Rev. Albert Bushnell. (WFMSPC 1906, 55)

Rev. Ira Preston and Mrs. Jane Preston (WFMSPC 1906, 56)

Rev. Epaminondas J. Pierce (Bond 1976, 459)

4

Corisco Mission 1850–1870

A DIFFICULT BEGINNING

Two AMERICAN MISSIONARY COUPLES embarked for Africa in late 1849, with the intention of beginning a new Presbyterian mission work in Equatorial Africa.[1] The Presbyterian Board already had a work in Liberia, and the new missionaries were seeking a location in what is now Gabon and Equatorial Guinea. Rev. and Mrs. James L. Mackey and Rev. and Mrs. George Simpson arrived at the ABCFM Gaboon Mission in late January 1850, as temporary guests. Seasoned ABCFM missionaries urged them to remain, to adjust to the tropical climate. Rev. William Walker noted their arrival in his diary, and expressed hope that their lives and health be long spared to labor for Africa.[2] While at Gaboon, Mrs. Mackey, who was in her ninth month of pregnancy, fell into a deep sleep, and died of what the missionaries termed *apoplexy*.[3] Her untimely death and burial at Baraka Mission forged an early and sad link between the Corisco and Gaboon Missions. Weeks after this loss, the remaining three missionaries inaugurated their mission on the island of Corisco, approximately fifty miles up the coast from Baraka station.

The first Report of the Corisco Mission, published in the Presbyterian Board of Foreign Missions Report for 1851, lists the Rev. George W. Simpson and his wife, and Rev. James L. Mackey, whose wife had died at Baraka

---

1. BFM, *Annual Report* [1850], 18
2. William Walker, *Diary*, January 31, 1850.
3. Nancy Sikes Porter, *Diary*, June 12, 1851

75

(Gaboon) Mission.[4] Tragedy again visited the mission when, a year after their arrival, the Simpson couple was lost at sea during a storm, leaving J. L. Mackey *alone* at Corisco. Months later, Miss Isabel Sweeney (a long-time acquaintance of Mr. Mackey) arrived on the field, and the two were married. In the 1852 Corisco report, only these two were listed, with no mention of any *assistant*.[5] Likewise, in the 1853 report, three missionaries were listed: Rev. James L. Mackey and his wife, and Rev. George M'Queen [*sic*].[6] Until its fifth year there was no mention, in the official reports to the Board, of the presence of *assistants* at the Corisco Mission. Private letters and journals, however, reveal that there was at least one other person who arrived in Equatorial Africa with the Simpsons and Mackeys in 1849, and remained with them during the early years of the fledgling mission. In an 1852 letter to the Board, Rev. James Mackey reveals her name, presence and role with the mission:

> There is a colored woman living with us who came out as an emi-grant to Liberia at the same time with our company in 1849. She was a member of the Methodist Church in [America]. She is a widow we believe her to be a Christian. *She has been employed as a domestic by us ever since we came down here* and has been taught to read and to write a little. We have had some thoughts of making her an assistant in the school. More particularly in taking care of the girls out of school. If you would approve of her appointment to such a station we would expect of course that she receive a support from the mission funds. *Her name is Margaret Webb.*[7]

Here, Mackey indicates his intent to prepare and promote Margaret from a private domestic role to that of mission assistant in the school.

Establishing Schools

The Corisco missionaries hoped to begin an educational ministry early on, but the deaths of three of the four founding missionaries severely compromised any development of the mission, beyond making initial contacts and erecting suitable buildings. With the arrival of additional missionaries in 1852, and the support and encouragement of their Gaboon

4. BFM, *Annual Report* [1851], 15.
5. BFM, *Annual Report* [1852], 20.
6. BFM, *Annual Report* [1852], 20.
7. James Mackey to Corresponding Secretary, December 2, 1852, italics added.

mission friends (a day's journey to the south), the small mission managed to maintain a foothold.

Francis Allison, one of the West African teachers serving at Gaboon, came to Corisco in June 1851 to inaugurate the boys' school.[8] Following Francis's departure, seven months later, James L. Mackey took over the teaching role. Though the school grew to seventy scholars within a month, Mackey found that he did not have the strength or the time to give it his full attention. He reluctantly disbanded the school, and wrote to the Board: "It was with much sorrow that I did it, for the instruction of the youth here is certainly the most promising part of our work. Can you not send two teachers?"[9] Because their pupils were coming from distant towns, the mission found it necessary to provide room and board for some, while those who lived locally were *day scholars*. At this time, Mrs. Mackey had a girls' school of about twenty pupils (eleven boarding), and there were three boys also being boarded. Mackey added that many more children hoped to be received into the school, but that circumstances did not permit the mission to increase enrollment. Education was expensive, and required a certain discernment, "so as not to expend the funds of the church on youth of little capacity or promise."[10] Mackey knew that such a school would also involve much care, labor, anxiety and confinement to those missionaries involved, all of which would tax and compromise their health in such a climate, but it was a necessary and "important means of training native youth for stations of influence in the evangelization of their own people."[11]

A Cooperative Effort with Liberia

Rev. Mackey went on to express his confidence in the future of the Presbyterian work at both Corisco and Liberia, and seemed to anticipate a cooperative effort, involving white Americans and those of African descent, in the evangelization of Africa:

> They are hindered by no obstacles of priesthood, caste, or prejudice; and they are likely soon to yield abundant fruits of the gospel culture. Their past and touching history; their sphere of labor, on a continent so benighted and yet separated from this country only by the Atlantic; and the residence among us of so many of

8. Rollin Porter to Corresponding Secretary, June 10, 1851.
9. BFM, *Annual Report* [1853], 19.
10. BFM, *Annual Report* [1853], 19.
11. BFM, *Annual Report* [1853], 19.

the children of Africa, many of whom are in the communion of our churches; —all seem to direct a large share of missionary strength of our body to be employed hereafter in connection with these missions, and in the general field of labor to which they are doors of entrance.[12]

For the next twenty years, Americo-Liberians were a vital part of the missionary work at the Corisco Mission and its mainland stations. Unlike the ABCFM mission at Gaboon, these assistants were *invariably female*, and most were hired on a short-term basis as personal assistants, particularly childcare workers. There was at least one orphan Liberian child who came to Corisco as a ward of one of the missionaries. The Liberian assistants were not mentioned in official mission reports, nor were their roles and salaries included in the mission budget, as they were likely employed privately by the missionaries. The one exception is Miss Charity Sneed, whose *name, role and salary* appeared in mission records and reports from the beginning of her service with the mission.

References to these persons have been drawn from missionary letters and diaries, some of which were compiled and published in books, such as *Crowned in Palm-land*, by Dr. Robert Hamill Nassau.

Seeking Teachers

The earliest indication that the Corisco Mission sought Americo-Liberian teachers was in an 1852 letter written by J. L. Mackey. After having requested that Margaret Webb be appointed as an *assistant* in the girls' boarding school, with mission support, Mackey mentioned that the boys' school was without a teacher since the departure of Francis Allison, who had returned to the Gaboon Mission. One potential candidate was Mr. McDonough, a man of color who was currently serving at the Presbyterian Liberia Mission. Mackay noted that Mr. McDonough would be very desirable, if he "is a man of industry and energy and exerts a good moral influence."[13] A few months later, Mackay received a letter from Brother Wilson, of Monrovia, which stated that Mr. McDonough had not responded, and was presumed to have declined. Wilson gave Mackay no ground of hope that they could procure any teacher from Liberia, suggesting that, even if there were

---

12. BFM, *Annual Report* [1853], 20.
13. James Mackey to Corresponding Secretary, December 2, 1852.

Liberian young men qualified to teach, their proper field was Liberia.[14] It is unclear whether the Corisco missionaries continued to seek teachers of African descent from Liberia or America. No such teachers were appointed or sent, and the mission eventually looked to their most promising pupils to serve as teachers.

"TWO EXCELLENT COLORED WOMEN"

Margaret Webb was eventually appointed as a caregiver for boarding mission schoolgirls. Her presence and role in the mission were absent from published mission reports, but for a tragic fire which took her life, and that of another African American woman, named Julia.[15] When a mission building caught fire in the middle of the night of April 3, 1854, the two women had run out of the building, to safety. Missionaries speculated that they then ran back into the building to salvage property, and the burning building collapsed in on them. Rev. George McQueen referred to the two as *servant women*, and noted that "if the alarm had sounded even minutes later they might not have saved the schoolgirls,"[16] which indicates that at least part of their role was to care for and protect the boarding pupils.[17] A short article appeared three months later, in *The Foreign Missionary*, reporting the extensive loss of property, and "the sad death of two excellent colored women connected with the mission."[18] The Annual Report for that year gave recognition of the "two valuable lives that were lost . . . two colored women from this country in the employment of the Mission, one of whom had been with the missionary brethren there from their first establishment on the island . . . Both of them were women of excellent Christian character, and their loss is severely felt and greatly lamented by the missionaries."[19]

In a detailed letter, published in the *Home and Foreign Record,* Rev. Mackey gave these details on the two women:

14. James Mackey to Corresponding Secretary, April 15, 1853.

15. Mackey, "Africa: Corisco Mission Report," 210.

16. McQueen, *Letter dated May 26, 1854.*

17. Mackey, "Africa: Corisco Mission Report," 210. Mackey also referred to the two women as *servants*. His account varies from that of McQueen. Fourteen girls were evacuated.

18. BFM, "Recent Intelligence [1854]," 58. The term *colored* is generally used for an African American, or a West Indian, while the term *native* is given for a local or foreign-born African.

19. BFM, *Annual Report* [1855], 28–29.

> Margaret was raised by Mr. Livingson, of Wilmington, North Carolina. She came out as an emigrant to Liberia in 1849, but never resided in the colony, preferring to come on with our mission company, which came from America at the same time, and she continued to live with us since. She was a woman of rare energy and force of character. I have rarely seen any one, white or black, who had more determination of purpose. When she came to Africa, she scarcely knew her alphabet, but by application and perseverance she had learned to read tolerably well, and she spent hours every day reading her Bible. Julia was raised by Mr. McDonough, of New Orleans, and was a resident of Monrovia for eleven years, but left there in November last to live with Mr. and Mrs. Williams, who came to join this Mission.[20]

Mackey referred to the loss of the "two precious lives" of the women, "who helped bear our burdens" and who were "snatched" from the mission community.[21] While it is not stated in mission archives, their graves were likely the first of the Corisco Mission cemetery. An 1863 article, written by former missionary, Mrs. Georgianna McQueen, notes that a "small stone . . . was erected for the two colored women who were burned when the first Mission House at Evangasimba was destroyed by fire."[22] Dr. Nassau also described their having been buried at the Corisco Cemetery, though he referred to them as "two African assistants."[23] Only J. L. Mackey mentioned the names and personal details of the two women, in two separate documents.

Aside from the two women who died in the fire at Corisco, there were no known *foreign* persons of African descent serving with the Presbyterian Mission at Corisco for nearly a decade.

Developing "Native Agency"

White missionary women, both married and single, came to Corisco to teach in the schools. The mission also endeavored to prepare and equip a *native agency* from among its more promising pupils. As young male and female pupils advanced in age and in spiritual maturity, the Mission

20. Mackey, "Africa: Corisco Mission Report," 210; see also ACS, "Late from Liberia [1850]," 155, which mentions that Margaret was a widow and verifies that she had united herself to a missionary family who had come on the same vessel.

21. Mackey, "Africa: Corisco Mission Report," 210.

22. McQueen, "Corisco Graveyard," 184.

23. Nassau, *Corisco Days*, 47.

assigned them to teach the younger, less advanced ones.[24] Mwambani, one of the advanced girls, was thus given responsibility for all but four of the largest girls, teaching them the alphabet, spelling, reading, basic geography, scripture memorization and catechism.[25] This particular opportunity—or promotion—came after the January 1858 departure of the teacher, Miss Caroline Kaufman.[26]

Mwambani flourished in her role as teacher, and her pupils progressed well in their studies. She was married that year to Andeke, a teacher in the boys' school.[27] They were among the earliest pupils of the mission, many of whom received training in academic, evangelistic and practical skills. Several young men were preparing for ministry. Missionary deaths and absences in 1857–58 thrust three of these young men into roles of greater autonomy and authority.[28]

The Board of Foreign Missions saw the advancements of the mission as signs of God's approbation, and inferred that any church mission organization who would "turn aside from work" would incur the charge of "want of fidelity to the great Head of the Church."[29] It further implied that the work in Liberia should be carried on "through the agency of colored men"[30] while Corisco, being a healthier location for those of *European constitution*, was to be enlarged through the enlistment of *those* laborers.[31]

When Miss Maria Jackson arrived on the field in 1859, she assumed the teaching role at the Girls' School,[32] and was assisted by Mwambani and a young Americo-Liberian colonist named Charity Sneed.

24. The *Lancastrian System* was commonly practiced in the mission schools.

25. Mackey, Isabella Sweeny, Report of the Corisco Girls' School.

26. BFM, *Annual Report* [1859], 41.

27. BFM, *Annual Report* [1858], 40.

28. BFM, *Annual Report* [1858], 42.

29. BFM, *Annual Report* [1858], 43.

30. BFM, *Annual Report* [1858], 44.

31. See Killingray, "Black Atlantic," 9, regarding *geography by race*, where missions considered separate fields for white and black missionaries, according to climate and health concerns.

32. BFM, *Annual Report* [1859], 41.

CHARITY L. SNEED—FIRST ASSISTANTSHIP (1858–1861)

Charity L. Sneed was between fifteen and sixteen years of age when she left her parents and traveled to Corisco,[33] for what was to be a limited time of service with the Presbyterian mission.[34] The details of her recruitment and date of arrival are not available, though she first appears in the published mission report for 1860.

Family Background

Charity and her parents, James and Lavinia Sneed, immigrated to Liberia in mid-1854. The Sneeds were active members in the Presbyterian Church in both Danville, Kentucky, and Liberia. Danville Presbyterian Church records show that James Sneed was converted in 1846.[35] The Sneeds were one of two African American couples whom the Danville Presbyterian Church formally "dismissed" in April 1854, to join the church in Liberia.[36]

EMIGRATION

The Sneed family appears on the passenger manifest of the *Sophia Walker*, as emigrants to Kentucky in Liberia (Clay-Ashland), which lists them as James Sneed, age 34, "purchased and set free to go with his wife," Lavinia [Sneed], wife, age 26, "Em[ancipated] by Chas. Henderson" and Charity [Sneed], age 11, [also emancipated by Chas. Henderson].[37]

---

33. Charity was born November 8, 1842, as per her gravestone inscription. She may have accompanied Rev. and Mrs. Ogden, in early 1858, or Miss Maria Jackson, in early 1859, as she assisted both Mrs. Ogden and Miss Jackson in the early years.

34. BFM, *Annual Report* [1860], 34.

35. See Bishop and Rice, *Outline*, 385–418, and Gaines, *Cub Creek Church*, 51. The Danville Presbyterian Church was begun by Rev. David Rice in 1784. Rice argued against slavery as the Constitution of Kentucky was being drawn. He previously pastored at Cub Creek church, in Virginia, an early multi-racial congregation which affirmed the spiritual and educational achievements of African Americans in their community. See also Fackler, *Chronicle*, and Brown, *Presbyterians,* both of which offer a history of this congregation.

36. Danville Presbyterian Church, "Minutes." See also Harrison and Klotter, *New History*, 167. In Kentucky, enslaved persons comprised 24 percent of population in 1830; they were 19.5 percent by 1860.

37. American Colonization Society, "List of emigrants," 217. See also Dunnigan, *Fascinating Story*, 43. The Kentucky Colonization Society sent 658 emancipated slaves to Liberia between 1829 and 1859. An 1851 law required newly-emancipated blacks to leave the state.

CENSUS INFORMATION

Available census records for 1840 and 1850 do not give names of enslaved persons, but list the racial designation (mulatto or black) as well as gender and age. Comparing the 1850 census records for the Charles Henderson slaves, and the ship's manifest for the *Sophia Walker*, one can conclude that Lavinia Sneed was considered *black*, while Charity was one of several *mulatto* girls of her age group.[38] Tracing James Sneed in the 1850 census is more difficult, as there were three Sneed households, each with a number of slaves unnamed in the census. Analyzing the available age estimates, and comparing them to the information given on the *Sophia Walker* ship manifest, James Sneed appeared to be part of the John Sneed household, and (if so) was listed as *mulatto*.[39]

VOYAGE TO LIBERIA

The Sneeds travelled with a number of former slaves who had been part of the Charles Henderson plantation, and were likewise freed to immigrate to Liberia. The *Sophia Walker* left the United States in late May 1854, and arrived in Liberia on July 30. A brief article in the *African Repository* noted that "[m]uch sickness prevailed on board during the passage out, especially among the children, twenty of whom died before reaching Grand Bassa, and eight or ten more soon after landing"[40] The American Colonization Society reported that, including the 252 passengers of the *Sophia Walker*, there were now 8,456 emigrants in Liberia.[41]

LIFE IN LIBERIA

Little is known about the town of Clay-Ashland, where the Sneed family first settled, though letters written by others that year described it as having "plenty of churches—one very fine Episcopal Church, one Baptist, one Methodist and one Presbyterian—and on the way to them four schools."[42]

38. 1850 U.S. Federal Census, Boyle County, Kentucky, 582.

39. 1850 U.S. Federal Census, Boyle County, Kentucky, 592.

40. ACS, "Later from Liberia," 340. There were about 120 children aboard the *Sophia Walker*.

41. ACS, "List of Emigrants," 219.

42. Rosabella Burke to Mary C. Lee, August 21, 1854, from Liberia, 92.

James Sneed served as elder at the church in Liberia.[43] This indicates that the Sneeds were a committed Christian family, and an active part of the church community, in both Kentucky and Liberia. It is not clear, however, whether they included themselves among those Americo-Liberians who felt that God had brought them to Africa in order to share the gospel, nor did Charity indicate what prompted her decision to serve with the Presbyterian mission in Equatorial Africa. Whether Charity had received schooling in America is also unclear, but it is certain that she received an education in Liberia, during her four to five years there, as she was fully prepared to assist in the classroom at Corisco.

Early Role

Charity's first reported role was that of *assistant* at the Evangasimba Girls' School, as per the Annual Report of 1859–60. At the time, Miss Jackson was the head teacher, while Charity Sneed and Mwambani were her *assistants*.[44]

In January 1860, Rev. Ogden sent a letter to the Board Secretary, to request "another young lady missionary to assist Miss Jackson at our girls' school."[45] He later added that "Charity Sneed is now assisting Miss Jackson in the instruction of the smaller girls, but she expects to return to her parents in Monrovia soon, and even should she remain could not be expected to maintain that authority over the girls and to render that assistance to Miss Jackson which a white lady would."[46] This particular correspondence was written to both ask for additional missionary teachers and to recommend a Miss Mary Latta, from Chestnut Hill, PA.

Perhaps due to her imminent departure in 1860, Rev. Ogden did not include Charity Sneed in the projected 1860–61 appropriations list (proposed budget), submitted in January 1860.[47] However, the *approved* list of appropriations, generated by the Presbyterian Board in April 1860, *did* include Charity.[48] That budget, which would begin in October 1860,

43. As per Peter Menkel, in a diary entry dated February 22, 1883. Menkel visited the grave of James Sneed, who died in 1861, and learned details of the Sneed family from their close friends, the Rev. Deputie, Mrs. Travers (née Ayshorn) and her mother, all still living in Liberia in 1883.

44. BFM, *Annual Report* [1860], 34.

45. Thomas Ogden to J. L. Wilson, January 4, 1860.

46. Thomas Ogden to J. L. Wilson, January 4, 1860.

47. Ogden, Estimated Appropriations.

48. John Leighton Wilson to the Corisco Mission, Appropriations for 1860.

listed the following appropriations: male missionaries, $400–500, single female missionary teacher, $250, native teacher $60. Depending on the roles (and likely time given) native assistants varied from $48 to $96 per year. Charity Sneed was appropriated an annual salary of $65, though her role was not clarified.[49]

Promotion

In her 1860 annual report for the Girls' Boarding School at Corisco, Miss Jackson wrote that the "morning session of school is [taught][50] by Charity L. Sneed, a colonist."[51] The published Corisco Mission Annual Report listed Charity Sneed by name on the mission roster, with the designation *assistant*. Charity's name was now positioned on that list *after* the appointed white missionaries, but *before* the four native assistants, both male and female, whose names and roles were also given.[52] Published annual reports often omitted names and details of the particular work of these assistants. For instance, the published 1861 Annual Report implied that *only* Miss Jackson taught at the Evangasimba Girls' School, until the arrival of Miss Latta in November 1860,[53] and did not include Miss Jackson's statement that Charity Sneed had been teaching at the school. Charity Sneed and Mwambani shared in at least some of the teaching. The Corisco Mission considered Evangasimba as one of its most important schools, as the education of females was "an indispensable element in the improvement of any community, but especially so to the elevation of a heathen population."[54]

Expanded Role

In January 1861, Maria Jackson married Rev. Walter Clark, who had transferred from the Gaboon Mission. With Miss Latta and Mrs. Clark both teaching at Evangasimba girls' school, Charity became "Mrs. Ogden's Liberian Assistant."[55] During Charity's first few years at Corisco, the mission suffered many illnesses and deaths, requiring all hands on deck to care for

---

49. John Leighton Wilson to the Corisco Mission, Appropriations for 1860.
50. Word obscured in the microfilm image.
51. Jackson, *Report of the Corisco Mission Girls' Boarding School*, 1860.
52. ACS, "Corisco Mission," 230.
53. BFM, *Annual Report* [1861], 35.
54. BFM, *Annual Report* [1861], 35.
55. Nassau, *Crowned*, 89.

the sick, as well as maintain the mission schools and boarding students, infirmary and store. As a personal assistant, Charity would have been involved in any of these tasks, as needed. Her role, however, appears to be that of *teacher's assistant*, if informally, during this period.[56]

"Nurse"

Mrs. Ogden's complicated pregnancy and childbirth, in early 1861, monopolized the time and attention of Charity Sneed, Mary Latta and Mrs. Clark, and necessitated the suspension of the girls' school for months.[57] Rev. Walter Clark complained of the devastating effect this crisis pregnancy had on the mission, noting that both Mrs. Clark and Miss Latta had become broken down in their own health by the added responsibilities related to her care. Clark described Charity as "a strong and faithfull [*sic*] colored nurse from Liberia who performed probably half of the work done for [Mrs. Ogden]."[58]

Miss Latta had hoped to regroup the girls and recommence the little school, despite a shortage of personnel. She suggested Charity's potential role in either teaching or caring for the girls.[59] However, in October 1861, Charity accompanied the newly-widowed Mrs. Ogden and her infant to America, and remained with them for an extended period.[60] While in America, and in the company of Mrs. Ogden, Charity made the acquaintance of Corresponding Secretary of the Board, Dr. John Lowrie,[61] and relatives of Miss Latta,[62] among others.

Charity's fluctuating role with the Corisco Mission was unusual, given that subsequent Americo-Liberian assistants were hired as private domestic employees of missionary families, or were *orphans* who were raised to be assistants.

56. Chauncey Loomis to John Lowrie, July 29, 1863.

57. Nassau, *Crowned*, 89.

58. Walter Clark to John Lowrie, October 15, 1862.

59. Nassau, *Crowned*, 90.

60. Mrs. Ogden gave birth in April 1861; her husband died of fever in May.

61. Charity Sneed to Walter Lowrie, October 31, 1871.

62. Nassau, *Crowned*, 244.

AMERICO-LIBERIAN ORPHANS

It was not uncommon for missionaries to *adopt* Liberian or African minors, with the intention of raising them to adulthood, while overseeing their education and training in life skills. Though missionaries sometimes implied a parent-child relationship, available correspondence suggests that these children were expected to be both helpful and *useful* to the family and mission. This type of arrangement might be more accurately labeled "apprenticeship," which was commonly practiced among Americo-Liberians who, in similar cases, took local native African children into their homes for the same intent.[63] John Leighton Wilson considered this system to be slavery in disguise.[64]

At least two orphaned Liberian girls accompanied missionaries to Corisco in late 1860. Warnetta Alvarez traveled with Rev. and Mrs. Walker, and remained with them for many years at the Gaboon mission.

The new missionary teacher, Mary Latta, brought with her a seven-year-old colonist child named Julia Goods, and requested that the child's support be taken from her own salary.[65] Subsequent references to Julia emphasized her domestic role in the household.[66] As Julia grew older, Mary Latta Nassau was increasingly frustrated with her, and disappointed that she was neither helpful nor reliable. Julia was eventually "sent from Corisco"[67] (to an unnamed destination) in October 1868, and there is no further information on her.

AMERICO-LIBERIAN DOMESTIC ASSISTANTS

As missionaries began to have families on the mission field, they recruited Americo-Liberian women to care for their babies and small children. Mary Latta Nassau's journal gives some detail of this type of employment, and describes several colonist women who came to the mission for this purpose.

---

63. See Shick, Tom, *Behold*, 65, and Ciment, *Another America*, 68, 69. In 1838, Liberia established rules for a *ward system*, which blended African peace-making traditions (enemy groups exchanging children to maintain peace) and European adoption laws.

64. John Leighton Wilson to Rufus Anderson, March 10, 1838.

65. Mary Latta to John Leighton Wilson, October 8, 1860.

66. Nassau, *Crowned*, 229.

67. Nassau, *Crowned*, 288.

Mrs. Jane Thompson

After giving birth to her first child in America, Mary Latta Nassau prepared to return to Africa well before his first birthday. She had originally hired a young woman in the U. S., hoping to travel with her to Corisco. The young woman, however, sailed as far as Liberia, and "left her service."[68] Mary then hired an Americo-Liberian woman, Mrs. Thompson, to accompany her to the mission field. They arrived at Corisco in late September, 1864.[69] Aside from her obvious role as baby Willie's nurse, Mrs. Thompson also assisted Mary Nassau with the household tasks, making her work much less arduous. In June 1865, the Nassaus sent their small son to live in the United States with relatives. After baby Willie left, the two women seemed to share the responsibility of caring for the boarding schoolchildren, and Mrs. Thompson's presence allowed the Nassau couple to eat their meals "alone together for the first time."[70] Mary Latta Nassau and Mrs. Clemens, the two missionaries responsible for the school, were both frequently sick and weak. Mary remarked that she couldn't get along as easily as she did if not for Mrs. Thompson.[71]

Mary Latta Nassau's July 1865 letter to a relative reveals some personal information on Mrs. Thompson. In the letter, Mary inquires whether there was news of Mrs. Thompson's husband, who had been out of contact for four years. Mary Nassau believed that Mrs. Thompson had "some notion of marrying on her return to Monrovia,"[72] as she had had several offers.

When the Nassaus left the island of Corisco, to occupy the new Benita station on the mainland, their "family" comprised Dr. and Mrs. Nassau, Mrs. Thompson, and two girls, one of whom was Julia Goods.[73] While Dr. Nassau worked to finish the mission house, his wife "commenced an evening school for adults and children, whom she taught while sitting sewing in the Ikenga (common room) with Mrs. Thompson."[74] Mrs. Nassau's letters indicate that both she and Mrs. Thompson were involved in the care of the girls, and of the household tasks. Mrs. Nassau was also training

68. Nassau, *Crowned*, 156.

69. Nassau, *Crowned*, 157.

70. Nassau, *Crowned*, 174.

71. Nassau, *Crowned*, 178.

72. Nassau, *Crowned*, 182.

73. Nassau, *Crowned*, 191–92.

74. Nassau, *Crowned*, 196.

a young male cook, and was occupied with food preparation.[75] On one occasion, Mary Nassau sent cook Ijabi to search for stones, "according to Mrs. Thompson's advice,"[76] and the three worked together to build a stone fireplace. Mary Nassau's letters also reveal Mrs. Thompson's willingness to adjust to her new environment, adapting familiar recipes to local products (such as making a cake from palm-oil) and trying an indigenous medicine for her toothache—and finding relief.[77]

Mrs. Thompson also seems to have established a warm relationship with persons in the local Benga community. Dr. Nassau's interpreter, Makendenge, provoked her fear of leopards by teasing her that they would "love the fat on her very much indeed."[78] According to Dr. Nassau, Makendenge was "a great friend of Mrs. Thompson." Apparently, many young local men had asked Makendenge if Mrs. Thompson intended to marry again. He discouraged them from asking so many questions, adding that "she would not have any of them; she would not marry in this part of the country, and if she did, it would be to no one but himself."[79]

Mrs. Thompson helped to care for the Nassaus' second baby, Paull,[80] who was born in July of 1866,[81] though she returned to Liberia in August, at the end of her two-year contract.[82] In a letter to her sister-in-law, dated Nov. 21, 1866, Mrs. Nassau stated that she would miss Mrs. Thompson, who had been "very faithful in all her allotted work," and joked that she would now have to do her own scolding, "instead of checking [Mrs. Thompson] for dealing reproofs on all sides with a very unsparing tongue."[83] Mrs. Nassau was then left with the care of her young infant, her "girls" and the household. In January 1867, Mrs. Nassau mentioned in a letter her three adolescent girls who "require a person to keep them in work and out of mischief, and I am the only person to watch them, and help the cook, etc."[84] This gives insight into the role filled by Mrs. Thompson in that household.

75. Nassau, *Crowned*, 197.

76. Nassau, *Crowned*, 197.

77. Nassau, *Crowned*, 199.

78. Nassau, *Crowned*, 201.

79. Nassau, *Crowned*, 201.

80. Nassau, George Paull, who died in May 1865 at Corisco.

81. Nassau, *Crowned*, 234.

82. Nassau, *Crowned*, 236.

83. Nassau, *Crowned*, 239.

84. Nassau, *Crowned*, 240.

Miss Louisa Carmey

Mrs. Nassau's papers also mention Louisa Carmey, a Liberian woman employed by the Clark family. The Clarks arrived with Louisa in May 1865, and left the field in March 1868,[85] due to their children's fragile health. It is not clear when Louisa's term of contract ended, but it appears that she had already left by 1868. Louisa seemed to have enjoyed a friendly relationship with both Mrs. Thompson and Mrs. Nassau.[86]

Mrs. Lavinia Sneed

After the departure of Mrs. Thompson, the Nassaus remained without household assistance until the following July, when another Liberian, Mrs. Lavinia Sneed, arrived with her daughter, Charity. Mary Nassau was delighted, and likely relieved, that she had come to assist with the baby and housework.[87]

The precious and rare details of Mrs. Sneed's early life are contained in a private letter written by missionary Laura Kreis Campbell, who served at the Baraka Station in the 1880s.

> She was born in America, both she and her husband were slaves, but with different masters. Mrs. Sneed's master set her free before the war, and also bought her husband's freedom. So we rightly judge that she was appreciated by her master. They immediately came to [Africa]. She spent most of her time after her arrival here in caring for missionaries and still continues in the service.[88]

Mrs. Sneed's presence in the household gave Mary Nassau both time and added strength to write, which she didn't have when she was "dependent on a few careless children for help about the house and baby."[89] The two women shared in the care of baby Paull, until his death, at age seventeen months, in December 1867. Mrs. Sneed also cared for baby Charley, who was born in late 1868.

Mary Nassau wrote to Mrs. Clark describing Mrs. Sneed as "a great comfort."[90] Both Mrs. Nassau and Mrs. Clark had faced crises as missionary

---

85. Nassau, *Crowned*, 303.
86. Nassau, *Crowned*, 199, 229.
87. Nassau, *Crowned*, 244.
88. Laura Campbell to the Family, December 21, 1881.
89. Nassau, *Crowned*, 246.
90. Nassau, *Crowned*, 288.

mothers, and both understood the value of a trustworthy and helpful *assistant*. Dr. Nassau's papers describe an incident where Mrs. Nassau, baby Charley and Mrs. Sneed were in a canoe, making the two-mile journey across the river to Bolondo station. The canoe was damaged and suddenly took on water. Mrs. Sneed held the baby above the inrushing water, "and sat helplessly praying"[91] as Mary Nassau stuffed the long gash with her shawl, and three boatmen tugged the swamped canoe to the shore.

MATERNITY NURSE

In January, 1870, Mrs. Sneed's role expanded beyond the Nassau household, when her expertise as a *maternity nurse* rendered her invaluable to the larger missionary community. Mary Nassau notes in a letter that her husband and Mrs. Sneed traveled to Corisco, while she and baby Charley remained at Benita "with the native children for assistants,"[92] Dr. Nassau went to Corisco for mission meetings, while Mrs. Sneed was needed to help Mrs. Menaul "until after her confinement."[93] While Mary Nassau knew she would be without Mrs. Sneed's valuable help for six weeks or more, she was concerned that Mrs. Menaul's health was poor, and she had "no good help."[94] Mrs. Menaul gave birth in early February 1870, and died two weeks later.[95] Mary Nassau noted that "Mrs. Sneed was a great comfort to [the Menauls], and it is a great comfort to me that we proposed her going."[96] Mrs. Nassau assumed full-time care of baby Bessie Menaul, while Mrs. Sneed resumed her charge of little Charley Nassau, until the newly-widowed Rev. Menaul and baby left two months later.[97]

In September 1870, Mrs. Nassau, herself, fell dangerously ill with fever. Dr. Nassau made the difficult decision to try to evacuate her by boat, on the open ocean, to either the Corisco or the Gaboon mission. In her delirium, Mary sparked to life, briefly, "when generosity spurred to an earnest charge for *the future care* of *a faithful nurse*,"[98] and also "when mother-love overheard and vetoed our intention of leaving behind two-year-old baby

91. Nassau, *Crowned*, 310.

92. Nassau, *Crowned*, 317.

93. Nassau, *Crowned*, 318.

94. Nassau, *Crowned*, 318.

95. BFM, "Recent Intelligence: Death of Missionaries," 129.

96. Nassau, *Crowned*, 326.

97. BFM, "Recent Intelligence, Notices [1870]," 177.

98. Nassau, *Crowned*, 338. Italics added.

Charley."[99] Both baby Charley, and his nurse, Mrs. Sneed, accompanied the Nassaus and their crew on this desperate journey. Mrs. Sneed held baby Charley in her arms in the open boat, while Mrs. Nassau lay unconscious under a makeshift shelter.[100] Mrs. Nassau died after midnight, and Dr. Nassau directed the boat crew to return to Benita. Mrs. Nassau was buried at the Benita cemetery, next to her second son, Paull. Mrs. Sneed cared for little Charley Nassau until his departure for America, months later. Her role as an employee of the Nassau family ended in 1871. Though she could have returned to Liberia, having many close friends there, Mrs. Sneed chose to remain with the mission, serving unofficially as an assistant. Her expanded role will be discussed further in the next chapter.

CHARITY SNEED—SECOND ASSISTANTSHIP (1868–1871)

It is not clear how long Charity remained in America with Mrs. Ogden, in 1861, but she was absent from the Corisco Mission for an extended period of time. Her name does not appear in mission Annual Reports for the years 1863–1869. She seems to have arrived with her mother, Mrs. Lavinia Sneed, in July 1867. At that time, Charity was designated to work for Mr. Clark,[101] perhaps to replace Louisa Carmey, though her role was unspecified.

Months later, in March 1868, Charity traveled with the Clark family as far as the Gaboon Mission. From there, the Clarks evacuated to America, for the sake of their children's health.[102] Charity remained at Gaboon for a short time, likely aiding with their work. Mrs. Lucina Bushnell, who was overseeing the Baraka girls' school, wrote to the Corisco mission to ask if Charity could remain with them. Charity, however, was expected to serve as teacher in the girls' school at Corisco, and returned to that ministry.[103]

Assistant to Miss Nassau

By August of 1868, Charity was associated with Miss Isabella Nassau, a new missionary and older sister of Dr. Nassau, who had come to the field to serve as a teacher and women's worker.[104] Miss Nassau wrote to the Board Secretary

99. Nassau, *Crowned*, 339.

100. Nassau, *Crowned*, 342.

101. Nassau, *Crowned*, 244.

102. William Walker, *Diary*, March 5–16, 1868.

103. William Walker, *Diary*, March 31, 1868.

104. Isabella Nassau to Dr. Lowrie, August 18, 1868.

that she was "thankful for the very efficient and devoted companionship in [the] work of Miss Charity Sneed, the Monrovian who has been so long in the employ of the mission."[105] At the time, Isabella Nassau was thirty-nine years old, and Charity was twenty-five. This relationship marked a significant turning point for Charity, as Miss Nassau recognized her potential, and accorded her greater autonomy, responsibility and recognition in her work. Miss Nassau, herself, was a strong-minded and independent woman, committed to the work of evangelism and discipleship.

After three months at the Girls' School at Corisco,[106] Miss Nassau and Miss Sneed transferred to join Dr. and Mrs. Nassau in the growing work on the mainland, at Benita station.[107] Six months later, they set up a separate ministry at the new station called Bolondo, two miles upriver from Benita.

It should be noted that *roles* of native mission workers were listed for each station, in the published Annual Report, but names were not given, with the exception of licentiate preachers. For the years 1868 and 1869, Charity—who was neither *missionary* nor *native*—was unnamed in the Annual Report, and her work not officially recognized. For example, the Annual Report for 1869 describes Miss Nassau's ministry work and relocation, but does not mention Charity Sneed by name. The mission roster simply states that the Reutlinger and Nassau couples and Miss Isabella Nassau were stationed at Benita, with "one native Christian teacher."[108]

Information on Charity's ministry is largely gleaned from unofficial records, particularly missionary correspondence to the Board, and published articles in the *Woman's Work for Woman* magazine, which show that Charity was present and actively engaged in the work of the mission, particularly in the years 1868–1871.

Personality and Character

Charity Sneed's personality and character emerge from a few anecdotal missionary stories, written in private journals and letters during the early years at Benita. Dr. Nassau wrote of a male intruder who entered their home while he was away. Mrs. Nassau was sleeping in her bedroom, and Charity was sleeping in the upstairs room with two native girls. Charity

105. Isabella Nassau to Dr. Lowrie, August 18, 1868.
106. Nassau, "Work for Corisco and Benita Women," 36.
107. Nassau, *Crowned*, 275.
108. BFM, *Annual Report* [1869], 18.

"woke suddenly, and saw a man's face at the head of the stairs; when he saw he was perceived he jumped down the stairs *and she after him*."[109] The intruder escaped and was never caught.

When newly-widowed Mrs. Reutlinger was reassigned to work with Miss Nassau at Bolondo, in 1869, a personality conflict developed between Charity and Mrs. Reutlinger. Both women were in their twenties, but Mrs. Reutlinger was particularly fragile, and described as "gentle" and "dependent" by her colleagues.[110] Dr. Nassau attributed the conflict to Charity's "unforgiving spirit," and her unwillingness to forget that "Mrs. R. had been the wife of one who at Corisco had assisted in perpetuating on her what I consider a piece of ecclesiastical wickedness."[111] Nassau gave no further explanation on the matter. Mrs. Reutlinger was soon transferred to Gaboon mission.

The published Annual Report for 1870, does not name Charity Sneed in the roster, but states that "Miss Isabella A. Nassau, and one Liberian assistant" were stationed at "Bolonda."[112] In her own report, Miss Nassau wrote that she was "assisted by a Liberia [*sic*] young woman of excellent character,"[113] and that they had opened up a school in May 1869, which had twelve resident pupils, and eight day students. The report stated that twelve women and girls had also been instructed in reading and sewing by Miss Charity Sneed,[114] while Miss Nassau was giving theological instruction to three young men. Shortly after this, Miss Nassau's health deteriorated. She and Charity journeyed to Old Calabar, to allow Miss Nassau to recruit her health. The two were guests of the Scotch Presbyterian Mission from December 1869 to March 1870.[115] Their absence necessitated the closing of the Bolondo School for that time.

Influence and Work

In July of 1870, Miss Nassau described their work in educating women and girls as the "first stage of society in this land" adding that it was "part of Charity Sneed's work and she has a good influence. I also make it part of

109. Nassau, *Crowned*, 283. Italics added.
110. Robert Hamill Nassau to Dr. Lowrie, April 6, 1870.
111. Robert Hamill Nassau to Dr. Lowrie, April 6, 1870.
112. BFM, *Annual Report* [1870], 19.
113. BFM, *Annual Report* [1870], 21.
114. BFM, *Annual Report* [1870], 22.
115. Nassau, *Crowned*, 317, 327.

mine."[116] Miss Nassau's handwritten 1870 Bolondo Report contained a brief description of their new outreach ministry:

> Added to the work of teaching in the school, we began, in May, a systematic visiting of the towns. Two afternoons a week were thus spent by Miss C. L. Sneed, the Monrovian assistant, in religious instruction in the towns, with the special hope of thus reaching the women. The effort proved increasingly interesting. The same kind of work was undertaken by the Benga assistant, Ijabi, though his teaching in the school prevented him from devoting more than one day in the week.[117]

Charity frequently appeared, without being named, in missionary publications. An example is taken from an article entitled, "The Work at Bolenda" [*sic*], published in the *Presbyterian Monthly Record*, and based on a letter written by Miss Nassau in September, 1869: "At Bolenda, Miss I. A. Nassau has the charge of a school and of other interesting efforts to spread a knowledge of our religion among the natives of this part of Africa. She is aided by an esteemed young woman of piety from Liberia, and by some native Christian helpers."[118]

The little school at Bolondo, which had resumed in April 1870, was suspended in September, when Miss Nassau returned to help her newly-widowed brother at Benita.[119] Dr. Nassau gave a gloomy report of the church at Benita, noting its being in a *low state*, with prominent church members falling into sin, small classes of inquirers, and poor reports from the native assistants.[120] Miss Nassau's report, however, describes a flourishing new work:

> Miss Nassau, Miss Sneed, her Monrovian assistant, and one of the native assistants, made visits to the native villages, extending on one occasion to a distance of thirty miles up the river, for the purpose of religious instruction. They were always well received, and

---

116. Isabella Nassau to Dr. Lowrie, July 11, 1870.

117. Isabella Nassau to Dr. Lowrie, September 28, 1870. Ijabi is likely the assistant who worked for Mary Nassau years earlier. This passage was later printed in the *Presbyterian Monthly Record*. See Nassau, "Bolenda School," 50.

118. BFM, "Work at Bolenda," 13.

119. BFM, *Annual Report* [1871], 34.

120. BFM, *Annual Report* [1871], 34.

interesting conversations were often held with people who had hardly ever before heard anything of the Gospel.[121]

Miss Isabella Nassau clearly gave Charity Sneed training, opportunity and recognition in her ministries of teaching and evangelism, while her brother, Dr. Nassau, simply referred to Charity as "an invaluable aid and most faithful *servant to sister*"[122] during this period.

MERGER WITH THE GABOON MISSION

The death of Mrs. Mary Latta Nassau, in September 1870, ended the tragic run of missionary deaths at Corisco 1869–70, but many more missionaries left the field in poor health, and those remaining were in need of rest and restoration. In late 1870, the missionary force was reduced to Dr. Nassau and Miss Isabella Nassau, aided by Mrs. Lavinia Sneed and Miss Charity Sneed. In 1870, both the ABCFM Gaboon Mission and the Presbyterian Corisco Mission faced an acute shortage of missionaries,[123] leading to the 1870–71 merger of the two missions, thus creating the Gaboon and Corisco Mission, under the direction of the Presbyterian Board of Foreign Missions. The Gaboon Mission had been reduced to the original station, at Baraka, with several outstations within a few miles. The Corisco Mission comprised the several stations on the island of Corisco, as well as the Benita and Bolondo stations, situated on the mainland.

---

121. BFM, *Annual Report* [1871], 34–35.

122. Robert Hamill Nassau to Dr. Lowrie, April 6, 1870.

123. Menaul, "Recent Intelligence," 10; BFM, "Recent Intelligence: Renewed Call," 105–6.

Mrs. Lavinia Sneed (Courtesy of Gault Family)

Mrs. Charity Sneed Menkel (Courtesy of Vincent Menkel)

Mrs. Mary Latta Nassau with Willie (Source: Teeuwissen website)

Dr. Robert Hamill Nassau (Courtesy of Amy Perry)

Cornelius and Reubina DeHeer (Courtesy of Holly Lemons)

Mrs. Louise Reutlinger (Courtesy of Laura O'Brien)

Miss Isabella Nassau (GAPC 1894, 70)

Rev. Graham and Laura Campbell and sons (Courtesy of Laura O'Brien)

5

Gaboon and Corisco Mission 1871–1895

OVERVIEW

AFTER TWO DECADES OF ministry, the Presbyterian Corisco Mission was decimated by missionary deaths and health crises. The ABCFM Gaboon Mission, by contrast, had not seen a missionary death in twelve years, yet their force was diminished due to chronic health issues and lack of new recruits. Only three seasoned couples remained at Baraka, in March 1864, and their number was reduced to two couples by June 1867.[1] The Bushnells departed for America in 1869, on a much-needed health furlough, leaving only the elderly and weakened Walker couple. Only Dr. Nassau and Miss Nassau remained at Corisco that year, assisted by Lavinia Sneed and her daughter, Charity.

The *Presbyterian Monthly Record* noted the merger of the two missions in mid-1870,[2] and continued to call for reinforcements at both their Gaboon and Corisco locations.[3] Dr. Nassau and his sister, Isabella transferred from Benita to the Gaboon (Baraka) mission station, which freed the Walkers to leave in March 1871, and left the Corisco-Benita work

---

1. Zorn, *Le Grand Siècle*, 84. Catholic mission schools saw tremendous growth as the ABCFM schools languished, under French colonial rule. Zorn credits the American Protestants for their prolific evangelism, translation work, and teaching in indigenous languages of Gabon.

2. GAPCUSA, *Minutes* [1871], 653. The official date of the merger was August 7, 1870.

3. BFM, "Renewed Call for Missionaries," 106; "Recent Intelligence: Gaboon Mission, 202.

"under the care of native assistants."[4] The Bushnells returned to Gaboon in mid-1871, having transferred from the ABCFM to the Presbyterian Board of Foreign Missions.[5]

Records indicate a high turnover of missionaries 1870–1880, primarily due to health concerns. A number of single women and a few couples came to the mission in that decade, though most lasted only a few years.

The severe shortage of foreign missionaries coincided with an increased reporting of the names and ministry efforts of the *native agency* associated with the mission. It was at this crucial time that the Presbytery of Corisco ordained Ibia J'Ikenge, in mid-1870, as their first indigenous minister of the Gospel. The published notice of his ordination stated, "In the absence of any other missionaries, he has now sole charge of the work on the Island of Corisco—a work altogether too great for him; indeed, one that has heretofore required the services of two missionaries from this country."[6] Dr. Nassau, in his 1888 historical overview of the Presbytery of Corisco, reveals that this landmark event was wrought with great hesitation, and only to preserve the Presbytery, in the absence of ordained missionary men.[7] Ibia had been a licentiate for a full ten years, prior to his ordination. Similar circumstances preceded the 1880 ordination of Ntâkâ (Toko) Truman, the son (or nephew) of the original Ntâkâ, mentioned in Chapter Two.

In the years following the merger, missionary losses allowed for greater contribution by, and recognition of, indigenous leadership. In an article published in the *Presbyterian Monthly Record*, Miss Isabella Nassau described the powerful praise and worship meeting at Benita station, followed by exhortation by their "very zealous and devoted elder, and also scripture reader or evangelist at Hanje, who has just returned from one of his long preaching journeys; weary enough in body, but refreshed in spirit."[8] Dr. Nassau also commented on the growth and health of the church that year at Corisco, and praised the newly-ordained Ibia and his wife, for their exemplary leadership and hospitality.[9]

4. BFM, "Mission House, June 25, 1871," 59.

5. GAPCUSA, *Minutes of the General Assembly* [1871], 652.

6. BFM, "Recent Intelligence: Ordination of a Native African" 225.

7. Nassau, *History of the Presbytery of Corisco*, 12. See also Hanciles, *Euthanasia*, 60. The CMS in Sierra Leone also ordained native men to fill needed numbers, though their role on the committee was *vestigial*.

8. Nassau, "Usual Prayer Meeting," 255.

9. Nassau, "Notices of Corisco and Benita Work," 278.

During this era, the Presbyterian Board appeared to be recruiting both white and black missionaries for Africa. The *Presbyterian Monthly Record* for February 1871 included their plea for more missionaries, particularly men, to be sent to Africa:

> It is chiefly the qualifications of health, mind and heart, and not complexion mainly, that we should consider in sending missionaries there. By all means let us send colored men, if we can find men of suitable qualifications, who are willing to go; but where shall we find them? In regard to health, however, it is a mistake to suppose that colored men from this country are exempt from acclimating fever, and from early death too often, when they go to Africa.[10]

As the two feeble missions united to economize resources and personnel, the Presbyterian Churches, "Old School" and "New School" were also reuniting for the same reasons, seeking healing and reconciliation after a long and bitter separation. The Board saw a direct connection between the unity of the Presbyterian churches in the United States, and the health of their overseas mission work; they encouraged churches to reconcile, reorganize and become self-reliant, that more funding be available for the support of foreign missions.[11]

The last quarter of the nineteenth century witnessed the sending of missionaries of color, particularly women, to fields in Africa—often with great celebration and generous support from women's organizations. Published reports and articles in missionary magazines give evidence that missionaries of color were both desired and needed in the work. Private correspondence, however, between the Gaboon and Corisco missionaries and the Board Secretary, reveals their discomfort and tensions regarding racial equality and inclusion in the mission hierarchy.

This era of the mission history offers the greatest detail in the lives and ministry of foreign-born persons of African descent, yet also reveals a "color line" within the mission, which was exposed, not by the foreign-born mission workers, but by the indigenous church leaders. Their indignant letters to the Presbyterian Board, in the 1870s and 1880s, protesting what they considered to be race-based discrimination, were followed by

10. BFM, "White and Colored Men Wanted," 48.

11. Board of Home Missions, "Union for Self-Support," 97. See also Brown, *One Hundred Years*, 216. There was a direct correlation between the reunion of the "Old School" and "New School" Presbyterians and the merger of the two missions into one Presbyterian work.

equally indignant letters, written in the mid-1890s by frustrated African American missionary candidates, and those who were preparing them for ministry in Africa.

MISSIONARY ASSISTANTS OF AFRICAN DESCENT

Despite the seeming openness to sending "colored brethren" to serve with the Gaboon and Corisco mission, only *one* African American man was sent, in 1872.

Mr. Wilber, Mission Boat Captain

Mr. W. R. Wilber was sent to the Gaboon and Corisco Mission to maintain and operate the mission cutter, which transported missionaries and goods between the Gaboon, Corisco and Benita/Bolondo mission stations. A brief notice, published in the 1872 Annual Report, described Mr. Wilber as a man of color and long-time sailor; he was a member of the Presbyterian Church of Superior, Wisconsin, and was highly recommended by his pastor. Mr. Wilber was to be employed on the mission vessel, *Elfe*, and was motivated to join the Presbyterian Mission "from a desire to do good to the people of his own race, especially in their spiritual interests.[12]

Within six months of Mr. Wilber's arrival, missionaries wrote to the Board Secretary, expressing their concern that Mr. Wilber, though pious, was deaf, and that his previous experience had been as a cook on a trading ship, and not as captain.[13] A brief update in the 1873 Annual Report, stated that "Mr. Wilder [*sic*] was not found to be well-suited to the care of the mission schooner, *Elfe*, and he will return to this country, still having the kind regards of all who know him."[14]

At least four women of African descent maintained consistent, long-term roles as mission assistants in various departments of the work. Three were Americo-Liberian: Warnetta (Wânâ) Alvarez, Charity Sneed and her mother, Lavinia Sneed; the fourth was Bessie Makae, who was said to be West African Kroo.[15] Though none of the four women were formally appointed, they filled vital roles in the mission and local churches, and

12. BFM, *Annual Report* [1872], 39.

13. Albert Bushnell to Dr. Lowrie, July 5, 1872; Samuel Gillespie to Dr. Lowrie, August 9, 1872; Samuel Murphy to Dr. Lowrie, August 1, 1872.

14. BFM, *Annual Report* [1873], 33.

15. Parsons, *Life for Africa*, 62.

received little or no recognition in the historical record. Yet, their work spanned decades, and touched the lives of countless others in that international community.

Warnetta Alvarez

Warnetta Alvarez came to Gaboon from Liberia, in 1860, with the Rev. William Walker and his wife, Catherine. She seemed to have been informally adopted by the Walkers, who had no children of their own.[16] Dr. Robert Hamill Nassau, however, described her as being "in Mrs. Walker's service."[17]

In 1868, when Wânâ was likely still in her teens, she was the subject of salacious rumors along the beach, among the white men who were involved in commercial trade. Rev. Walker considered this to be a "great catastrophe which had happened at Baraka."[18] Yet, he stood up for Wânâ, and sought to protect her honor in the community; he also used the occasion to lecture the young men on their sinful attitudes toward women, in general. His discourse included a direct accusation that they "had determined beforehand that a person who has any tinge of African pedigree has no rights which a white man is bound to respect."[19]

When the elderly Walkers returned to the United States for a needed rest, in 1871, Wânâ likely travelled with them. The Walkers eventually settled permanently in the state of Wisconsin, while Wânâ returned to Gaboon in mid-1873, in the company of two new single women missionary teachers. A brief notice in the *Presbyterian Monthly Record* reported on the departure of the three women, noting the names and sending churches of the two missionaries, and adding that a "young Liberian woman, Miss Warnetta Alvarez, who has been in this country for a year received a good part of her education in the mission school, accompanied them, expecting to be useful in the same school in that place."[20]

In the year following Warnetta's return to Gaboon, the mission built a new seminary building for the girls' school, which gave instruction to forty pupils. The school flourished under the care of missionaries Mrs. Lucina Bushnell and Miss Lydia Jones, who were "assisted by a native

16. Nassau, *Crowned*, 287; William Walker, *Diary*, January 4, 1869.

17. Nassau, *Crowned*, 287.

18. William Walker, *Diary*, September 20, 1868. Other diary entries indicate that Wânâ actively pursued these attentions, and the rumors were likely substantiated.

19. William Walker, *Diary*, dated September 20, 1868.

20. BFM, "Notices of Missionaries [1873]," 153.

teacher, and the last half year with Warnetta Alvarez as matron."[21] That year, Warnetta was appropriated a salary of $60.00, which was given through the Woman's Foreign Missionary Society of the Presbyterian Church, by the Troy Church Auxiliary Society in Ohio.[22] Three years later, in 1876, the same auxiliary society sent a donation of $40.00 towards her support.[23] The initials "B. R." after her name may indicate that she was serving as Bible Reader at that time.

Though "Wânâ" was virtually invisible in official mission reports, she was mentioned many times throughout Rev. Walker's diary, especially in his lists of regular communicants of the church at Baraka. Wânâ had come to the mission from Liberia, yet Rev. Walker referred to her as one of the "native members of the church."[24] She seemed to disappear from the mission record and church roll sometime in the mid-1870s, while she was still a young woman. There is no reference to her marrying within the community or leaving Gaboon; neither is there mention of her in Walker's journal during his extended stay at Gaboon in the early 1880s.

Mrs. and Miss Sneed: Integral Mission Roles

Mrs. Sneed eventually left Dr. Nassau's employ in early 1871, and joined her daughter and Miss Nassau in their work at Benita.[25] However, both Nassaus left for furlough in the United States in late 1871.

Correspondence with the Board

Just prior to the Nassaus' departure, Charity Sneed wrote to the Corresponding Secretary, Dr. Lowrie, to express her sincere appreciation and admiration for Miss Isabella Nassau, and to describe her ministry and simple lifestyle at Bolondo. She also recognized Dr. Nassau's kindness and devotion to the work in Africa.[26] Having met Dr. Lowrie during her stay in the US ten years earlier, in the company of Mrs. Ogden, Charity addressed him with warmth and familiarity. It is the one known letter in the mission correspondence archives, handwritten by Charity Sneed.

21. BFM, "Gaboon and Corisco Mission, 1873," 176.
22. WFMSPCUSA, "Receipts, April 7, 1873," 127.
23. WFMSPCUSA, "Receipts, February 1, 1876," 58.
24. William Walker, *Diary*, September 28, 1868.
25. Bushnell, "Arrival at Gaboon," 306.
26. Charity Sneed to Dr. Lowrie, October 31, 1871.

OFFICIAL RECOGNITION BY THE WOMAN'S FOREIGN
MISSIONARY SOCIETY

From the time the two women began working together, in 1868, Miss Nassau was intentional about highlighting Charity's work and accomplishments in her own reports. Prior to her departure for America, in 1871, Miss Nassau also "introduced" Presbyterian women readers to Charity Sneed, whom she described as "a young colored woman from Monrovia, a devoted Christian, who has lived with me during my residence in Africa, is employed by the mission, and goes to the towns and talks with and instructs them. She speaks the native language well, and understands the customs of the people".[27]

Miss Nassau explained that the work is often interrupted, due to the many missionary deaths and absences in the past ten years. Though they did not have a white missionary to superintend the work at Corisco mission, there were several "most capable Christian women,"[28] who had been educated and trained in the mission school in the past decade. At the end of her letter, Miss Nassau returned to the subject of Charity Sneed, describing her work as Bible Reader: "With Benga Scriptures and primer and hymnbook in her satchel, she goes from house to house. This is her afternoon work; in the mornings the women come to her to have their sewing cut out and basted, and she teaches them to sew. They are very apt as a rule in learning both letters and sewing."[29]

The Women's Foreign Mission Society supported the work of missionary women and indigenous workers, giving them both recognition and "voice" in their magazine, *Woman's Work for Woman*, which was first published in 1871. The rich details of Charity Sneed's ministry throughout the 1870s were shared with the readers of this magazine, while the published Annual Reports for the Gaboon and Corisco Mission largely overlooked her work.

OFFICIAL RECOGNITION IN ANNUAL REPORTS

In late 1871, two new missionary couples, Kops and Murphy, arrived at Benita to serve in theological educational and women's ministries, replacing Dr. Nassau and Miss Isabella Nassau. Charity remained with the two

27. Nassau, "Letter from Miss I. A. Nassau," 102.
28. Nassau, "Letter from Miss I. A. Nassau," 103.
29. Nassau, "Letter from Miss I. A. Nassau," 103.

new couples at Benita/Bolondo. The Annual Report for 1872 recognizes Charity Sneed by name, and describes her role as *aid to Miss Isabella Nassau*. However, Rev. Samuel Murphy gave special mention to her work in his own written report, noting that in Miss Nassau's absence, Miss Charity L. Sneed had conducted the Bolondo School with good success.[30]

EXTENDED ABSENCE FROM THE MISSION

The Sneeds also took time away from their mission work, leaving in November 1871 for an extended visit to Liberia.[31] Charity was now twenty-nine, and had been assisting Miss Nassau for more than three years, in evangelization and teaching ministries. Mrs. Sneed, who had originally come to serve as caregiver for the Nassau children, seemed to have become indispensable as a nurse/midwife at the mission, if informally. Both Mrs. Kops and Mrs. Murphy became pregnant within six months their arrival to the field. Anticipating Mrs. Sneed's return from Liberia in July of 1872, both women were counting on her to help them during their *confinement*. When Mrs. Sneed's visit in Liberia extended beyond the anticipated date of return, Rev. Kops and Rev. Murphy made the difficult decision to send their wives back to the US, lacking confidence in the French physician available at Gaboon. Rev. Albert Bushnell lamented the loss of these valuable women, but understood the choice to err on the side of caution.[32]

STEPPING UP

Though Mrs. Kops and Mrs. Murphy departed for the US, their husbands would remain at the Benita mission station. Rev. Bushnell, in a letter published in the *Presbyterian Monthly Record*, noted that the mission expected Mrs. Sneed and Miss Charity Sneed to join the two missionary men at Benita when they return from Monrovia."[33] The occasion of their return, in late 1872, was published in the Gaboon and Corisco Mission Annual Report, which mentioned *Mrs. Sneed* for the first and only time: "Since the return of Mrs. and Miss Sneed at Benita last October, the influence

---

30. BFM, *Annual Report* [1872], 41.

31. Jones, "Extracts," 242–43. The Sneeds returned to the mission in September 1872.

32. Albert Bushnell to Dr. Lowrie, July 5, 1872.

33. Bushnell, "Excerpt, July 11, 1872," 312.

among the females, which was lost by the departure of Mrs. Murphy and Mrs. Kops, is being regained."[34]

In these two instances, Mrs. and Miss Sneed are mentioned as *integral* (if not appointed) members of the mission community, whose roles are crucial to the ongoing ministry, and not directly subordinate to a particular missionary.

Charity Sneed as Missionary to Benga Women

During the two years of Miss Nassau's absence in America, Charity Sneed emerged as an independent worker, whose ministry was a vital and necessary part of the mission work at Benita. For those two years, 1872 and 1873, "Charity L. Sneed" is listed in the mission roster at the beginning of the Annual Report, and not categorized as an *assistant*.[35] By this time, she had gained proficiency in teaching, preaching, literacy training and women's ministry, raising her to a practical level of missionary, even if she had not been formally appointed. She was now a mature woman of thirty, who had gained the trust and respect of her host community.

Mrs. Sophia Murphy had known and observed Charity Sneed's work at Benita for several months prior to Charity's departure for Liberia. In a letter published in *Woman's Work for Woman*, in May 1873, Mrs. Murphy marveled at the changes evident among the new believers at Benita (in late 1871), as many women were now adopting the Christian mode of dress and coming daily to Miss Charity Sneed for sewing instruction. "Miss Charity is a young colored woman from Monrovia, and lived with Miss Nassau. She is a true missionary, does much good among the women, and they all respect her."[36]

In the absence of their wives, Rev. Murphy and Rev. Kops continued the work, though both returned to the United States, after only two to three years of service. Kops departed for America in April 1873. Murphy "was then left alone, having the assistance of Miss Charity L. Sneed, who continued her work among the women with very great encouragement."[37] Murphy appreciated Charity's impact in the community, and her having won their trust: "Miss Charity Sneed has instructed the women in reading and

---

34. BFM, Annual Report [1873], 36.
35. BFM, *Annual Report* [1872], 38; *Annual Report* [1873], 33.
36. Murphy, "Extracts, January 19, 1873," 87.
37. Murphy, "Benita," 177.

sewing, and has had several girls under her care. The people are anxious and willing to send their girls to the mission."

"Bible-Reader"

At the encouragement of Miss Nassau, Charity wrote a letter to potential sponsors in the United States, giving them a vivid description of her work as Bible-woman and women's worker, at Benita. It was published in *Woman's Work for Woman*, along with a brief introduction: "Letter from Charity L. Sneed, *a native Bible-reader*, to the Martin Luther Mission Band, Wheeling, West Virginia."[38]

> Dear ladies: Miss Bella [Nassau] told me of your desire to support a Bible-woman in the Corisco Mission, also that you would like her to write you sometimes. As my work here agrees with it more than that of any one else connected with the mission, I shall feel very glad to do so as long as I am living at Benita, and thank you very much for your very kind interest. But I feel almost afraid to undertake it, fearing my description may not prove satisfactory to you. I hope that the love to Jesus prompts me in doing my work. It has been my custom for some time to visit the women in their different towns. I at first tried to get them to come every afternoon to the mission-house and let me teach them, but they did not continue this long, giving many excuses for not coming. I now go to them. Some are glad to see me and try to learn their letters [;] others will not try, as they say they cannot see. I also read to them from one of the Gospels and a hymn-book in the Benga language. Generally they are very quiet until I have finished, then they say, "You must come often, we like to hear, but are too tired to walk to you after we come from our gardens. We have so many things to do" . . . I could add many other incidents, but there is only a short time before the letters are to be sent. Please allow me to add that these poor dark sisters are very, very ignorant and miserable. My heart aches for them. Will you not, dear ladies, pray for them and for me, that the little I try to do for them may be blest in leading many of them to light, to heaven? Yours, gratefully, Charity L. Sneed.[39]

38. Sneed, "Africa: Bolonda-Letter," 159.

39. Sneed, "Africa: Bolonda-Letter," 159, 160. See also Bliss, *Missionary Enterprise*, 88–89, 160; also, Pruitt, *Looking Glass*, 1. Nineteenth-century women's work in India, China, and Muslim countries described women's suffering, resulting in greater interest and support from American women, and a significant "feminizing" of the nineteenth century mission movement.

As per Miss Nassau's recommendation, the "Martin Luther Band" of the Second Church at Wheeling, sponsored Charity for the next several years, at $60 per year,[40] which was likely half of her yearly salary.

BREACHING BARRIERS—1870s

The chronic health problems and high attrition rate of appointed missionaries, during the 1870s, gave way for the promotion and empowerment of *native agency*, the stated goal of the both missions. The historic ordination of Ibia J'Ikenge, in 1870, would finally end the clergy/laity division that prevailed between the mission and the native church, a division which Pastor Ibia believed was perpetuated by racial discrimination. This race-based separation in the Christian community was further breached with the interracial marriage of Charity Sneed and Peter Menkel, both American-born mission workers. That same decade, there was a concurrent breach in the gender barrier, as female mission workers took on roles traditionally limited to ordained men. All three breaches served to destabilize the mission power structure which had long prevented the development and consecration of native leaders, and the ultimate goal of an autonomous indigenous church.

Breaching Barriers—Native Clergy

For several years, particularly since the long-delayed ordination of the first indigenous pastor, Rev. Ibia J'Ikenge, there were racial tensions between local Christians and certain missionaries. While such tensions may have been brewing during the early decades of both the Gaboon and the Corisco Missions, there is no documentation on the subject. The events in the first decade of the combined Gaboon and Corisco Mission brought these tensions to the surface, and opened a frank conversation between the Board, the Mission and local Church leaders.

CRITICISM OF MISSION HIERARCHY

When Rev. Cornelius DeHeer returned from furlough in 1872, he was uncomfortable in his *subordinate position* to Rev. Ibia, who had been placed in charge of the Corisco mission during DeHeer's absence.[41] DeHeer, who

40. WFMSPC, "Appropriations," 360; "Receipts, Feb, 1874," 76; "Receipts, March, 1876," 91.

41. Albert Bushnell to Dr. Lowrie, July 5, 1872.

had long mentored Ibia, asked that Ibia be relocated to another mission site, and that his place be given to a white missionary. Ibia, frustrated after serving nearly two decades with the mission, spoke out against the mission's hierarchy. In a letter to the mission, forwarded to the Board Secretary by Rev. Samuel Murphy,[42] Ibia stated that he desired to be "the slave of no missionary,"[43] adding,

> I do not know whether it is the rule of the mission that black men
> [should] be in perpetual pupilage to white men. I know that it is
> the rule of some Missionaries and some have no sympathy in it.
> Some of you teach plainly that the training up of native laborers
> the aim should not be to govern them perpetually like children or
> let them be as dependent as children, but while governing them
> for a season to develop their manliness and self-dependence, teach
> them what and how they ought to do and then tell them to work
> in Jesus. Depending on him for every needed help and hold them-
> selves responsible . . . to him! This is sound and scriptural.[44]

In the latter portion of this same letter, Ibia remarked that he had been "in the Old School Experience some years,"[45] indicating his familiarity with controversies within the Presbyterian Church in America. In this instance, Ibia implied a relationship between the mission's apparent race-based subordination to Old School Presbyterianism,[46] which did not support social equality for blacks, though it asked Christians to be "pitiful" and "courteous" toward them.[47] Five years later, Ibia continued to discuss this subject in his correspondence to the Board Secretary, expressing his confidence that Dr. Lowrie would act fairly towards the indigenous church, and "adopt a course that tends to secure the great, single and ultimate aim of all missionary efforts, the establishment of an *independent, self-sustaining and self-propagating Christianity*,"[48] indicating both his knowledge and approval of the original mission goal of church autonomy.

42. Samuel Murphy to Dr. Lowrie, September 3, 1872.

43. Ibia J'Ikenge to the Mission [Dr. Lowrie], 1872.

44. Ibia J'Ikenge to the Mission [Dr. Lowrie], 1872.

45. Ibia J'Ikenge to the Mission [Dr. Lowrie], 1872.

46. See Moore, "Black Presbyterian Clergy," 54. Archives of black Presbyterian leaders show that both slavery and theological concerns were the basis for the schism between "Old School" and "New School" Presbyterianism, and that Black clergy were as divided as Whites on the issues.

47. BFM, "Negro Race," 170. See also Schweitzer, *On the Edge*, 131–35.

48. Ibia J'Ikenge to Dr. Lowrie, August 8, 1877. Italics added.

SUPPORT OF WOMEN'S MINISTRY

Pastor Ibia championed the work of both native and missionary women workers, and expressed a desire for a female missionary presence at Corisco, to build up the ministry among women. Ibia opened a direct line of communication and collaboration with women's mission organizations in America, likely through the liaison of Miss Isabella Nassau. Ibia's 1872 invitation indicates not only his openness to working collaboratively with white missionaries, but also with women as full colleagues in the work: "Tell the ladies that we are ready to welcome them and to give them the right hand of fellowship to take part of this work with us . . . ..Tell them to come and help to destroy the works of the Devil."[49] Two lady missionaries arrived five months later, and were stationed at Corisco, but both left the field after a short duration, due to failing health. One of the ladies, Sadie Hendricks, stated that Ibia was doing all he could to keep the girls' school going, and to keep the female missionaries there at Corisco. She affirmed that the mission showed more interest in educating and building up *young men* and that the men were "in their shortsightedness, very indifferent to the advancement of women."[50] The local men also feared that their women would become dissatisfied with their position.

VOTING POWER

Just two years after the combined mission ordained its first native pastor, Rev. Bushnell expressed concern to the Secretary of the Board that if native pastors became a majority, *they might out-vote the missionaries*.[51] He also reported the "ambition" of the local Christians (at Corisco) to do their own Mission work, as well as their "obstinacy" [sic] in refusing the missionaries' advice.[52] According to Bushnell, Rev. Ibia was leading this movement.

Rev. Bushnell expressed similar concern to the Board Secretary, a year later, when the mission was considering allowing unmarried lady missionaries to vote, as well as attend the session meetings. Bushnell feared that this looked "too much like the women's rights movement at home and might lead to trouble in the future, you might by mistake send us some strongminded women, I fear there is in some cases a tendency for

49. Ibia J'Ikenge to the Mission [Dr. Lowrie], 1872. See also Hill, *World*, 46.
50. Sarah Hendricks to Dr. Lowrie, August 1, 1873. Italics added.
51. Albert Bushnell to Dr. Lowrie, June 17, 1872. Italics added.
52. Albert Bushnell to Dr. Lowrie, October 30, 1872.

ladies sent out by the Ladies' Boards to feel that they are independent of the Mission and the Board."[53]

For a brief period in the 1870s, the mission hierarchy was challenged by both independent native leadership and a number of equally independent women missionaries who appeared to work collaboratively in evangelism, education and women's ministry, even as the male missionaries lamented their weak influence and poor progress in the work.

When Miss Isabella Nassau returned from her furlough in 1873, she and Charity Sneed resumed their collaborative ministry at the Benita Station. That year, several missionaries left the field, largely for health reasons. The mission also welcomed a number of new missionaries, including Mr. Peter Menkel, a lay missionary appointed to serve as captain of the mission schooner, and Rev. William Schorsch, who would be stationed at Benita with the Misses Nassau and Sneed.[54]

Breaching Barriers—A Mixed Marriage

Charity Sneed had been serving with the Corisco mission (on and off) some fifteen years when Peter Menkel was appointed to the Gaboon and Corisco mission, in mid-1873.[55] Peter was in his early twenties, and had apparently been counseled by the Board Secretary to find a suitable helpmate. Just five months after leaving New York, Peter wrote to him to announce that he had found such a person:

> one who would not be a drawback on me in regard to the work and learning of the language, of which you were afraid I would do (marry some young lady before I came out). I did not do that, but am about to marry a Lady here (the 25th of December, 73) who will not be a drawback to me either in the language or work, as She has the first, as to the second has been brought up in it, *the care and work in some measure have been left to Her charge, nor is the number few of those who give a great deal to Her judgment*

53. Albert Bushnell to Dr. Lowrie, September 22, 1874. See Beaver, *American Protestant Women*, 108. Women's Mission Boards raised great sums of money, supported single missionary women and the work of indigenous church workers throughout the world. This movement was a threat to the major boards, which sought to either subordinate or absorb the women's societies.

54. BFM, *Annual Report of the Board* [1874], 27–29.

55. BFM, "Recent Intelligence [1873]," 221. Peter Menkel left the US in May 1873. He was a member of the South Third Street Presbyterian Church in Williamsburg, Long Island.

and care, one who has been the Companion to Miss Bella Nassau for a long time, and is well known by Her, it is Miss Charity Loisa Sneed, of Benita.[56]

Despite Charity's longstanding service with the mission, and the respect that she had earned from her missionary co-laborers, the scandal of an interracial marriage caused great consternation in the mission community. The couple may have been dissuaded for a time, as the December marriage date was not realized. Months later, in March 1874, missionary Albert Bushnell, of Gaboon, wrote to the Board Secretary:

> We learn incidentally that Mr. Menkel against the well-known wish of almost every member of the Mission . . . married Charity Sneed!! He was at Corisco, expecting to come up here next week on business, but of what kind I know not—Our Ladies are concerned lest the evil will not cease there, from some intimations they have heard. If our German brethren have come out here to establish this leveling of all . . . distinctions it is a sad pity that they ever came, for they will not only destroy their own influence, but imperil that of others. Already some of our native young men as a consequence and say they are then equal . . . begin to demand the same salary. The influence here has been evil and only evil. But I have not time to write more, I think you will have to write very plainly against these radical ideas.[57]

Here, Bushnell not only reveals perceived superior-inferior relationship between foreign missionaries and their native co-laborers, but also implies that Mr. Menkel is of higher status than Charity Sneed. As both were American-born, and had had at least a common education, this status difference seems to be purely based on ethnicity.[58]

Bushnell did not clarify his reference to the "German brethren," but there had been interracial marriages between German missionary men and women of African heritage in the Basel Mission at Accra, two decades earlier.[59]

56. Peter Menkel to Dr. Lowrie, October 29, 1873.

57. Albert Bushnell to Dr. Lowrie, March 1874.

58. See Bucher, *Two Women*, 9. Mrs. Bushnell told a young Mpongwe woman that it was wrong for blacks and whites to marry; the woman then refused an offer of marriage, believing Mrs. B. would not consent.

59. Both Menkel and Schorsch were German-American. See also Predelli and Miller, "Piety and Patriarchy," 84–85. The Basel Mission was likewise uncomfortable with the marriage of Johannes and Catherine Zimmerman, in the mid-nineteenth century,

POTENTIAL "CONSEQUENCES" OF THE MENKEL MARRIAGE

American fears over interracial marriage had peaked during the civil war years, a decade earlier, and many believed such unions to be a violation of nature, and socially abhorrent for both races.[60] In his remarks to the Board Secretary, Bushnell correlated interracial marriage with the threat of economic and political equality between the two races. This, too, was a prevalent notion of the time.[61] Bushnell later met with Peter Menkel, who was visiting the mission station. In a letter to the Board Secretary, Bushnell reported on their conversation, noting that Menkel

> said it was done hastily as they did not intend it three or four days before but they found the people were talking about them and I told him that while we all disapproved of, and regretted it, we would say nothing; but make the best of it we could since it was done. In reply to Mr. Schorsch's announcement that he had had the pleasure of marrying them, I replied that I did not see how it could have been a pleasure to do what he must have known would have been a doubtful pleasure to every member of the mission and of the Board, and to our patrons generally, we hope the innovation will not be made a precedent. Mr. M. has placed himself on a level with the natives, in public estimation; some of whom before considered themselves his equals, which caused no little friction between them and him.[62]

Bushnell added that Charity had her work and a salary of $120 at the Benita station; Menkel's salary was $400, which was more than adequate for them; Bushnell was certain that "if their salary should be changed by this union, it would give dissatisfaction and trouble here."[63]

Though missionary marriages on the field were typically included in Annual Reports, the Menkel marriage was not mentioned in the Annual Report for 1874–75. Subsequent reports would include Peter Menkel in the

---

indicating that Europeans also felt strongly on the matter of mixed marriages. Peter Menkel visited Accra in March 1883, and met the biracial adult children of Zimmermann, one of three Basel missionary men who had married interracially. Menkel diary entry for March 29, 1883, Accra, Ghana.

60. Walker, "Walker's Appeal," 19; Anonymous, "Amalgamation, Part 2," 102; Bryce, "Thoughts," 644, 651.

61. Lemire, "Miscegenation," 2.

62. Albert Bushnell to Dr. Lowrie, April 10, 1874.

63. Albert Bushnell to Dr. Lowrie, April 10, 1874.

mission roster, but Charity was never again listed by name, neither was her work mentioned in the body of the report.[64]

Breaching Barriers—Women in Men's Work

While Pastor Ibia welcomed missionary women as co-laborers in the ministry, many of the missionary men expressed despair and frustration that there were comparatively few male missionary recruits. By necessity, some missionary women took on responsibilities that were traditionally limited to ordained men. Rev. Schorsch expressed his disapproval that Miss Isabella Nassau was training native men for church leadership. During this same time period, Rev. Albert Bushnell expressed his reluctance to take a much-needed health furlough, as his departure would necessitate leaving his work, cares and responsibilities "*to the Ladies* and the Lord."[65]

Rev. Schorsch, who described himself as an "extreme German" in the gender debate, soon found himself at odds with his two co-laborers, Miss Nassau and Mrs. Menkel, whom he regarded as "high-styled American ladies."[66]

SETTING PRECEDENCE—A MISSIONARY FAMILY

The Menkels welcomed their first child, Katie, in March, 1875, a year after their marriage. Dr. Nassau attended the birth, and likely performed her baptismal ceremony in July 1875.[67] A second child, Alec, was born a year or so later. Two more daughters would be added in the coming years.

Charity and Peter Menkel were the first missionary couple, in the history of both the Gaboon and Corisco Missions, to successfully raise their small children on the mission field in Africa. The high mortality rate for missionary mothers and their babies caused missionary families to leave the field when they began to have children, or to send their children home to America, to be cared for by others. Though the Menkels are not credited

---

64. The 1875, 1879, 1880, 1881 annual reports listed "Peter Menkel *and his wife*" in the roster (BFM 1875, 26; 1879, 30; 1880, 26; 1881, 31). The reports for years 1876–1878 listed only Peter Menkel, eliminating Charity and her work altogether (BFM 1876, 27; 1877, 27; 1878, 29).

65. Albert Bushnell to Dr. Lowrie, July 5, 1875.

66. William Schorsch to Dr. Lowrie, June 20, 1874. See also Ibia J'Ikenge to Letter to Dr. Lowrie, August 8, 1877. Schorsch was recalled in 1875. Ibia J'Ikenge attributed it to Schorsch's not getting along with the women, and causing division at Benita.

67. Menkel, *Diary*, March 12, 1875 (birth) and July 15th 1875 (baptism).

with the remarkable "first," it is noteworthy that missionary couples began to have, *and keep*, their small children with them on the mission field, beginning in the early 1880s.

The Menkels seemed to have a warm relationship with their fellow laborers, especially with Miss Nassau and Miss Dewsnap, who were stationed nearby and enjoyed visits with the Menkel children.[68]

Maternity and Ministry

After her marriage to Peter Menkel, Charity kept up her ministry activities, and received both recognition and support from the *Women's Foreign Missionary Society*, as a "Bible Reader," a role that was generally filled by native evangelists.[69] Miss Dewsnap and the Menkel family were serving at Benita, with full approval and cooperation from the local community, whose king and headmen expressed a willingness to help the two women missionaries, though they were waiting for a white gentleman to come.[70] While Peter was a white man, he was not an ordained missionary.

Miss Nassau continued to give recognition and validity to Charity's work, and a positive perspective on the development of *native agency*. In an 1879 letter published in *Woman's Work for Woman*, Isabella described her visit to the Bolondo Girls' School:

> Mrs. Charity Menkel has had entire charge of the school since February 14 of this year [1878]. She began with four pupils; Charles G. Makâmgâ, one of my best pupils, who is an enthusiastic teacher, was appointed her assistant. The number of permanent pupils is now 12, and from far and near there is increased desire on the part of the people to send more. Mrs. Menkel, you recollect, was supported before her marriage under the name of Miss Charity L. Sneed, by the "Martin Luther Band," of Wheeling W. Virginia . . . I was greatly surprised and delighted with the progress, not only in the native language among the pupils, but also in English reading and writing. But this will interest you less than what I may say of the prayerful spirit of these little girls.

68. Peter Menkel, *Diary*, various entries mention Charity and the children visiting Miss Nassau (January 10, 1879), and Miss Dewsnap visiting the children (January 25, 1879).

69. WFMSCPC, *Seventh Annual Report* [1877], 41. Charity was supported in 1877 by the Henderson Band, Wilkinsburg, Pennsylvania.

70. Nassau, "Kombe Licentiate Preacher [Extract of Miss Nassau's Letter]," 151.

When Charles told me of their prayer meeting by themselves, I thought, dear little seekers after Jesus![71]

Charity's commitment, competence and autonomy in the women's ministry freed Miss Nassau from that work, and allowed her to give focused and consistent effort to the training of indigenous pastors and teachers at Bolondo.[72]

UNREMARKED

Charity Sneed Menkel's ministry likely continued through 1881,[73] though she was unnamed and unrecognized in the Annual Reports from 1874 until her death in 1882. Other sources, published after Charity's death, also exclude her. One notable example is a list of Gaboon and Corisco missionaries for the years 1871–1883, published by The Presbyterian Board. In this document, Charity is neither mentioned as the unmarried Miss Charity Sneed, nor the married Mrs. Charity Menkel, though she had served with the mission during ten of those twelve years.[74] Her husband, Peter Menkel was included in the list.

Mrs. Lavinia Sneed's role was also unspecified for the period of the 1870s, except for the references to her helping Charity and Miss Nassau in their work, or her potential role as midwife for the missionary women. There were no missionary babies born on the field during the 1870s, with the exception of three of the four Menkel children. It is likely that Mrs. Sneed remained near her daughter and her growing family during that period. Those missionaries whose journals trace her movements were either absent (Rev. Walker) or had relocated to another mission location (Dr. Nassau), or had not yet arrived to the field (Laura Campbell). As Mrs. Sneed was an unofficial member of the mission, her name did not appear in the Annual Reports or other published documents.

1880s—DIVERSITY AND CONFLICT

The decade of the 1880s saw a dramatic increase in missionary families, as couples arrived, and single men and women married on the field. These couples would remain on the field much longer than their predecessors,

71. Nassau, "News from the Field," 407–8.
72. Nassau, "News from the Field," 408.
73. Reutlinger, "Appended Report," 200.
74. BFM, *Annual Report* [1883], 175.

allowing them to invest more fully in the ministry, and with greater confidence. For the first time, the mission received a college-educated single woman of mixed racial heritage as an appointed missionary. Her coming coincided with sweeping French colonial restrictions on mission education, and growing tensions between local church leaders and the mission on matters of equality and autonomy.

Extended Missionary Families

Like the Presbyterian [Corisco] mission families of the 1860s, this generation of missionary couples chose to remain on the field for pregnancy and childbirth, though they did not recruit Liberian women to care for their children. Curiously, this vital role was filled informally by the older missionary widows, who were stationed with young families, giving them support in both their household and ministry responsibilities. Mrs. Lucina Bushnell and Mrs. Phebe Ogden gave significant amounts of time and energy to the children of their colleagues, their roles looking very much like those of the Liberian women who came in the 1860s.

Lavinia Sneed as "Maternity" Nurse

As families increased, Mrs. Sneed once again became a midwife/nurse to expectant and new mothers. Dr. and Mrs. Bacheler were expecting their first child in late 1881; his wife having already suffered one miscarriage, Dr. Bacheler felt that Mrs. Sneed's presence was needed.[75] He arranged to have her relocate to their remote interior mission station, Kangwe, where she cared for Mrs. Bacheler during her last trimester of pregnancy and first few months of motherhood. A month prior to the baby's arrival, Mrs. Sneed also helped to nurse missionary Susanna Dewsnap during a fatal case of "African Fever."[76]

Private missionary letters and journals give insight into Mrs. Sneed's social position within the mission family. Mrs. Laura Campbell, who served in the early 1880s, mentions her periodically, and always within the context of warm fellowship and hospitality. In late 1881, she wrote in a letter that "Mrs. Sneed nursed Mrs. Nassau and her children over fifteen years ago, and always has done a great deal for our missionaries, *so much so that she*

75. Henry Bacheler to Dr. Lowrie, June 23, 1881.
76. Reading, *Ogowe Band*, 188.

seems like one of us."[77] The Campbells were very glad to have Mrs. Sneed in Gaboon, as she was a good nurse.

Gaboon and Corisco Mission, January 1882. Seated, L to R. Rev. W. H. Robinson, Mrs. Janet Marling, Dr. Bacheler, Rev. William Walker, Mrs. Lucina Bushnell, Mrs. Mary Foster Nassau, Dr. Robert H. Nassau (on ground), Rev. Cornelius DeHeer. Standing, L to R: Rev. Arthur Marling, Rev. William Gault, Mrs. Lizzie Gault, Mrs. Laura Campbell, Rev. Graham Campbell, Mrs. Phebe Ogden, *Mrs. Lavinia Sneed*, and Mr. Peter Menkel. Six of the couples represented here had children on the mission field in the 1880s. Mrs. Sneed is included in the photo, indicating her integral—if informal—role in the mission family.

Menkel Family Crises

In the early months of 1882, Peter Menkel left for an extended health furlough in America, taking with him his eldest daughter, Katie. During his absence, Charity Menkel and her two younger children moved from Benita station to Baraka Mission at Gaboon.

---

77. Laura Campbell to the Family, December 21, 1881.

Relocation

Charity and her children were given temporary lodging in one of the mission houses for several months, during which time a small house was being built for them on the premises. Rev. William Walker remarked in his diary, in late December 1881, that "Mrs. Menkel came, and stops at lower Baraka (residence), and I hear of no council of war to keep her out, as when she came before."[78] This private and cryptic remark was not further explained, nor is there any other source which mentions the incident.

In April of 1882, Walker made further notes in his diary that the treasurer was "trying to get a house for Mrs. Menkel. And there will be an expense of fifty or a hundred dollars on the Mission."[79] The house would be occupied by the Menkels as well as the Kroomen (West Africans) who worked for the mission. Walker added, "I object, but it is of no use."[80]

Despite Walker's complaints, other missionaries seemed pleased that the Menkel family, including Mrs. Sneed, was living among them. Mrs. Laura Campbell noted in her diary that her husband had built the Menkels' new house "about a minute's walk from our house. T'will be very pleasant to have them so near. Mama Sneed came down with the Bachelers and is with us. We will have her here as much of the time as she can be spared from home. She is such good company."[81] At the time, both Charity Menkel and Mrs. Campbell were expecting babies, and Campbells were counting on Mrs. Sneed's help with the birth and care of their baby, expected in August.[82] By June 1882, Mrs. Sneed and Mrs. Menkel were situated in their own comfortable little house at Baraka Mission.[83]

Racial Discrimination in America

The first indication of racial discrimination recorded in Peter Menkel's diary appeared when he and seven-year-old daughter Katie arrived in New York City, where his adult siblings lived. Menkel felt welcomed by them, "but found there was feeling about Katie's color."[84] Menkel's German-American

78. William Walker, *Diary*, December 30, 1881.

79. William Walker, *Diary*, April 6, 1882.

80. William Walker, *Diary*, April 10, 1882.

81. Laura Campbell, Diary, entry dated May 10, 1882.

82. Laura Campbell to Dr. Lowrie, September 13, 1882.

83. Graham Campbell to R. H. Nassau, June 1, 1882.

84. Peter Menkel, *Diary*, May 2, 1882. New York City. The Menkel family liked Katie,

family, afraid of their neighbors' reproach, refused to take her in. When Menkel tried to find Katie a placement at The Industrial Home for Children, he was told that "as the child had colored blood she could not be received."[85] Menkel finally sent Katie back to Africa, with Miss Lydia Walker, a single lady missionary,[86] just weeks before his own departure, in January 1883.[87] He received word of his wife's death in that interim.[88]

DEATH OF CHARITY SNEED MENKEL

Rev. Walker tersely noted in his diary the birth of another daughter to Mrs. Menkel on July 10, 1882,[89] and her weeks of discomfort and illness from kidney disease, leading to Charity's death in late August.[90] While Rev. Walker seemed to have little empathy for Charity Menkel in these diary entries, he shows great sympathy for her grieving mother: "Mrs. Sneed, Mrs. M's mother, is deeply affected by the loss of her last child, and relative, except for four little grandchildren, the oldest of which is with her father in the U. States."[91] Walker's diary also gives indication that it was primarily the local church members and friends who ministered to Mrs. Sneed in her sorrow. Among them was Mary Clealand Dorsey, now known as "Mrs. Kirkwood."[92] Dr. and Mrs. Bacheler considered it "their duty to move into Mrs. Menkel's house and keep house and help Mrs. Sneed take care of the children until Mr. Menkel's return,"[93] thus reciprocating the devotion and care that they had received from Mrs. Sneed the previous year.

Rev. Campbell, in a letter to the Board Secretary, remarked on the need to inform Mr. Menkel, in America, of the death of his wife. Campbell noted that his heart was sad thinking of "the poor husband anticipating soon meeting *the one that he has loved so tenderly and one that was worthy of such*

---

but feared scandal, should neighbors learn that Katie's mother was *colored*.

85. Peter Menkel, *Diary*, May 3, 1882. New York City.

86. Peter Menkel, *Diary*, October 24, 1882. Lydia Walker Good.

87. Peter Menkel, *Diary*, January 22, 1883.

88. Peter Menkel, *Diary*, November 2, 1882.

89. Laura Campbell, *Diary*, July 10, 1882.

90. Laura Campbell, *Diary*, August 28, 1882. Charity's death and the Campbell birth coincided.

91. William Walker, *Diary*, August 29, 1882.

92. After the death of Josiah, Mary Clealand Dorsey wed a Scottish trader, Mr. Kirkwood.

93. Laura Campbell to the Family, September 13, 1882.

love."[94] Mrs. Campbell expressed admiration for Mrs. Sneed's fortitude in the midst of grief: "Poor Mama Sneed bears her great sorrow remarkably well. She has such a childlike faith in God. It is beautiful to see her so calm and trustful. She wonders why she was not taken instead of Charity."[95]

Charity's death was noted in the Annual Report for 1882–83:

> Mr. Peter Menkel came to [the US] on a visit for his health, and af-
> ter some months returned. In his absence Mrs. Menkel was called
> to her rest. She was held in much esteem as a faithful and excel-
> lent missionary, and deep sympathy is felt for the four children
> deprived of her care, and also for their father. Everything was done
> for them that could be done.[96]

Mrs. Sneed was not mentioned in the obituary, though she remained at the mission and was the mother of Mrs. Menkel.

Missionary Graves: Dr. Henry Ford (d. 1858), Miss Susannah Dewsnap (d. 1881) and Mrs. Charity Sneed Menkel (d. 1882). Charity Menkel's daughter, Lou, was buried next to her mother in January 1885. Baraka Mission Cemetery, Libreville, Gabon. (Courtesy of Laura O'Brien).

---

94. Graham Campbell to Dr. Lowrie, September 13, 1882.
95. Laura Campbell to the Family, September 13, 1882.
96. BFM, *Annual Report [1883]*, 39.

Mrs. Phebe Ogden (above). Charity Sneed was her assistant and caregiver in the early 1860s, at Corisco. Mrs. Ogden, likewise, cared for Charity and her children in late 1882, prior to and after Charity's death, at Baraka. (USCDL, 1890–1900)

THE "MOTHERLESS MENKEL CHILDREN"

During the January 1883 session meetings, the mission assigned Mrs. Ogden to "take charge of Mrs. Sneed's house and the Menkel children."[97] Mrs. Ogden had given much devoted care to Charity in her final weeks,[98] just as Charity had done for her twenty years earlier, at Corisco. Because of her distress and objection to the proposed assignment, the mission assigned Mrs. Ogden to teach in the boys' school.[99] Mrs. Sneed then assumed (by default) the care of her four grandchildren, receiving a small *salary*, from the mission accounts, for the care of the Menkel children.[100]

97. William Walker, *Diary*, January 10, 1883.

98. William Walker, *Diary*, July 18, 1882.

99. William Walker, *Diary*, January 10, 11, 12 and 15, 1883.

100. Peter Menkel to Dr. Lowrie, dated September 16, 1884; Letter to Rev. Walker, dated November 1, 1884.

On his journey back, along the coast of Africa, Peter Menkel stopped at Monrovia to visit with close friends of the Sneed family, noting their names and details of their conversations in his journal. After a visit to his father-in-law's grave, and reading the inscription Charity had had engraved on the tombstone, Peter was overcome with grief, and wrote in his journal, "Oh how miserable [and] unworthy I feel of the love of such a woman and character as my Wife, that I had appreciated Her more and loved Her better when She was Mine. Hers was a loveing [sic] nature, kind and true . . . "[101] During one port visit, he encountered missionaries who were the children of interracial couples of the Basel Mission. Menkel seemed relieved and pleased to see these biracial adults, who had received an education and were serving in the mission. His own four children (ages three months to seven years) seemed to have a precarious future.

On Sending "Colored Brethren"—1882

Near the time of Charity Sneed Menkel's death, the Presbyterian Board asked the Gaboon and Corisco Mission their opinion on the sending of "colored brethren" to the field. Graham Campbell hesitated to give a definite opinion, but noted his "wavering faith in this people's stability."[102] He was aware of similar cases elsewhere and his impression is not favorable.

Rev. William Walker, who had arrived with the multi-racial team at the birth of the Gaboon Mission, stated that he could work with colored brethren "just as well as with white men."[103] His one overriding concern was that the Mpongwe pastor, Ntâkâ (Toko) Truman, would try to gain an influence over such persons. Walker believed that if they were men of candor and common sense, they would resist his influence; "otherwise it might be bad."[104] Mr. Joseph Reading had a much stronger opinion on the matter, entreating the Mission Board to "never send a colored man to this field, unless you send all colored."[105] Mr. Reading also cited the mission's problems with Rev. Ntâkâ Truman, and believed that it would only lead to more discord and contention. In Reading's opinion, it was an issue of

101. Peter Menkel, *Diary*, February 21, 1883.
102. Graham Campbell to Dr. Lowrie, September 13, 1882.
103. William Walker to Dr. Lowrie, September 14, 1882.
104. William Walker to Dr. Lowrie, September 14, 1882.
105. Joseph Reading to Dr. Lowrie, September 15, 1882.

equality: such a man would have to be treated equally to the white missionaries, so they would have to extend the same privileges to every one of the mission's non-white employees.

The previous year, Pastor Ntâkâ Truman, of Gaboon, had sent a number of letters to the Corresponding Secretary, to complain about the white missionaries. Truman wrote that white missionaries had been keeping vital information from the black ministers,[106] and that correspondence addressed to them was being opened by missionaries prior to their delivery to the African pastors.[107] He noted the inadequacy of their provisions and salaries, which were insufficient to support a family, and the reason why so many trained native Christian leaders went into trade, and left the ministry.

Rev. Ntâkâ Truman felt that many missionaries had only come for their pay, while others were led by the Spirit of God. He cited *Murphy*[108] as a person who "cared for the black man because he came to teach them,"[109] and noted that the people discern that missionaries are often sinful. Rev. Truman complained that missionaries would hold meetings without inviting or notifying himself and Pastor Ibia, and was convinced that this was due to racial bias on the part of the white missionaries: "We are all Ministers of the Gospel but how is it that white ministers keep us away from that meeting? We all teach the same doctrine and preach the same Gospel, but what is the difference between them and we? Is it because we are black and they are white?"[110] Truman, who had left trade in 1870 to enter into full-time ministry, was licensed in 1874 and ordained in 1880. He now contemplated leaving the mission because of the way the white missionaries treated him.[111]

A subsequent letter, in January 1882, indicated that the local believers were considering breaking away from the missionaries to follow their African pastors. Echoing Pastor Ibia's sentiments of a decade earlier, Ntâkâ added, "we are trying the best we can to help our white ministers to carry the work but they don't please our hearts."[112] He had not received

---

106. Ntâkâ Truman to Dr. Lowrie, October 10, 1881.

107. Ntâkâ Truman to Dr. Lowrie, June 24, 1882. Rev. Ibia J'Ikenge and Rev. Ntâkâ Truman were the only two ordained native pastors at the time.

108. Samuel Howell Murphy.

109. Ntâkâ Truman to Dr. Lowrie, October 10, 1881.

110. Ntâkâ Truman to Dr. Lowrie, October 10, 1881.

111. Ntâkâ Truman to Dr. Lowrie, October 10, 1881.

112. Ntâkâ Truman to Dr. Lowrie, January 21, 1882.

reply to his previous letters, and reminded the Board Secretary that they awaited his response.

In a letter also dated January 21, 1882, Rev. Ntâkâ Truman detailed the inaccuracies in published mission reports regarding personnel placement, missionaries keeping him "in the dark" about the responsibilities and authority given to him, and a complaint that the white missionaries do not invite black pastors to their tables, which he attributes to racial discrimination: "This is a bad example that they set—showing that there is a difference between black and white"[113] Ntâkâ further argued that missionaries were treating Ibia, an ordained pastor, as "a boy" and that he should not be treated in this way. He repeated his earlier claim that the people were discouraged, and some were hesitant to enter ministry because of the way whites were treating black people. Ntâkâ ended the letter by stating that the Corresponding Secretary's lack of response to his many letters indicated that he had put them aside, and that he "cares for the white ministers, and ought to see what is right for [African ministers], too."[114]

Rev. Ntâkâ Truman wrote the Board Secretary, in April 1882, to again protest that missionaries were preventing him from reading correspondence from the Board which pertained to him, insisting, "*I am one of them and why is it that these people hide it from me?*"[115]

A month later, missionary Graham C. Campbell wrote to the Board Secretary, responding to all of the complaints expressed by Rev. Ntâkâ Truman. In the letter, Campbell described Ntâkâ as an Mpongwe gentlemen and a man of influence, who only wants to draw a salary and ask for more. Campbell assured Dr. Gillespie that he had given Ntâkâ both *brotherly counsel* and *fatherly admonition*[116] Campbell also lamented the difficulties they had with other young men currently serving in leadership, that, if he was rightly informed, "the training of these young men was such as would naturally lead to the self-esteem, pride and arrogance that is certainly pretty fully developed in two of these young men."[117]

113. Ntâkâ Truman to Dr. Lowrie, January 21, 1882. See also McArver, "Salvation of Souls," 124, for a similar case in Liberia. *Sharing a table* seemed to be a clear indicator of whether the Body of Christ was truly integrated. In both missions, this exclusion was deemed offensive.

114. Ntâkâ Truman to Dr. Lowrie, January 21, 1882.

115. Ntâkâ Truman to Dr. Lowrie, April 1882. Italics added.

116. Graham Campbell to Dr. Lowrie, May 10, 1882. Rev. Campbell was thirty-five years old, and Ntâkâ Truman was approximately *five years older*.

117. Graham Campbell to Dr. Lowrie, May 10, 1882. He alludes to Miss Nassau, who

African pastors of the Corisco Presbytery, early 1890s. Rev. Ibia J'Ikenge is seated at lower left. Others in this photo are Itongolo, Etiyani, Ntâkâ Truman (Jr), and Frank Myongo. (Courtesy of Godduhn Family)

Though the Board asked for the missionaries' opinions on the question of sending *colored brethren* from America, there is no indication that they sought the opinions of the African leaders on this important issue. During this year of mission-church racial tensions, and debate about sending *colored brethren* to the Gaboon and Corisco field, the Presbyterian Women's Board appointed a young, college-educated *woman* of color, to that same field.

Miss Mary Lucy Harding

Mary Lucy Harding came to the Gaboon and Corisco Mission as a full missionary, in late 1882. Originally from Detroit, Michigan, Miss Harding had just graduated, with honors, from Ann Arbor University, with a four-year degree. Much was made of Miss Harding's being a *colored missionary* who was returning to the *land of her ancestors* with the light of the gospel.[118] She was also touted as the first colored female missionary in that

---

not only trained African men in theology, but also affirmed and empowered them in their ministry.

   118. Isabella Nassau to Dr. Lowrie, June 24, 1882.

part of Africa. Ironically, she was so light in complexion that she appeared European, according to Dr. Nassau.[119]

Background and preparation

Miss Harding's personal life and thoughts remain a mystery, as there are no known personal papers or journals available. The US Federal Census for 1860 shows Basil Harding (carpenter, age 51) with his wife, Frances, (age 39) and 2-year-old Mary, living in Detroit, Ward 6, Michigan.[120] Ten years later, Mary was twelve, and her sister Ann was nine.[121] The Harding family was listed as "mulatto" in the 1860 census, but "white" in the 1870 and 1880 censuses. Basil remained in Detroit when his wife and daughter left for Ann Arbor. The 1880 Federal Census shows Francis [sic] Harding, and her daughter, Mary L. Harding (age 22), living near Ann Arbor University. Both women were listed as *white* on the census. Mary was listed as a student, while her mother (age 59) was described as a laundress. Mrs. Harding was designated Head of Household, and they were sharing their residence with an English immigrant couple in their thirties, and their five children, ages eight and under.[122] The University of Michigan-Ann Arbor has scant records, which indicate that Mary and her mother, Frances Harding, were from Detroit,[123] and that Mary lived at 35 Ingalls during her freshman year.[124]

Mary Harding was said to be one of the first two black women to graduate from the Ann Arbor University, both of whom "chose to put their brains and skills to work to help their own people."[125] Shortly after her June, 1882 graduation from Ann Arbor, Miss Harding received her missionary appointment, through the Women's Branch of the North-west, to be a teacher at the Presbyterian mission school at Batanga.[126] Apparently, her appointment

119. Nassau, *My Ogowe*, 420.

120. Ancestry.com, *1860 Federal Census, Detroit, Wayne, Michigan*.

121. Ancestry.com, *1870 Federal Census, Detroit, Wayne, Michigan*. Ann appears in this census year only, and may have died prior to 1880. Name spellings vary (Basael, Franzes, Maria).

122. Ancestry.com, *1880 Federal Census, Ann Arbor, Michigan*.

123. Lofy, Email, November 3, 2008.

124. UMAA, *Palladium*, 54.

125. Bordin, Ruth, *Women at Michigan*, 75.

126. SCA–UM, "Our Recent Missionary Recruits," 2. Batanga is now part of Southern Cameroon.

caused much interest and excitement, as described in a magazine published by the Christian Association of the University of Michigan:

> Miss Harding early consecrated herself to the missionary work, and after the appointment looked joyfully forward to her entrance upon her difficult labors in the "dark continent." The preparation for her departure was the occasion of stimulating interest in the cause of missions among a large circle of friends in this city and elsewhere, who have become interested in her. One lady in Detroit has agreed to pay her salary yearly, and other friends of the cause have vied with each other in contributing to her outfit and other necessary expenses. The impulse that her departure has given to the cause of mission at home is, we believe, an omen of the bless-ings that await her on the foreign shore.[127]

Sending *the first single colored woman from America* was an important distinction claimed by the Women's Presbyterian Board of Mission of the Northwest, as evident in an indignant correction written by Mrs. G. A. Har-mount, of Chicago, who disputed a later claim by the supporters of Miss Fleming, a Baptist missionary sent to the Congo.[128]

One particularly admiring article, printed in a New Zealand news-paper, *The Otago Witness*, on 2 December 1882, gives great insight into Miss Harding's sense of calling and her commitment to preparation for the mission field. The article, which seems to be based on a personal interview (though this is not stated), notes that "this coloured girl obtained an edu-cation in one of the first institutions of our land, equal to that which the wealthiest citizen could give to his sons, and under difficulties which would have been greatly discouraging to any one but one of a heroic character."[129] The article states that Miss Harding's widowed mother relocated to Ann Arbor several years before, so that her daughter could pursue her studies in preparation to become a missionary teacher, either in Africa or among the freedmen in the south. Miss Harding

> was poor, and supported herself by washing for the students dur-ing the University year, and labouring as a servant during the vacation. During her college course, she has stood foremost in

127. SCA–UM, "Our Recent Missionary Recruits," 2–3.

128. Harmount, "Note of Correction," 331. See Jacobs, "Three African American Women Missionaries," who were contemporaries of Miss Harding, with similar educa-tion and honors.

129. *Otago Witness*, "Young African Missionary," 27. The original source was not cited.

her class as a student, obtaining the respect of her professors, and the confidence and good will of her class mates. During her four years, she was a faithful member of the pastor's Bible-class, and proved herself well versed in the Scriptures, and an earnest Christian disciple, modest in her deportment, and ready for every good work. During these years her zeal for the missionary work had been steadily increasing, and she has had her heart set on carrying the gospel to the land of her forefathers.[130]

The article, written just prior to Miss Harding's departure for Africa, noted her church's participation: "the church of Ann Arbor has always taken a warm interest in this young woman, whose course commended itself to their highest approbation, and the ladies are preparing her outfit, working with joy in the thought that one of their number is to be their representative on the dark continent."[131] Nearly all notices of Miss Harding's appointment as a missionary to Africa mention her being *colored*, and some imply that this gave her unique qualification for that role, despite her academic achievement and *calling*. The 1883 annual report of the Woman's Presbyterian Board of Missions of the Northwest called readers' attention to:

all the hindrances which have fettered her, and the toil she has cheerfully borne, in completing a course of education in one of our noblest universities. Intellectually she is abundantly equipped, and not less so, it is believed, for spiritual work, in the land and among the peoples from whom her ancestors came, and to whose service in the name of her master, she has consecrated all her rich spiritual, mental, and physical endowments.[132]

An article in *The Gospel in All Lands* describes the farewell services for a number of departing missionaries, in Chicago, on Sept 16, 1882. Miss Harding is described as "the young colored girl, who has lately graduated with such high honor at the University Ann Arbor, Mich., who is to accompany Miss Bella Nassau on her return to Africa."[133] *Woman's Work for Woman* magazine mentions the outgoing missionaries and the countries to which they were appointed; Miss Harding's appointment is described as *"to her dusky sisters in Africa."*[134] Among Miss Harding's supporters was a Mrs. Z. Chandler, who

130. *Otago Witness*, "Young African Missionary," 27.

131. *Otago Witness*, "Young African Missionary," 27.

132. WPBMN, *Annual Report* [1883], 16–17.

133. Helm, "Farewell Meeting to Missionaries," 168.

134. WPBMN, "Farewell," 429.

contributed $350 towards her salary, and the Wing Lake church, who gave five dollars towards her outfit and traveling expenses.[135]

Miss Harding was one of twelve Presbyterian missionary women serving in Africa, in early 1883. Of these, eleven were appointed to the Gaboon and Corisco Mission, and one to the Liberia mission. Nine of the women were representing the Women's Foreign Missionary Society of the Presbyterian Church, and the remaining three were sent by the Woman's Presbyterian Board of Missions of the North-West.[136] Though no distinction is evident in this list of twelve women, two were persons of color, both of whom were sent by the WPBMN. In their twelfth annual report, this regional organization claimed to be "a factor in the aggressive mission of the church militant,"[137] having taken up the work and carried it forward through faith and their unceasing prayer. Part of their strategy in Africa was to support the sending of persons of African descent, and to sponsor trained native evangelists and teachers in their work. Having appointed Miss Harding to Gaboon and Corisco Mission, and Mrs. Rachel Wardsworth (a native teacher) to Liberia, the WPBMN hoped to send additional persons of African descent, for the multiplication of Christian schools, and dissemination of the truth, proving that "many a little child shall lead parents and friends to the knowledge of their Saviour."[138] They named Scotia Seminary, in North Carolina, as a "feeder" for this supply, as it provided education to African American youth. Because of their intentional sending and support of women of color, this particular organization made much of Miss Harding's ethnicity, as well as her spiritual and academic qualifications to serve as a missionary in Africa.

First Experiences in Africa

Miss Harding arranged for her mother to accompany her to Africa, though Mrs. Harding was not appointed by the Board, and would not be considered a missionary.[139] During their ocean voyage to Africa, Miss Harding

135. WPBMN, "Receipts," 431. See Thorne, *Congregational Missions*, 93. Many women's organizations formed direct relationships with foreign fields, circumventing the male-dominated institutions, and with emphasis on sending single women missionaries overseas.

136. WPBMN, *Annual Report [1883]*, 185.

137. WPBMN, *Annual Report [1883]*, 18.

138. WPBMN, *Annual Report [1883]*, 16–17.

139. Nassau, *My Ogowe*, 420.

applied herself to the study of the Benga language, as she and Miss Nassau were expected to work at Batanga, the northernmost site. Miss Nassau, who was already fluent in that language, expressed her admiration and confidence: "Miss Harding and her mother are very well, and I think Miss H. will be able to teach at once in the Benga, as soon as she is stationed. She has a well-disciplined mind, and will, I trust, do noble work in Africa."[140] By the end of the voyage, Miss Harding could read fluently in Benga.[141]

The three women arrived in Gaboon on November 21, 1882, along with another new missionary, the Rev. Adolphus C. Good.[142] The next day, Miss Harding recorded her first impressions of the local culture and customs: "the nights are hideous with fetish dances carried on by old women, who curse everybody, even the mission, which is called Baraka. Mother and I thought at first that the noise must be caused by wild animals."[143]

Miss Nassau noted Mrs. Frances Harding's positive impact during her first weeks at the mission: "Mrs. Harding is filling a large place, and one which only her good motherly self can fill."[144] One month later, Miss Nassau again complimented Mrs. Harding, with a thinly-veiled slight to her daughter, "Miss Harding and her mother are both well and happy . . . I think in that most important part of missionary work the daily life, good Mrs. Harding will do as much for the people she lives among as her highly-educated daughter."[145]

Two months later, at their session meetings, the mission leadership decided not to send Miss Nassau and Miss Harding to begin a pioneering work at Batanga. Instead, they appointed the two women to Kangwe mission, on the Ogowe River, deep in rainforest.[146] In a letter to her constituents, Miss Harding expressed her willingness to learn another dialect, though added her concern that she would, at first, be unable to understand her pupils, or they, her. She asked them to "pray that in all things the love

140. SCA–UM, "Our Missionaries," 4.

141. WFMSPC, "Africa: Woman's Work on the Dark Continent," 182.

142. Nassau, "Baraka, Gaboon River," 197.

143. Harding, "W. Africa," 125.

144. Nassau, "Baraka, Gaboon River," 197–98.

145. Isabella Nassau to Dr. Gillespie, January 12, 1883.

146. Now the town of Lambarene. Dr. Nassau pioneered the Presbyterian mission there in the 1870s. Catholic priests opened a mission station nearby, in 1880. The old Kangwe Mission site is adjacent to Schweitzer Hospital.

of Christ may constrain me."[147] In a subsequent letter, Miss Harding further explains this change of assignment: "We did not go to Batanga, because that is on the coast and the policy of the mission is interiorward. Moreover the people at Batanga have been provided with a native preacher, and must be made to respect him and not expect a white missionary."[148]

Miss Harding was put in charge of the Kangwe Girls' School, while Miss Nassau did *town visitation* along the river. Curiously, Miss Harding lived with Mr. and Mrs. Reading at the bottom of the steep hill, while her mother lived at the hilltop house with Miss Nassau.[149] Mr. Robinson, then a single man, lived with the boarding school boys, also at the top of the hill. Miss Harding was occupied with studying the Mpongwe language, and teaching "her girls" to read, write, count and sew.[150] She regularly visited the towns in the area, in order to attract more pupils for her school, noting in her report that she was interested in her girls and enjoyed her work, and asking her readers "pray for me that my light may not be dim."[151] She observed that early marriages often halted the education of her young pupils, and that women and girls were "looked upon as property."[152] She also perceived that the Galwa people around her were terrified of evil spirits, making them slow to understand the love of Jesus Christ.[153]

Miss Harding described her itinerating work, preaching and teaching, in a letter to Dr. Lowrie, the Board Secretary, in late 1884. In it she expressed her view on the purpose of mission education: "We must teach these people enough to enable them to read their own Bible, otherwise our work will be very unsatisfactory work and our progress slow."[154] Despite these cultural obstacles, Miss Harding was pleased with the success in her work, finding both comfort and delight in it. She assured him that she was in good spirits and perfect health.

147. Harding, "Africa: Miss Harding [1883]," 186.

148. Harding, "Kangwe Girls' School [1883]," 305.

149. Miss Harding later moved up on the hill, living for a time with Miss Nassau. Eventually, the Hardings occupied the hilltop house.

150. Harding, "Kangwe Girls' School [1883]," 305.

151. Harding, "Kangwe Girls' School [1883]," 305.

152. WPBMN, *Annual Report* [1884], 18.

153. WPBMN, *Annual Report* [1884], 19.

154. Mary Harding to Standing Committee, December 10, 1884.

Interpersonal Relationships

It is difficult to trace interpersonal relationships from mission reports and official documents. These details are usually found in private letters or journals. Mary Harding left no private collection of papers, and other missionary writings mention her rarely, if at all. Available Presbyterian Mission archives indicate that she spent her entire seven years in the remote interior Ogowe River region. Only the missionaries who were present when she arrived at Baraka Mission, in late 1882, and the few who made the difficult river journey to the interior stations, would have met her. In her letters to the Board Secretary, and to other missionaries, Miss Harding gave evidence of her respect, appreciation and warm regard for her colleagues. She noted the departure of elderly William Walker, and the Campbell family, all from the Gaboon (Baraka) station: "Mr. Walker has taken his fatherly presence from us, but I am glad that he has concluded to rest, after his arduous, long-continued labors . . . I am exceedingly sorry that Mr. and Mrs. Campbell are compelled by Mr. Campbell's sickness to go home. We shall miss them very much. Mr. Campbell's activity is equaled by his fervent zeal in the work for Christ, and I am afraid his zeal has consumed him, or the climate must conquer our best men."[155]

There is indication that Miss Harding and her mother were fully involved in social interactions, hosting as well as being hosted, in small gatherings of the missionary community and the larger, secular community on the Ogowe River.[156] Among their secular visitors were riverboat captains and European business owners.[157]

Miss Harding often referred to her mother's helpful presence in the mission. She also signed her correspondence to the Board Secretary with added greetings from her mother,[158] and invariably reported good health for both of them.

While Miss Harding's correspondence reveals only positive aspects of missionary interpersonal relationships, other correspondence indicates mounting tensions between missionaries. Often, these conflicts are attributed to temper, personality and the debilitating climate. In the case of Peter Menkel, mission concerns about Menkel's mental health and "usefulness"

155. Harding, "Report from Kangwe Mission [1883]," 309.
156. Nassau, *My Ogowe*, 431–443.
157. Nassau, *My Ogowe*, 556.
158. Harding, "Items of News," 309.

on the field give way to underlying tensions about his biracial family: their status on the field, their ethnic identity, and their appropriate "home."

Peter Menkel's Conflicts and Recall

Peter Menkel's irascible temper and interpersonal conflicts with missionary colleagues led to discussion of recalling him to America. The various letters from the missionaries to the Board reveal great concern about the future of his biracial children (either in America or in Africa)—their education, well-being and moral development.

MISSIONARY INPUT TO THE BOARD

Joseph Reading, who argued that Menkel ought to *leave with his children*, expressed his view on the matter: "His marriage with a Negro woman was a great mistake. As usual in social sins the heaviest misfortune falls upon the children and so in this case. In any country, they must be classed as "negroes" for they are certainly not white. In America, they may grow up to usefulness, but not here. It is almost absolutely certain that here they will grow up to a life of sin and shame."[159]

In a subsequent letter, Reading continued to argue for Menkel's recall, due to his health and state of mind. Again, he mentioned Menkel's children, noting that they were mulatto, *half-Africans*, and were not the same as the white American children. Reading claimed that their mother was a not missionary, though employed by the mission. While he respected Charity above her husband, Reading believed that race and social standing make a difference.[160]

Peter Menkel was grateful to his mother-in-law for caring for his children, but also questioned their future. Two years after his wife's death, Menkel wrote to the Board:

> now as regards to family, for Mrs. Sneed's sake I have great cause for gratitude. Her life and strength being spared thus long and the children are doing nicely. So with the bright outlook for their future I feel quite lighthearted, for a long time it was not so, for I tried every way I could think of but nowhere here could I find what was needed, till through the kindness of Mrs. Good I learned

159. Joseph Reading to Dr. Lowrie, February 8, 1884.

160. Joseph Reading to Dr. Lowrie, December 9, 1884. The letter was damaged and some words (those at the right margin) are obscured.

of the Scotia Seminary in Concord, N.C., in the care of Rev. Mr. Dorland there and a like institution for boys is my hope for my children centered.[161]

Retired missionary, Mrs. Lucina Bushnell, also responded to the question regarding Menkel and his children, and seemed to imply that either option—to keep them in Africa or send them to America—would have pros and cons. Mrs. Bushnell questioned whether Menkel could find a place in America where he and the children could live, and where Menkel could find a place in society where he would be both useful and happy. Like Reading, she was concerned about the children "falling into the net which will most surely be spread for them,"[162] referring to the moral climate of Gaboon.[163] Mrs. Bushnell anticipated the difficulties of separating the Menkel children from their grandmother, especially two-year-old Grace, and questioned whether Mr. Menkel should stay and "take care of his mother-in-law, who is now quite advanced in years."[164] The missionaries likely did not expect Mrs. Sneed to return to America; they presumed the family would be separated, due to the children's educational needs and/or Peter Menkel's recall by the Mission Board.

CHILDREN'S EDUCATION

At Peter Menkel's request, Mrs. Lydia Good wrote a letter to the Director of Scotia Seminary, regarding the placement of Katie Menkel in that school:

Rev. Luke Dorland: Dear Sir. I have been advised to write to you concerning a little molatto [sic] girl that we wish to have in school. Her name is Kate Menkel aged 8 years. Her Mother was an American negro and came to Liberia many years ago. Has been employed in our Mission for 20 yrs at least . . . a faithful earnest Christian and in every way exemplary. Nine years ago was married to Mr. Menkel, a German-American, employed as Capt. of a schooner. Last year the Mother died leaving 4 children, Kate being the eldest. The grandmother, a good old colored Auntie cares for

161. Peter Menkel to Dr. Lowrie, September 16, 1884.

162. Lucina Bushnell to Dr. Wells, July 19, 1884.

163. Many biracial children at the mission schools were born to African mothers and European fathers, out of wedlock. The girls were often enticed by European traders into immoral lifestyles. See also Jordan, *White Man's Burden*, 85, and Stoler, *Carnal Knowledge and Imperial Power*.

164. Lucina Bushnell to Dr. Wells, July 19, 1884.

them as well as she can. These children have better minds than the native[s] and while the Missionaries are willing to do all they can for them, yet it seems they should have a better education and the Father has asked me to assist in this. Kate will probably have the allowance from the Board in N. Y. of $100.00 and the father will try to add from his salary. He would wish Kate educated with idea of returning here as a helper in Mission work, and also to have some employment by which she could earn her own living.[165]

The letter gives great insight into the missionaries' perspectives on this racially mixed family, revealing some stereotyping, but also genuine concern and positive expectation as to the need and practicality of a solid education.[166]

Katie was not sent to Scotia Seminary. A year later, Mrs. Good re-marked in a letter to Rev. Walker, who was now in Wisconsin, "Mama Sneed is always so glad to hear from you. She is well at present, but poor old creature I wonder how she endures the care of those [four] wild, noisy children."[167] Her letter reflects the warm affection and sympathy that Mrs. Sneed received from various members of the mission community during this period, and hints at the difficulties Peter Menkel was facing, regarding the care and education of his children.

In mid-January 1885, Peter Menkel wrote an anguished letter to his former missionary colleague, Rev. Walker, to apprise him of his family cri-sis and ask his help in the matter. Remembering Walker's kind words of sympathy when he was bereaved of his wife and left with his four mother-less children, Menkel wrote,

> But now a worse difficulty stares me in the face, While here, their ever kind and loveing [*sic*] Grandmother has been . . . in Her self-sacrificing efforts for the children all a mother could do at Her age. She has been faithful and Her reward is sure in Heaven at least. But our little home is to be broken up this time into fragments, for we must part. The Mission have requested the Board to recall me at Mr. Reading's instigation, I believe.[168]

165. Lydia B. Good to Rev. Luke Dorland, October, 23, 1883.

166. See Killingray, *Black Atlantic Missionary Movement*, 18. Children of Black missionaries were less likely to receive the education opportunities available to white missionaries.

167. Lydia B. Good to Rev. William Walker, June 11, 1884.

168. Peter Menkel to Rev. Walker, January 15, 1885.

Menkel's visit to America, three years earlier, gave him reason to believe that it would be difficult to secure homes for the older children, and Mrs. Sneed couldn't bear to part with little Grace. Menkel wondered where in America he could settle with them without the prejudice of color.[169]

"Misrepresented"

Concerned that he might have difficulty finding work in America, Menkel asked the mission to draw up a letter attesting to the *legitimacy of his children*, and that he had been *lawfully married* to their mother. The letter would state that Mr. Menkel was "*not a missionary* but a very useful man discharging faithfully all that [he] considered [his] duty,"[170] that Charity "had been *a faithful servant* to all who employed her. And that while the wisdom of the marriage might now be questioned it was countenanced, if not urged, by some of our missionar[ies]."[171] This statement that Menkel was *not* a missionary is puzzling, as he had been officially—after long and intense debate—declared "a full missionary, with full privileges" at the session meetings, held December 13–21, 1881.[172] That same year, in a letter to the Board confirming Peter's need to recruit his health. Dr. Bachelor gave his opinion on Peter's character, assuring them that he was a man of great usefulness, and had, perhaps, been misrepresented:

> he does more work and gets less thanks for it than any member of the mission. Above all he is a good, continuous Christian. And yet is ridiculed (or has been) by <u>ministers</u> in consequence of his "burden for souls," as they derisively call the habit of speaking with everybody concerning their spiritual welfare, which he possesses. Would to God we all had more of this . . . element in our Christian make-up! When such a man as Mr. Walker says "He is a good deal more efficient in his sphere than I in mine" it is a good recommendation, I think.[173]

Dr. Bachelor noted that older missionaries observed wonderful improvement in Peter's demeanor, since his 1873 arrival. Bachelor then made

169. Peter Menkel to Rev. Walker, January 15, 1885.

170. Peter Menkel to Dr. Wells, February 10, 1885. Italics added.

171. Peter Menkel to Dr. Wells, February 10, 1885. Italics added.

172. Robinson, Summary of the Minutes. Charity Menkel was not on the roster for 1881 annual meeting. All other missionaries were named, and counted as either *absent* or *present*.

173. Henry Bacheler to Dr. Lowrie, June 23, 1881.

reference to Peter's having had "many lessons of patient endurance under, and forgiveness of, wrongs he has been obliged to suffer."[174]

Miss Jones asked Mrs. Sneed about her son-in-law, in light of the decision to dismiss him, to which Mrs. Sneed replied that it was "nothing but his temper and strong will" and that "his mind is right."[175]

FAMILY LOSS AND SEPARATION

In the middle of the crisis regarding Peter Menkel's possible dismissal, his third child, little "Lou," died of kidney disease. Considering Menkel's difficulty in finding a home (or homes) for his biracial children, Mrs. Sneed saw the child's unanticipated death as a blessing in disguise, exclaiming, "Thank the Lord she is safe"[176]

It was finally decided that Mrs. Sneed would keep little Grace, while the two school-age children, Katie and Alec, would go to America. Mrs. Ogden accompanied the two of them on their journey in August 1885.[177]

Besides tensions among missionaries, there were equally devastating conflicts between the missionaries and the multiple communities in the region. This period was particularly trying for those serving in the interior along the Ogowe River.

Challenges in the Ogowe Region

Missionaries serving in the Ogowe region experienced multiple challenges in the 1880s, including a notable increase in French Colonial restrictions, deadly inter-ethnic conflicts, and recurrent missionary illnesses, which debilitated the whole mission community, as they cared for one another and maintained the evangelistic, discipleship and educational ministries.

FRENCH COLONIAL OPPOSITION

The mid-1880s were difficult for the missionaries, due to the increasing restrictions placed on their work by the French colonial authorities.[178] In

174. Henry Bacheler to Dr. Lowrie, June 23, 1881.

175. Lydia Jones to William Walker, May 23, 1884.

176. Lydia B. Good to Rev. Walker, January 23, 1885.

177. Menkel, Peter, *Report for the Year 1885*, January 7, 1886. Menkel was not recalled, but served for many more years; his children were raised in the US, but in separate locations.

178. See also Ratanga-Atoz, *Histoire du Gabon*, 18, and Zorn, *Les Chemins*, 476,

April 1883, colonial powers announced the official decree that all teaching must be done in French, at the exclusion of all other languages.[179] From Miss Harding's first arrival in the Ogowe, the mission schools were threatened with closing, and evangelistic work was being curtailed. Miss Harding noted that the French were "making themselves troublesome. They do not want the blacks to preach in the villages, which means stopping the work of our Bible readers. They do not want English taught in the schools, or even Mpongwe, but French only.[180] They will not allow Protestant ministers to perform the marriage ceremony."[181] Miss Harding and other missionary teachers circumvented these restrictions by teaching only a few boarding pupils at a time, on a personal basis;[182] and continued to preach the gospel to the people living along the Ogowe River and its tributaries.

INTER-ETHNIC CONFLICT

A second challenge for the missionaries during this period was the inter-ethnic conflict between the diverse peoples of the region, which was tied to increasing trade with Europeans.

Miss Harding offered cultural insights and observations to her constituents in America, gleaned during her preaching and teaching ministry among at least two significant groups on the Ogowe: "the Fangwe tribe [is] a fierce, warlike, buccaneering, cannibal, thievish tribe, who care nothing for learning or for God—who care for nothing, indeed, but Mammon."[183] The Fangwe would gather to hear her gospel presentations, however, and some indicated a desire to learn to read. Miss Harding predicted that the Fangwe, "though ignorant of Bible truths, are susceptible to them, and, if they are taught properly, will embrace Christianity at no distant day."[184]

Miss Harding also described the nearby Galwe people, who lived along the lakes of the region. To reach this population, she made journeys of two

---

regarding the bitter disputes between French colonial powers and the American protestant mission in Gabon.

179. Zorn, *Le Grand Siècle*, 84.

180. See also Zomo, "Le Travail des Mission Chrétiennes," 54–61, regarding the *politics of language*, and French colonial scorn and annihilation of indigenous languages.

181. Harding, "Items of News," 309. Protestants were American, Catholics were French; the restriction was based on nationality, not church affiliation.

182. BFM, *Annual Report [1885]*, 49.

183. BFM, *Annual Report [1885]*, 53.

184. BFM, *Annual Report [1885]*, 53.

weeks or more, seemingly alone. Miss Harding reported that many had given up their idols and fetishes, and were seeking a faith that would elevate them. She noted the Galwe people's interest in the gospel teachings, and their many questions. She regarded them as a noble tribe, though polygamy, which was prevalent among them, was making them effeminate. The Galwe were docile, hospitable and industrious, courteous, and respectful towards elders, as their culture was patriarchal. They were also eager to learn how to read. This particular passage is further developed in Miss Harding's handwritten report, but edited out of the published Annual Report. She actually reported that the Galwa were eager to learn to read *in both the English and Mpongwe languages, but were disinterested in French.*[185]

Miss Harding observed that both the Galwe and Fanwe resented the French: "the Galwas dislike them because they do not protect [them] from the Fans. The Fans do not like them because they destroy Fanwe villages and kill the inhabitants for shooting at the traders. So the missionaries are increasing in favor with all tribes, for the people are beginning to realize that the missionaries have come to benefit them."[186]

As an educator, Miss Harding was delighted that the Galwe were eager to learn, and anyone among them who could read was asked to teach in the towns until other learners could read fluently. Many were self-taught, and could read from the Bible, as well as write. Miss Harding saw the Galwe people as too peaceable, and frightened by the Fanwe and their guns, "until they give up to them their towns, gardens, and houses. The latter tribe has been very aggressive lately, and have taken one large town by going to the town and shooting at the inhabitants, and ordering them to leave their town and find another place."[187] The Galwes retaliated, on occasion, and had gone to a Fangwe towns and killed them, as well.

Excerpts from Miss Harding's handwritten report, which were not printed in the Board's Annual Report, also included her opinion that the pupils should *not live for a long time on the mission premises, as it caused adjustment difficulties when they returned to their towns*: "they are unable to practice civilized ways in the towns and get to be above the ordinary duties of the heathen, which duties are not heathenish in themselves, though rude."[188]

185. Mary Harding to the Standing Committee, December 10, 1884.

186. Mary Harding to the Standing Committee, December 10, 1884.

187. BFM, *Annual Report [1885]*, 53–54.

188. Mary Harding to the Standing Committee, December 10, 1884. See also Sanneh,

In the same report, Miss Harding expressed her desire to impact the women of the region:

> I enjoy my work very much but have not yet accomplished what I intended to accomplish and that is to get the women interested in their own salvation that they will sustain a woman's prayer meeting. But the power is not with me, but this Christ who turns men's hearts as the rivers of water are turned. I can do all things through Christ who strengthens me, and who will give me all the wisdom and courage I need in this stronghold of Satan.[189]

Miss Harding's work among women would eventually bring about transformation, though it drew opposition from the foreign traders and the Catholic priests in the region.[190]

Missionary Illness

A third challenge to the Ogowe mission, in the mid-1880s, was the frequency of illnesses which necessitated the departures of several missionary couples. The Readings, the Robinsons and the Goods all served at the interior Ogowe stations, and were absent for significant periods of time, to restore their health, or to cover for those who returned to the United States.

Miss Harding, in contrast, remained at the Kangwe mission station, often alone, to conduct all religious meetings, including Sabbath school services,[191] in addition to her regular teaching and evangelizing work.[192] This was unusual, as missionary women did not ordinarily "fill in" when the ordained men were absent or too weak to conduct services. There had long been concern about leaving missionary women alone on any given station,[193] due to heathen and immoral influences of the surrounding community. There is no known record of the missionaries expressing concern about *this particular female missionary* operating the mission alone, despite the known conflicts and dangers prevalent at the time. Nor is there record

---

"Yogi and the Commissar," 4. Separating children from their heathen villages, or "en-clavement" was common among missions. Sanneh exposes its weaknesses.

189. Mary Harding to the Standing Committee, December 10, 1884.

190. Stoler, *Carnal Knowledge and Imperial Power*, 43. Where European women were few or absent, colonized women were solicited for domestic services, prostitution or concubinage. This sexual submission substantiated colonial racism.

191. Harding, "Gaboon and Corisco Mission Report," [1886]," 7.

192. BFM, *Annual Report [1886]*, 64.

193. Clemens and DeHeer, Report of the Corisco Mission [1860];

of her having taken a health furlough, or any other leave of absence, during her tenure as missionary at Kangwe.

In 1885, Rev. Graham Campbell reported on the health crises which caused two missionary couples to suddenly leave Kangwe station, leaving Miss Harding alone at the mission, "*but Mr. S., one of the traders, has promised to render all possible assistance.*"[194]

Dangers, Conflict and Opposition

Miss Harding showed evidence of her tenacity and courage in opening up a *vernacular school* for a duration of three months, "which had thirty scholars, eager to learn, and the prospect of a large increase; but French interposition compelled it to be closed."[195] She had been authorized by Rev. A. C. Good to open the school, and so it was with mission sanction, though in defiance of colonial restrictions.[196] In her 1885 year-end report, Miss Harding noted that in one of the towns where she had been preaching and impacting the women, men from the trading factories protested, and threatened to "get the French priest" to stop her.[197] The priest came, and the two argued about the content of her preaching messages. He also challenged her at the next town, at the insistence of the men from the trading factories. Miss Harding noted that both Mr. Good and Mr. Robinson were away at Madeira, and had been absent for the past four months.

Miss Harding described in detail a dangerous *palaver* which began when a Fangwe boy stole a bird from one of the Galwa mission boys, and quickly escalated into an armed intertribal conflict. Miss Harding intervened just as the situation was coming to a head, and prevented certain bloodshed. *At her appearance, the Fans left.* The trader whom Mr. Good had asked to "look in on the mission" was unavailable to intervene, and sent word to the French Commandant instead. Miss Harding reported that the Commandant's only response was to declare that "the mission folks had no business to keep taking small boys and he would not come to help us even if the Fans killed us all."[198] Rev. G. C. Campbell happened

194. Campbell, "Illness of Missionaries in Africa," 455. Italics added.

195. BFM, *Annual Report [1886]*, 64.

196. Mary Harding to Standing Committee, December 19, 1885.

197. Mary Harding to Standing Committee, December 19, 1885.

198. Mary Harding to Standing Committee, December 19, 1885. Spelling varies in reports: *fan, fañ, fanwe, fangwe*. The current English spelling is "Fang," while the French is "Pahouin."

to arrive the next day from Gaboon,[199] but it doesn't appear that it was to intervene in the palaver, but rather to pack a trunk for Mr. Robinson, who needed to return to the United States, for his health. The French authorities were alarmed by Campbell's sudden arrival, and apologized for not coming to the aid of the mission. They also advised that the school be closed. The French then bombarded the (implicated) Fangwe town the following day. Miss Harding ends the story,

> the commandant sent to me for a written complaint of the trouble with the Fans and I replied that *I had no complaint against them whatever*. But I finally sent it on Tuesday to shield the aforesaid trader who has been very kind to us missionaries. The Fans then went to the commandant to ask him to cease hostilities . . . Since then I have had charge of the station and have preached every Sunday morning and held Sunday School in the afternoon for all the natives in the stations, mine and those at Andende at the foot of the hill.[200]

The accounts in Miss Harding's report were accepted as *true and accurate* by the Mission Standing Committee,[201] as the only line struck from the entire report was the phrase "to pack a trunk for Mr. Robinson," pertaining to Mr. Campbell's reason for coming to Kangwe from Gaboon.[202] Miss Harding's expanded role was reported in the June 1886 issue of *The Foreign Missionary*, which noted that "in the absence of the other missionaries she has conducted religious worship and Sabbath School services"[203] in addition to teaching in the school and continuing her town visits. These official reports were among the many sources which confirm details and claims presented by Miss Harding in her personal correspondence and reports.

ON SENDING "COLORED" MISSIONARIES—1885

By 1885, the Board assessed the many obstacles and dangers—particularly related to health—for missionaries serving in Western Africa, which they saw as a *preparatory work* and the beginning of an effort that would

199. The trip from Baraka Mission to Kangwe was a journey of several days, by ocean and river.

200. Mary Harding to Standing Committee, December 19, 1885. Italics added.

201. The Mission Standing Committee consisted of the ordained male missionaries of the field.

202. William Gault to the Corresponding Secretary, January 7, 1886.

203. BFM, "Missions in Western Africa [1886]," 6.

eventually spread to the interior of the continent. They recognized that the church's interest in Western and Central Africa was due to their proximity to America, and also because there was "a large body of people in our country whose forefathers came from Western Africa. *Many of their now Christian descendants may be expected to become missionaries there, not a few of them from the membership of our Church.*"[204] The Board had made a similar statement, several years earlier, that the Gaboon and Corisco field was still vital, as it was easily accessible and inhabited by "tribes from which many of the colored people in our country were originally taken by the hand of violence. It has, therefore, claims of special interest on the churches of this land."[205]

The *Presbyterian Monthly Record* brought these questions to light in their August 1886 issue, giving a history of both the ABCFM Gaboon Mission and the Presbyterian Corisco Mission, prior to their merger, and noting the deaths and permanent departures of missionaries due to ill health. After the 1870 merger, this trend continued through the mid-1880s. While many questioned whether the work should continue, given the loss of life and health, the writer reminded readers that "the gospel must be preached to people who live in climates unfriendly to foreign missionaries."[206]

As to the question of laborers, the writer wondered whether the Church should rely on white missionaries, "or should colored people be sought for, as missionaries in this trying climate? Of course, eventually native laborers must be the chief agents in the spread of the gospel everywhere in Africa, as in other parts of the world; but for the present foreigners cannot be dispensed with. Shall they be white or colored?"[207] Citing the common arguments that the African climate was deadly to both whites and blacks, and that missionary recruits must have proper qualification, the writer suggested that, while they hoped to find good missionaries from the various "colored" Presbyterian congregations, they couldn't expect to do so at present.[208]

One suggestion was to send missionaries on two-year trial deployments, to see if they could adapt to the climate, given that several of the white missionaries had served between eighteen and thirty-one years. The writer

---

204. BFM, *Annual Report* [1885], 56.

205. BFM, *Annual Report* [1880], 28.

206. BFM, "Gaboon and Corisco Mission," 295.

207. BFM, "Gaboon and Corisco Mission," 296.

208. BFM, "Gaboon and Corisco Mission," 297.

referred to two men and three women (likely Dr. Nassau, Miss Nassau, Mr. and Mrs. DeHeer, and Mrs. Reutlinger), while overlooking the parallel cases of the two African Americans (Sneeds) who served for twenty or more years in the same missions. The conclusion, in 1886, was that there were more missionaries lost through death and illness than were spared.[209]

MISS HARDING'S SCOPE OF MINISTRY

Mission appropriations for 1886–87 show that Miss Harding and Miss Nassau each received $400 for the year, while married couples received $800. Curiously, Miss Harding was additionally appropriated $300 for a crew,[210] though there is no indication that Miss Nassau, or any other Ogowe missionary, received the same.[211] This appropriation, *requested by the Mission Standing Committee*, gives evidence that her extensive preaching and teaching journeys were recognized and approved by the both the mission and the Board.

Excerpts from Miss Harding's ministry reports reveal the scope of her ministry, as well as her keen observation of, and appreciation for, her host communities.[212] She observed that the local population was fond of music, and had *sweet voices*—chanting as they rowed or during processions. An organ, provided by her supporters, allowed her to play music, to the delight of the people around her. Miss Harding encouraged the children's natural love of music, and some pupils invested in hymnbooks, despite their "scanty means."[213] As she went in her canoe, teaching in the many towns, she would carry a concertina, to accompany her singing. When she came in sight, the children would gather, shouting, "the musical instrument! the musical instrument!"[214] and join her in song. Miss

---

209. BFM, "Gaboon and Corisco Mission," 297.

210. Hired boatmen who traveled with her on her river-based preaching and teaching itineration.

211. William Gault to the Corresponding Secretary, January 7, 1886.

212. See Jacobs, *Three African American Missionary Women*, 323. Sylvia Jacobs claims that missionaries showed contempt for African culture, and sought to increase contributions by invoking *pity*, describing Africans as debased, degraded or depraved. Miss Harding's negative descriptions invoked prayer and hope for their salvation. She often praised Gabonese culture.

213. WPBMN, *Annual Report* [1886], 25.

214. Harding, "African Children," 108.

Harding added, "Some of them will never let me touch them, but others will nestle contentedly in my arms."[215]

The Women's Presbyterian Board of Missions of the Northwest, who regularly supported Miss Harding's work, financed the tuition of many schoolgirls, and at least one Bible woman under her care.[216] In her report to them, Miss Harding credited her health to her mother's good housekeeping which gave her "more comfort in her little home, and time and strength for her work in the villages and for the children."[217] The report described her difficulties with the Catholic priest, who forbade her to visit the women, and attempted to injure her character among them; she ignored him when possible, and continued her visits to the women in their huts.[218]

"Marked Encouragements"

The Gaboon and Corisco Annual Report for the year 1886 noted the continued *embarrassment* of the missionary labors, due to the health-related absences of so many missionaries, the French restrictions on the use of the vernacular languages (which inhibited education and translation work), and the continued interference of the Catholic priests. The Board of Foreign Mission, giving consideration to the climate and the unanimous vote of the missionaries, consented to the eventual withdrawal of the Gaboon and Corisco Mission from the regions under French colonial rule.[219]

Despite these dire conditions, the annual report also included some notable encouragements. Rev. A. C. Good reported both growth and a religious movement in the Ogowe region: "Large numbers of Galwas from far and near have attended the communion services, coming at much inconvenience, and without the least expectation of any personal advantage; and no less than

215. Harding, "African Children," 108.

216. WPBMN, *Annual Report* [1886], 25. See also Seat, *Providence*, 112. Women missionaries' close relationships with women in nineteenth- and twentieth-century Japan increased respect for that nation, and helped transform American attitudes of condescension and discrimination towards non-white persons. See also Stoler, *Carnal Knowledge*, 57. Western women's presence in colonized areas reduced concubinage, though it increased racial separation. Such women championed the cause of colonized women, raising moral standards which protected them.

217. WPBMN, *Annual Report* [1886], 25.

218. WPBMN, *Annual Report* [1886], 25. See Ambouroue-Avaro, *Un Peuple Gabonais*, 234–35, regarding the contribution of the American Protestants among the Galwa people.

219. BFM, *Annual Report* [1887], 60.

one hundred and sixty were admitted to the roll of catechumens, or inquirers, of whom many are women, —a new and most encouraging thing."[220]

The report credited this growth to "the reading and preaching of the Gospel, largely on visits to their villages on the rivers, by the missionaries in their boats."[221] Miss Nassau's report, which was included in the published Annual Report, also remarked on the encouraging "spirit of inquiry that is awakened in all parts of this Ogowe district, especially among the Galwa tribe," which she attributed to the Bible readers, noting that their written quarterly reports to Mr. Good showed diligence in journeying and preaching the Gospel.[222] This Annual Report is notable in its absence of *any reference to Miss Harding's work*, and the omission of her name, except for the roster of missionaries at the beginning of the report. The Kangwe mission report only included the reports of Mr. Good and Miss Nassau, neither of whom acknowledged Miss Harding's role or ministry in the Ogowe, and the certain impact she had among the Galwa people that year. Mr. Good described the continued aggression of the Catholic priests, and the large number of Galwa inquirers, all without mentioning Miss Harding, who was directly involved with both. Miss Nassau wrote glowingly of their progress in the region, but gave recognition and credit only to Mr. Good, and the native Bible readers. Again, Miss Harding was neither mentioned nor credited with her role in this religious awakening in the region.

Rev. A. C. Good reported, in early 1887, that "one hundred and sixty men and women have this year decided for Christ on the Ogove."[223] While the missionaries rejoiced in these record numbers for 1886–87, they felt the increasing stronghold of the French colonial government, and its restrictions on their work.[224] The mission speculated that if the Gaboon work was transferred to French Protestant missionaries, it would be uninhibited by the colonial powers.[225] The Presbyterian Board hoped to transfer their work to the Campo River region, in German territory,

220. BFM, *Annual Report* [1887], 61.

221. BFM, *Annual Report* [1887], 61.

222. BFM, *Annual Report* [1887], 62.

223. GAPC, "Monthly Concert [1887]," 554. Now, "Ogowe" (English), or "Ogooué" (French).

224. See Zomo, *Le Travail des Missions Chrétiennes*, 59, 60. American missionaries were early ethnographers of the local population, though their motivation was religious, rather than cultural.

225. See Hastings, *Church in Africa*, 416. Colonial powers favored missions representing the colonizing nation, and not religious denominations.

in what is now southern Cameroon. The French Protestant Mission later sent delegates and teachers to the Ogowe interior stations.[226]

Opposition and Persecution

Miss Harding, in an 1887 report to the Women's Board, described herself as being in "excellent health and with undaunted spirit,"[227] despite the French authorities having nominally closed her school, and the continued persecution by the Catholic priests. Miss Harding added that one of the priests "became so violent that he was reproved by the commandant, and the result of this excessive zeal on his part, is a more friendly attitude of the official toward the missionary."[228] A fuller description of this incident was included in Miss Harding's handwritten report, giving insight into her courage and tenacity:

> so the commandant instead of giving me a hearing began grumbling about our English school. I told him that we had no school whatever and that I had no scholars at all and that I had only four work boys to paddle my canoe. He showed me my English book and I showed him that it was only a hymn book and that I only used it for the music that I looked at while playing my concertina. Then he grumbled some more about the colony being anglicized and returned my books to me. I then grumbled some more about the defencelessness [sic] of an American woman in his colony. So he said he would report the priest to the head commandant at Gaboon.[229]

In 1887, Miss Harding was visiting three to six towns per day, five days per week, teaching and reading to the people who came to listen. She was printing materials in Mpongwe language, and had acquired enough of the Fangwe dialect to teach her inquirers the Lord's Prayer in their language, as well as answers to over a hundred Catechism questions. She reported that the Fangwe were proud to think that she could speak in their language, and listened to her with delight. They especially appreciated the hymns, as they were very great lovers of music. One day, after Miss Harding had taught them about the woman who was a sinner, who washed Jesus's feet with her tears, and was forgiven her sins, one of the Fangwe women followed her to the river

226. GAPC, "Monthly Concert [1888]," 600.

227. WPBMN, *Annual Report [1887]*, 27.

228. WPBMN, *Annual Report [1887]*, 27.

229. Mary Harding to Unknown Recipient, 1887; Report to the Standing Committee, 1887.

landing, and said 'He is kind . . . what must I do to be saved?' These incidents more than repaid Miss Harding for her arduous labors.[230]

Revival was now happening on the Ogowe River, and many were added to the church family. Miss Harding was holding a regular women's prayer meeting, with good attendance, and her first pupil at Kangwe (school) was baptized.[231] In her year-end report for 1887, Miss Harding described traveling with a boat and Fangwe crew, "from town to town along the river, scattering the word of life and endeavoring to lead souls to Christ."[232] On Sundays, Miss Harding taught a large class of Fangwe, likely a mixed group of men and women.

Interpersonal Conflict

Robert Hamill Nassau, in his book, *My Ogowe*, mentions Miss Harding multiple times, generally in the context of mission social gatherings and hospitality. Twice in the book, Dr. Nassau alludes to interpersonal tensions between Miss Harding and her colleagues—specifically Miss Isabella Nassau and Rev. Adolphus C. Good. The first instance was in 1885, when Nassau's sister, Isabella, intimated to him that her working relationship with Miss Harding had not been a positive one since their arrival at Kangwe mission in 1883,[233] and that the imminent transfer of Rev. A. C. Good to that mission would further add to her discomfort, as (Dr. Nassau noted) "Mr. Good was a very able man and efficient worker. But, his natural constitution was such that anyone associated with him had to submit under his direction."[234] Miss Nassau asked her brother to allow her to transfer to *his* mission station at Talagouga, several hours' journey upriver from where she and Miss Harding had been stationed. The second instance was in February 1888, when Dr. Nassau accompanied Rev. A. C. Good on a "formal call on Miss Harding on the Hill, relative to some difficulties between him and her, *as to station control*."[235] These are the only two (of fifteen) mentions of Miss Harding in this book which indicate any personality conflicts, and Nassau does not mention the great mission

---

230. Mary Harding to Standing Committee, December 12, 1887.

231. WPBMN, *Annual Report [1887]*, 28.

232. BFMCUSA, *Annual Report [1888]*, 66.

233. Nassau, *My Ogowe*, 472.

234. Nassau, *My Ogowe*, 472.

235. Nassau, *My Ogowe*, 571.

palaver which followed, leading to Miss Harding's recall from the mission field, at the request of her male colleagues.

MISS HARDING'S RECALL

After concluding the meeting with Miss Harding and Rev. Good, Dr. Nassau wrote to the Corresponding Secretary that the Mission Standing Committee was requesting that Miss Harding be recalled. Rev. Good had earlier asked that the mission remove Miss Harding from the Ogove, and send her to the Benita station on the northern coast. Nassau noted that *all the mission* was aware of the difficulties with Miss Harding, but "no one was willing to *relieve Mr. Good of Miss H.'s presence.*"[236] The mission decided that Miss Harding must remove herself from Kangwe and relocate to Gaboon (Baraka), to await their decision on her future work and location. They hoped she would either voluntarily return to America, or that she would alter her conduct and be accepted at Benita. Nassau went to great length detailing Rev. Good's written requests that Miss Harding report to the Mission Standing Committee, and her *refusal* to go, despite adequate time and the availability of transportation from Kangwe to Gaboon. Nassau listed the charges by the mission against her: "her brutal treatment of the natives, her unjust suspicions, her bitter hostilities, her unchristian disharmony and the scandalous exhibitions of them before the heathen and the injury of Peace, and the hindrance of our work."[237]

Several missionary men related a story about Miss Harding's confrontation with Miss Isabella Nassau, during which she accused Miss N. of being a *liar* and said *she would go to hell*. However, there is no written testimony by Miss Nassau, and none of these men were eyewitnesses to the event, which seems to have happened in 1884, as per Mr. Reading. Dr. Nassau, years later, admitted that Mr. Reading had wanted the Session to investigate the incident at that time, but Dr. Nassau felt the matter should not be made public.[238]

---

236. Robert Hamill Nassau to Board Secretary, February 23, 1888. Italics added. It is difficult to assess whether Miss Harding's ostracism was based on her ethnicity or her alleged personality conflicts with fellow missionaries.

237. Robert Hamill Nassau to Board Secretary, February 23, 1888.

238. Robert Hamill Nassau to Board Secretary, February 23, 1888, A. C., Letter dated February 24, 1888;

In one of the first letters detailing Miss Harding's interpersonal conflicts, Mr. Reading described her as having "too much temper and tongue,"[239] which he predicted would cause problems with the French colonial authorities. Reading used Miss Harding's example as a reason why the mission should never again send them a person of mixed parentage nor any person of color, as he believed it would produce only evil results. Reading admired Miss Harding's language skills and desire to do ministry, but believed that she carried, as a person of color, too heavy a burden to serve well in that stressful climate. Reading added that it was common knowledge that children resulting from a cross between races possess the evil qualities of both parents, and none of the good. "What then of a girl that has Negro, White and Indian in her veins?"[240] Mr. Reading felt sympathy for Miss Harding, but believed she could be more useful in ministry elsewhere.

Dr. Nassau asserted that Mr. Good bore Miss Harding's behavior with great patience, despite her "disregard for his position as *master of Kangwe*,"[241] and reminded the Board Secretary of the mission policy that *one gentleman* is given charge of a mission station.[242] Nassau related more complaints against Miss Harding, involving excessive corporal punishment of female pupils, though mission leaders apparently asked the complainant to remain quiet on the matter, and there was no investigation. Dr. Nassau, like Mr. Reading, pointed to Miss Harding's station in life, the insecurity of her social status, her sensitivity to unintended and misinterpreted actions or words of others, and her *unchristian conduct*.[243]

Dr. Nassau did not side with his sister in these controversies, as her personality was also difficult. He did make the *only* reference to what may be the *root* of the tensions between Miss Nassau and Miss Harding—that Miss Harding was originally expected to be *subordinate to Miss Nassau*: "As soon as she arrived at Gaboon in 1882, she resented the position that which

239. Joseph Reading to Dr. Lowrie, August 7, 1884.

240. Robert Hamill Nassau to Board Secretary, February 23, 1888. See also ACS, "Our Colored Population," 266–83. An 1843 study purported to show a high rate of insanity among biracial persons, due to their physical weakness (compared to pure blacks), their lack of congenial society, and the painful contrast between themselves and their neighbors.

241. Robert Hamill Nassau to Board Secretary, February 23, 1888.

242. See Bowie et al., *Women and Mission*, 9. Details on Frances Davidson, who faced many of the same gender-based mission tensions as the Harding case. She also left the field for these reasons.

243. Robert Hamill Nassau to Board Secretary, February 23, 1888.

she had been appointed by the W.F.M.S."[244] Miss Nassau recognized this while they were still en route to Gaboon; she knew that this arrangement was not possible, and did not wish to be in a superior role over Miss Harding. When the two women arrived on the field, Miss Harding was then given an independent work, and equal status with Miss Nassau and every other missionary woman on the field. Both Dr. Nassau and Rev. Good noted the tacit friction between the two women, especially during public communion services, though Rev. Good "preferred to delay action."[245]

It should be noted that Miss Nassau also had personality conflicts with fellow missionaries prior to Miss Harding's arrival on the field. In late 1881, while Miss Nassau was on furlough in America, Dr. Bacheler wrote a letter to the Board Secretary to question their decision to send Miss Nassau back to the field, without consulting her co-laborers, as all the other missionaries were opposed to her return. None of the women would live with her, and many believed her to be *insane*. Bacheler witnessed Miss Nassau's frequent bouts of hysteria; she was often prostrated with mental crises, which were "terrible for herself and for all around her."[246] Dr. Bacheler cited her return as one of the incentives for his own departure from the field.

When the Mission Standing Committee suggested the transfer of Miss Harding to Benita station, there were strong responses from the missionary women serving there. Mrs. Reutlinger responded in protest, fearing that Miss Harding would destroy their harmony at Benita station; Mrs. DeHeer also refused. Dr. Nassau, in relating these responses to the Board secretary, reveals that only the Ogowe missionaries were witnesses of the charges against Miss Harding, while the other mission personnel (likely those at Benita) had *never met Miss Harding* and knew *only what their colleagues had told them about her*. Mr. Marling generously offered to build a little place for her two miles from his Angom station. His wife, however, was so strongly opposed to the idea that Marling immediately withdrew his offer.[247]

---

244. Robert Hamill Nassau to Board Secretary, February 23, 1888.

245. Robert Hamill Nassau to Board Secretary, February 23, 1888.

246. Henry Bacheler to Dr. Lowrie, June 23, 1881.

247. Robert Hamill Nassau to Board Secretary, February 23, 1888.

Restrictions, Recollections and Repercussions

The Mission Standing Committee resorted to withholding Miss Harding's appropriations and gave her no appointment, thinking she would then resign voluntarily. Dr. Nassau reported that Miss Harding was determined to stand her ground, and they could not restrict her salary without orders from the Board. She remained at Kangwe at her own expense, and seemed to be gaining sympathy for what appeared to be persecution. Dr. Nassau felt that, while Miss Harding could influence her supporter, Mrs. Chandler, she must remember that she occupied a property belonging to the Mission.[248]

After relating these details in a letter to the Board Secretary, Dr. Nassau speculated that Miss Harding would "probably deny all this, or most of it, and write you a very nice letter.[249] He then pleaded that the Board send four more men to the mission, as the current male missionaries were likely to leave in the near future.

Charges against Miss Harding

Rev. A.C. Good sent a letter to the Corresponding Secretary, relating his account of the difficulties with Miss Harding. Good acknowledged that he had been "unwilling to ventilate so disagreeable a subject until absolutely necessary,"[250] and he, too, described their multiple requests that she attend meetings at the Gaboon, and her "refusal" to come, despite written requests and multiple opportunities for travel to Gaboon. Good had hoped that "a consultation with her might lead to some arrangement by which she could be removed from the surroundings and circumstances which in the Ogove have rendered her life a hindrance instead of a help to the work. No charges or complaints were put on record."[251] At their January 1888 meetings, Rev. Good felt bound to reveal facts which convinced nearly all of the Mission Standing Committee that, whatever was decided, Miss Harding should no longer be allowed to remain in the Ogowe region. Good's knowledge of the difficulties between Miss Nassau and Miss Harding, dating back to their ocean voyage in 1882, was based on *hearsay*, as he was stationed at Gaboon (Baraka) for his first two years on the mission. Good felt that Miss Harding, in her behavior toward Miss Nassau, had "shown a violence of temper

248. Robert Hamill Nassau to Board Secretary, February 23, 1888.
249. Robert Hamill Nassau to Board Secretary, February 23, 1888.
250. Adolphus Good to Board Secretary, February 24, 1888.
251. Adolphus Good to Board Secretary, February 24, 1888.

and language, which is utterly unwomanly and unchristian, and *which puts her in the wrong no matter what the merits of the quarrel*."[252] Good regretted that he had destroyed the one written piece of evidence which would prove his accusations against Miss Harding. In 1884, while Rev. Good was still at Baraka, Miss Harding had sent him a letter concerning a quarrel "of which I can only remember that the language was so violent, unwomanly [and] unchristian that I was horrified and disgusted. I remember that it was full of such expressions as 'devil,' 'liar,' and 'she will go to hell' referring to Miss N. Unfortunately I tore the letter up at once. If I could today lay that letter before you I would not need to write anything to convince you that Miss H. is not fit to be a missionary of the Gospel of Christ."[253] Rev. Good added that Miss Nassau pursued friendship and reconciliation, but was repeatedly (and publicly) rebuffed by Miss Harding. Good pleaded with Miss Harding to forgive Miss Nassau, but she responded with visible passion and a loud voice, "I will never forgive Miss Nassau, she has wronged me too deeply for me ever to forgive."[254]

Good recounted to the Board Secretary several of Miss Harding's complaints: that Miss Nassau has, from the time they came to the Ogowe, told the natives to call Miss Harding a "nigger" and "slave;" told them not to greet her and that they should curse her; that Mr. Reading and Miss Nassau told the "natives" to call her "Mary" rather than "Miss Mary"; that Rev. Good's "boys" insulted her and made racial remarks about Miss Harding and her employees, that Good's "people" openly curse and disrespect her in his presence (with no rebuke from Good), that Miss Nassau or Mr. Reading told the "slaves" who work on the hill across the river from Kangwe, to shout curses at her, and that Mr. Reading was at the bottom of the affair with the Catholic priests interrupting her work, by writing to local traders that they should ask the priests to do so.[255]

Rev. Good felt that Miss Harding's fits of passion and her constant brooding over perceived wrongs had had a negative effect on her Christian character. He expressed surprise at Miss Harding's sudden denial of all of her longstanding complaints, now that the mission was addressing them. Good anticipated that Miss Harding would write to the Board to deny that she had

252. Adolphus Good to Board Secretary, February 24, 1888. Italics added.
253. Adolphus Good to Board Secretary, February 24, 1888.
254. Adolphus Good to Board Secretary, February 24, 1888.
255. Adolphus Good to Board Secretary, February 24, 1888.

quarrels with the natives or with missionary colleagues. Good then ended his long letter with an acknowledgement that it was her word against his:

> I have only this to say. It is a question of veracity between me and Miss Harding. If you believe her then your opinion of me must be such that you should lose not a day in recalling me to America. If you believe my statements then it seems to be you must admit that Miss H. ought not to stand on a mission field as a representative of the meek, loving, longsuffering Jesus of Nazareth. I therefore not hastily, but after three [years] patiently enduring these scandals on this station, now at last join my brethren in asking you to remove Miss Harding from the mission field.[256]

Mr. Joseph Reading added his own reflections on the Harding controversy, in a letter to the Board, dated March 1888. He regretted having anything to do with it, though expressed some concern about monetary questions. Reading candidly recommended that the Board proceed slowly in Miss Harding's case, noting that Dr. Nassau had been equally troublesome, at times. While the mission might do better without her, Reading felt it wasn't fair to recall her in disgrace, based on a complaint from Dr. Nassau, until she had had fair warning or opportunity to improve. Reading recommended they consult the ladies who sent her out.[257]

Public Perception of the "Palaver"

The situation worsened in the next two months, as Mr. Reading's subsequent letter to the Board noted that the mission's action toward Miss Harding was now bearing its *legitimate fruit*. Apparently her being confined at Kangwe with no appropriation had become a subject of gossip among the secular community along the coast, and a scandal to the mission. Reading described how the case appeared to those outside the mission:

> that Miss Harding and Mr. Good have quarreled. Mr. Good has written home to have her sent away in disgrace. In the meantime, he will not let her have anything and so she is a prisoner in her home and its immediate premises. The latter statement is true, as they can see for themselves. You can easily see what an occasion this gives to the enemies of the Cross of Christ to draw all sorts of comparisons and say all sorts of hateful things. But the evil does not stop there. The *educated natives* who are employed about the

256. Adolphus Good to Board Secretary, February 24, 1888.
257. Joseph Reading to Corresponding Secretary, March 1888.

factories and steamers *add their comments* and so it goes thro' the native communities up and down the river and along the coast.[258] In a bachelor community like this, public opinion takes the lady's part, especially as *they cannot understand what Miss H. has done that she [should] deserve to be thus treated* . . . I doubt not in the least that this whole affair was gotten up by the arch enemy to counteract the effect of the splendid revival that has been going on at Kangwe.[259]

Reading then admitted that there was no place where she could serve, within the mission, yet away from the *brethren,* "where no one will trouble her and yet she can have the comfortable home she deserves."[260] Reading added that they (his family and Miss Harding) had once lived at Kangwe in the same home and had been very happy in that arrangement.

The Board's Perspective

Corresponding Secretary, Dr. John Gillespie, wrote a response to the mission, expressing his pain and disappointment at the Mission's request for the withdrawal of Miss Harding. He urged them to proceed cautiously, and noted that the Board would have to hear Miss Harding's side of the issue before making a decision on the matter. Gillespie wondered whether they could find for her a work within the bounds of the mission, but separate from that of her colleagues, and out of immediate contact of them, stating, "if some field of usefulness could be found where she could do something for the Master it would avoid the humiliation of her recall, which, of course must be attended with a great deal of personal feeling, and more or less publicity."[261]

Miss Harding's Response

Miss Harding's perspective on all of these events is expressed in a letter to the Board, dated August 9, 1888; a full eight months after the Mission Standing Committee began their campaign to have her recalled. Miss Harding thanked Dr. Gillespie for his communication about the mission's

258. The *educated natives* would be former pupils of the mission schools, whose opinions of the mission were informed by their own experiences and the collective memories of their community, dating back forty-six years.

259. Joseph Reading to Corresponding Secretary, May 22, 1888. Italics added.

260. Joseph Reading to Corresponding Secretary, May 22, 1888.

261. John Gillespie to the Gaboon and Corisco Mission, May 15, 1888.

called meeting of February 13, and added that she was "very sorry that the Mission Meeting did not forward to you my letter to it explaining my inability to attend that meeting. *It was very unjust to me and to my side of the case to suppress that letter.*"[262]

In response to the charges that she refused to attend called meetings, at Baraka, Miss Harding gave a detailed account of the unavailability of steamers passing to and from Kangwe. She had never attended mission meeting since her arrival in the Ogowe, and was told that it wasn't necessary for ladies to attend these meetings, which involved only men, who transacted all business. She could not leave her belongings behind, in an old bamboo house, which could be easily broken into; she knew that if she went to Gaboon, the gentlemen would not allow her to return to the Ogowe to pack her things. She then defended her desire and right to remain, as she had worked long and faithfully, and was attached to the people. She had given herself unreservedly to the mission work and had wearied herself, mind and body, in the daily discharge of her work. Miss Harding asserted that the actions against her by the mission were unnecessary and unjust, and felt that some of the members ought to apologize to her for their untrue statements about her. She then added her theory that "the real reason of their hostility is that I have shown *no matrimonial inclination.*"[263]

Miss Harding believed that the decision of the mission to stop appropriations had done more harm than anything she had ever done, and that the natives were anxiously asking her why she no longer visited their towns, and begged her to return. She expressed surprise at the January mission meeting actions against her, noting that she had often been helpful to Rev. Good in his mission work, such as making a long canoe journey down the river to procure food for him and his workers, and printing materials for his French boys' school. She felt that she, herself, ought to have had a school for the past two years. She could pronounce French well and was familiar with French idioms; "Besides I am the best teacher in the mission, so far as I am acquainted with the missionaries. When the French Commandant last visited me he was surprised that I had no school, and said that I ought to have one. It has [been] kept from me only on account [of] personal prejudice."[264] Miss Harding had working knowledge of both Mpongwe and Fangwe dialects, and reminded the Board Secretary that

262. Mary Harding to Dr. Gillespie, August 9, 1888.
263. Mary Harding to Dr. Gillespie, August 9, 1888. Italics added.
264. Mary Harding to Dr. Gillespie, August 9, 1888.

she had often been left as sole missionary in the station. She had held all religious services during the five months that her colleagues were absent, and these were well-attended.[265]

MISSION REPRISAL

Rev. A. C. Good sent an August 1888 letter to Dr. Gillespie, in response to the Board's earlier letter asking to hear Miss Harding's side of the story. While he agreed that the Board had pursued the right course, Good argued that Miss Harding had deliberately kept them in the dark, and that they might have acted differently if they were more aware of the full story. Good's view was that Miss Harding had been fully informed and knew all that was being done, yet she had "kept consistently to the policy of doing nothing."[266]

Good noted that Miss Harding had received Dr. Gillespie's letter, and that if he (Gillespie) didn't receive a response from her, acknowledging receipt of that letter in the same mailing, that he (Gillespie) should know that he is being treated with contempt. Good then speculated on what Miss Harding might write, or leave out: "I fancy she will just deny in toto that there is or has been any difficulty between her and her fellow missionaries."[267] Good then went on to discredit Miss Harding's mastery of the Fangwe language, as well as her printing work in the indigenous languages.

A note, written by Miss Harding to Mr. Reading (enclosed in Good's letter), relates some details of the mission on the Ogowe, and an account of a pupil and French missionary pulling out weapons against one another. Miss Harding adds, "since mission meeting stopped my work it is surprising how much stronger I have grown. The roses are returning to my pale cheeks. I was breaking down my health unconsciously before kind Providence procured me a rest. Mother joins me in sending you our best respects. Please remember us to all the missionaries."[268]

Missionary Joseph Reading commented on what he termed the *Nassau-Harding palaver*, attributing the entire problem to Miss Harding's

---

265. Mary Harding to Dr. Gillespie, August 9, 1888. The Fangwe people were fierce warriors and cannibals, and many were terrified of them. In hiring Fangwe paddlers, preaching to Fangwe crowds, and teaching them hymns, she proved she was not afraid of them.

266. Adolphus Good to Corresponding Secretary, August, 20, 1888.

267. Adolphus Good to Corresponding Secretary, August, 20, 1888.

268. Mary Harding to Joseph Reading, August 21, 1888.

"mixed blood."[269] The following week, Reading wrote that the Hardings would depart the next day, stating, "this whole day has seemed to me like a funeral—I can hardly keep from crying. Here is a strong, healthy young woman who knows the work and can speak the language fairly well; contented, willing to work, no home ties, —going home in disgrace to gratify personal spite—these things ought not to be."[270]

THE HISTORICAL RECORD

Because the Gaboon and Corisco Mission history has been documented and written by men, much of the material lauds the work and accomplishments of missionary men, while largely ignoring the presence and work of the women. A careful gleaning of available Presbyterian archives, coupled with extensive research in online public and genealogical records have yielded further details on Miss Harding and Mrs. Sneed, both of whom returned to America.

Mary Harding

Miss Harding's work in the Ogowe has been remarkably understated, if not ignored, by Presbyterian annals and historical documents.

Much of what has been written about the Gaboon and Corisco Mission was preserved, compiled and written by Dr. Robert Hamill Nassau, who said very little about Miss Harding and her work on the Ogowe, during her six years in that remote region. In an article written a decade after Miss Harding's departure, Nassau described his having inaugurated the work in the Ogowe River region, and that the work was "carried on during later years by my associates, Rev. W. H. Robinson, H. M. Bacheler, M.D., Mrs. J. M. Smith, Miss I. A. Nassau, *and others*, until the grain began to ripen in 1886, just as Rev. A. C. Good, Ph.D., joined us to help gather in the sheaves."[271] Considering that those missionaries mentioned by name had spent three or less years in the work, and most were debilitated by recurrent fevers or other health issues, it is significant that Miss Harding's name is not mentioned in this article.

Miss Harding's sending church, the Ann Arbor Presbyterian Church, summarized her missionary career in Africa in their 1961 history:

269. Joseph Reading to Corresponding Secretary, March 29, 1889.
270. Joseph Reading to Corresponding Secretary, April 5, 1889.
271. Nassau, "Sowing Beside All Waters," 345. Italics added.

One member of the church, Mary Harding, a colored girl who worked her way through college, wanted to go to Africa as a missionary. She was accepted by the Board of the Northwest and, with the aid of the Presbyterian Society, she and her mother went to Africa. She did her best but the natives did not like her. After five years she returned and found work with the Freedman's Board among the negroes in the South.[272]

Miss Harding began a new work immediately after her return to the US, serving as a teacher for the Presbyterian Freedman's Bureau, among the African American families in the southern states. In one of her earliest reports, Miss Harding noted her surprise at seeing African American Christians engage in what she considered *ecstatic* and *heathenish* dance: "I am surprised to find so many relics of barbarism in the midst of civilization as I have found since I came here."[273] She was delighted to be teaching children and adults, including married couples, two preachers and one elderly man in spectacles.[274]

Women missionaries assigned to teach in the Freedmen's Bureau schools were supported financially through the WMPF. Scant records show that Miss Harding taught in at least two schools in Arkansas, though there are no records of her after 1910.

Lavinia Sneed

Lavinia Sneed remained with the mission for a total of twenty-four years (1867–1891), the longest record of service among the African Americans, and longer than most of the white missionaries.[275] She was also the last African American to serve with the Gaboon and Corisco Mission.

272. Goodrich, *Historical Facts and Events*, IV–3). See also Brown, *One Hundred Years*, 1098. Arthur Brown's lengthy history on the Presbyterian mission in West Africa makes no mention of Miss Harding, but for her name on the missionary list. The letter "C" designated *missionaries of color*; Miss Harding is not thus designated. Missionaries listed with the "C" designation are Charity Sneed Menkel, and the Underhills, who were sent in 1928.

273. Harding, "Freedmen [1890]," 231.

274. Harding, "Freedmen, [1891]," 156.

275. Rev. Albert Bushnell, Rev. William Walker, Rev. Cornelius DeHeer and Rev. Robert Hamill Nassau, MD all served thirty years or more. Mrs. Louise Reutlinger, Mrs. Reubina DeHeer, Miss Isabella Nassau, and Mrs. Phebe Ogden also put in between twenty-five and thirty-five years. All of these took periodic furloughs of one or more years during their tenure.

In 1882, Mrs. Sneed was fully engaged in support work for the mission, and was paid a modest sum for the full-time care of her four grandchildren, while they remained in Africa. By contrast, Mrs. Bushnell and Mrs. Ogden, both elderly widows serving in supportive roles, were given formal appointments and full missionary status.[276] Mrs. Sneed's appropriation in the 1888 mission budget was $50, at a time when Mrs. Ogden, also an elderly widow, was receiving $400—equal to what the younger, single missionary women (Harding, Jones) were earning at the time.[277] Mrs. Sneed's last grandchild, Grace Menkel, left for America circa 1889. At that point, mission treasurer, J. H. Reading questioned whether Mrs. Sneed's $50 allowance would be considered a "pension," as no *white missionaries* could receive a pension.[278]

Lavinia Sneed remained with the mission until 1891, when she learned that Dr. Nassau was leaving with his small daughter, Mary. He includes this account in his book, *My Ogowe*,

> When good old Mrs. Sneed heard my plans for going to the United States, she felt as if the last of her friends would be gone. Her daughter had died; the children had been sent to homes in the United States; the husband had re-married, and she exclaimed to me, "O Doctor! I wish I could lay my old bones in America!" "Do you really mean it?" "Sure I do!"[279]

Nassau had already anticipated this decision, and had contacted a friend in Philadelphia, who located for him a home for aged colored people in that city.[280] By that time, Mrs. Sneed was about sixty-four years of age and had no formal role with the mission. At Nassau's suggestion, the Board paid for Mrs. Sneed's passage, and her placement in the home. The Board Secretary authorized the treasurer to "meet the charges growing out of this action in both cases."[281]

Dr. Nassau's private journal records their ocean voyage and early weeks in the US. The two accompanied one another on various family and social visits, indicating the enduring familial bond established decades earlier. Mrs. Sneed had been "nurse" to the Nassau boys from 1867 until 1870, and also had a close relationship with little Mary Nassau, who was seven in 1891.

276. Joseph Reading to Dr. Lowrie, January 12, 1883.

277. Gillespie, Estimates for 1888 for the Gaboon and Corisco Mission.

278. Reading, *Letter to the Corresponding Secretary, dated July 6, 1889.*

279. Nassau, *My Ogowe*, 693.

280. Nassau, *My Ogowe*, 693.

281. John Gillespie to Gaboon and Corisco Mission, July 7, 1890.

Honoring the wishes of his first wife, Mary Latta Nassau, Dr. Nassau looked after Mrs. Sneed as she transitioned to America, thirty-seven years after her departure as an emigrant to Liberia. Mrs. Sneed lived out her final years at the Stephen Smith Home, in Philadelphia, where she died in October 1906. Her official death certificate lists her occupation as *missionary*.[282]

Full Circle

Interestingly, the Bible Woman who succeeded Julia Green was Mrs. Sarah Dorsey Lewis,[283] daughter of Americo-Liberian Josiah Dorsey and West African, Mary Clealand Dorsey.[284] Both Sarah and her sister, Celia, were considered Mpongwe, due to their birth and assimilation into the local culture.[285] Missionary Jean Kenyon Mackenzie wrote of "Ma Sara" in her book, *Black Sheep*, which was printed in parts in the Atlantic Monthly.[286] Sarah appeared in Mary Kingsley's famous work, *Travels in West Africa*,[287] the author having been invited to a church ladies' meeting. "Ma Sarah" was still serving at the Baraka Mission in 1911—nearly seventy years after her father, Josiah Dorsey, arrived with the original A.B.C.F.M. missionary party—when the last of the American missionaries withdrew from the work, leaving Baraka church and schools in the hands of the native Christians.[288]

---

282. Eden, Eden Cemetery Interment Book, 1906, 236. Lavinia Sneed was buried at the Eden Cemetery, "Smith Home" section. The log notes "Lavinia Snead" age "45 years" [*sic*]. Burial October 30, 1906. As she was 26 in 1854, Mrs. Sneed was in her seventies at her death. Her grave is unmarked, and unknown. The Ancestry.com website includes the "All Philadelphia, Pennsylvania, Death Certificates Index, 1803–1915" (FHL Film Number 1319472), which states that Lavinia Sneed died October 27, 1906. This record lists her occupation as *missionary*.

283. BFM, *Annual Report* [1895], 21.

284. MacKenzie, *Black Sheep*, 795.

285. Nassau, *My Ogowe*, 315.

286. Mackenzie, "Black Sheep: Part III," 795.

287. Kingsley, *Travels in West Africa*, 116–17.

288. BFM, *Annual Report* [1911], 63–64.

Mrs. Sarah Dorsey Lewis, daughter of Josiah and Mary Clealand Dorsey
(Albert I Good Papers)

Fanwe Warrior (R. Nassau 1914, 681)

Fanwe Woman (R. Nassau 1914, 380)

Galwe women (R. Nassau 1914, 258)

Kangwe Mission schoolgirls carrying firewood. (R. Nassau 1914, 512)

Mr. Peter Menkel, husband of Charity Sneed Menkel
(Courtesy of Menkel family)

Rev. Adolphus C. Good, who led the effort to dismiss Miss Harding
(Parsons 1897, 75)

Mr. Joseph H. Reading, his wife, Mary, and daughter.
(Courtesy of Laura O'Brien)

Lydia Walker Good was helpful to Peter Menkel in his distress. Mrs. Good
was full Native American, but did not suffer the race discrimination that
Miss Harding did (Courtesy of Laura O'Brien)

6

Epilogue: The Unsent

"ON SENDING COLORED BRETHREN" —1888

THE PRESBYTERIAN BOARD ONCE again asked the missionaries, in late 1888, their opinion on the sending of *colored brethren* to the Gaboon and Corisco Mission.

Input From Missionaries

Joseph Reading, who had arrived on the field in 1875, gave his opinion:

> Twice since I have been connected with the mission this has come up and been settled. I have my doubts of colored men from America being valuable in mission work here; the native resents their superiority, and themselves find the superstitions and [obscured] customs appealing very powerfully to them coming as they do from their own race. Whatever good they may do will be best developed by grouping them in missions by themselves. We have such a mission in Liberia, let them go there. We have all we can stagger under with these Frenchmen. Thrown so completely upon one another as we are here, we need to be of a kind as far as possible. The Nassau-Harding palaver came in the first place from Miss Harding's mixed blood. But there is another question—the effect it will have on our native brethren. They are the peers of these men. If the American negro is not a member of our Standing Committee there will be endless trouble; and if he is, then the

native minister must be, too, then what of the funds? I [would] regard it a calamity, and not a light one either, to send even one.[1]

Dr. Nassau also replied to this query by the Board, indicating that the question pertained to recent or future Lincoln University graduates who were seeking placement on the mission field in Africa. Nassau had visited Lincoln University (formerly Ashmun Institute) in the early 1870s, and had been offended that a mulatto speaker had made the following statement in a commencement address: "We admit no claim on us of duty to Africa other than lies on any other educated Christians. We are American; of American soil; with no fore-fathers graves in Africa."[2] Nassau felt some bitterness regarding Lincoln, which was originally founded for Africa, yet had done so little for Africa. Nassau argued that Lincoln made much ado about ten native African students who were to be educated and sent back as missionaries among their own people. Nassau estimated that this cost ten times as much money than if they were educated in humility at such a school in Africa. Nassau questioned whether they went back in such a capacity among their own people, and asked, "Did not the [two] who went out under the Board claim to be put on a footing with American missionaries in salary and expenses?"[3]

Dr. Nassau agreed that colored brethren should come to the Gaboon and Corisco field, though he was not sure whether they would be successful; he felt that American blacks are similar to whites in their physical adaptation, though they do not have the same *will-force* or *indomitable purpose* needed to withstand the climate and hardships in Africa. Nassau refuted the idea that American blacks would have more sympathy with, or accomplish more among, the native Africans, due to their common ethnicity, because they were foreigners, just as the whites were foreigners. Nassau believed that there would be tensions between American blacks and *native* Africans, partly due to the insecurity of American blacks, and their unwillingness to *come down to* the level of the native, and partly due to the free-born African's scorn of those who were (or had once been) slaves. Nassau believed that American Negro brother would be *neither fish*

1. Joseph Reading to Corresponding Secretary, March 29, 1889.

2. Robert Hamill Nassau to Dr. Gillespie, April 24, 1889. See Walker, "Walker's Appeal," 68; Richard Allen: "This land which we have watered with our tears and our blood is now our mother country, and we are well satisfied to stay where wisdom abounds and the gospel is free."

3. Robert Hamill Nassau to Dr. Gillespie, April 24, 1889.

nor fowl— even with fraternal acceptance from fellow missionaries, they would likely be discriminated against by the native population; Nassau was certain that the native would prefer to be governed by a white man, and consider a black foreigner lower in status than their highest class of natives. Nassau added that certain missionaries did not associate closely with natives and had never invited Pastor Ibia to eat with them. Nassau held himself in stark contrast, stating that he associated closely with his native brethren, and would "if need were . . . marry a Negress."[4] Nassau ended the letter stating that an American Negro missionary would fare better among the *freedmen* in Liberia, though he did not object to his coming to the Gaboon and Corisco Mission:

> Let him come; he shall have the fairest chance for success that I can aid him to. But I do not think he is coming very fast. Rejoicing in his citizenship, and the dream of a Presidential Chair, he is thinking only of doctors, lawyers, legislators. To ask him to go back and down to his "brethren" in Africa is an insult![5]

Rev. A. C. Good also replied to the *colored brethren question* with an emphatic "yes"—but on certain terms: he felt they should come as members of the local Presbytery, yet subject to the mission as to location and finances. Good also felt they should come for life, identify themselves with the native population and have a status equal to the native ordained ministers; they would not be members of the Mission.[6]

Input From the Indigenous Church

There is no indication that the Board posed the question to the African pastors, or to the indigenous church in Gaboon, regarding the sending of *colored brethren* from America. Yet, in April 1889, the indigenous Gaboon Church communicated directly to the Board Secretary, Dr. Gillespie, their strong feelings and opinions about missionaries sent by the Board, and indicated their preferences for future missionaries. The primary purpose of the letter was to express their disapproval of Mr. Reading: that they had never wanted Mr. Reading to be their leader or preacher, that his sermons were theologically questionable, and that his motive for coming was not for the sake of the Gospel, but for secular, commercial gain. The indigenous

4. Robert Hamill Nassau to Dr. Gillespie, April 24, 1889.
5. Robert Hamill Nassau to Dr. Gillespie, April 24, 1889.
6. Adolphus Good to Dr. Gillespie, May 12, 1889.

Gaboon Church accused Reading of serving both God and mammon, and attempting to lead the Gaboon Christians to do the same. The church then pleaded with the Board to send out missionary leaders of the caliber of Murphy, Pierce, Best and Campbell. Lastly, they intimated that Reading (whose wife and child had returned to the United States) was luring Gabonese churchwomen away from their husbands.[7]

Question of Sending White Missionaries to Liberia

Rankin, in an 1890 article on Presbyterian missions in West Africa, listed missionaries, both black and white, who were sent by the Board to Liberia. Three ordained graduates of the Ashmun Institute (later Lincoln University) went in 1859, and all three died within the following six to ten years. Another decade passed before another graduate of that institution, Rev. Darius E. Donnell, was sent out as a missionary. He died within six months of his arrival in Africa. The last *white* missionary sent to Liberia was German-American, Rev. Edward Boeklen, who died there in 1868, after two years' service. Rankin reported that, as of 1890, there were five ordained ministers and five lay teachers—*all colored*—the largest number ever having served in Liberia. Rankin cited the 1888 Annual Report, which posed the question, "Why should not the Board return to its former usage of sending white missionaries to Liberia?"—adding his reply that the statistics over the previous thirty years showed "little difference between white and colored laborers."[8] Rankin advocated for the sending of another white missionary leader, citing the example of David A. Wilson three decades earlier, and reminded readers of J. L. Wilson's opinion that natives had great respect for the white man.[9] Rankin's views indicate that the rapidly-multiplying white missionary force would potentially reclaim Liberia, the one field open to missionaries of African descent.

Several years later, in 1894, the Board of Foreign Missions faced criticism from several fronts, pertaining to racial discrimination on the part of its missionaries serving in Africa. The first was a public revelation, by Dr. Nassau, of the Gaboon and Corisco Mission's policy of subordinating, and discriminating against, African church leaders; the second was the mission's apparent unwillingness to received *colored* missionary

---

7. Gaboon Church to Rev. John Gillespie, April 18, 1889.
8. Rankin, "Incidents of Missions," 540.
9. Rankin, "Incidents of Missions," 541.

candidates from America, despite the availability of qualified and conse-crated *colored brethren*.

GABOON AND CORISCO MISSION "COLOR LINE"

The Board of Foreign Mission sent yet another inquiry to the Gaboon and Corisco missionaries, in 1894, asking their opinion on the possibility of sending *colored missionaries*, and apprising them of a potential candidate, a young woman of nineteen, named Miss McLeod.

Regarding the Appointment of "Colored Brethren"

Individual missionary responses to the Board's question on sending Afri-can American missionaries were written and sent in 1894, and compiled by the Board in early 1895. Several of the letters refer to the application of Miss McLeod, though most answer the question more broadly.

R. H. Milligan felt that any appointed colored men should be equal in salary and position as the whites. He based this on scriptural teach-ing, the mission policy of maintaining equal status between ordained and unordained men, as well as professional and unprofessional personnel; blacks could not live on less than the whites' salaries, which were very basic. Milligan felt that black missionaries could not *condescend* as the whites do: "for we never may act toward the natives as kindly as we feel, it is so easy for an African to become familiar and impudent, and they would more easily become so to one of their own color."[10] Milligan also felt that blacks would be more likely to fall into "certain kinds of immorality,"[11] particularly because of skin color. Native people had a superstition that white men had powerful charms which protect them from harm; they would likely not fear the black missionary in the same way.[12]

Milligan noted that it was *proper* to compare the colored missionary with the native worker trained by the Mission. While the colored mission-ary would have superior training, both intellectual and spiritual, the native worker would be able to live as the local people do, and would either know the language, or be able to learn it rapidly. Milligan estimated that the native worker would cost one-sixth as much as the missionary, including salary, transportation and other costs. Milligan expressed concern that

10. BFM, Colored Missionaries [1895], 2.
11. BFM, Colored Missionaries [1895], 2.
12. BFM, Colored Missionaries [1895], 5.

white and black missionaries would find it difficult to maintain *congenial fellowship* with one another, due to their difference of taste or temperament. He also felt that the native would certainly treat a *colored missionary* as inferior to the whites.[13]

Dr. Laffin asserted that black missionaries would not necessarily fare better than whites in the climate. He cited the example of missionaries in Congo, where the black missionaries

> certainly were not more acceptable to the natives. They seemed to be continually afraid the natives would not fully appreciate their superiority over them (the natives). I noticed this frequently irritated the natives. Then again, with the exception of one, they seemed to be always looking for slights from the white missionaries and we had to be quite careful in their presence not to do or say any things that could be construed into an insult. This prevented hearty cooperation in the work.[14]

While Laffin was willing to work alongside black missionaries, he felt it was not in the best interest of the mission work to send them.

Mr. Roberts felt that black missionaries "should come as regular missionaries . . . if they have the qualification of missionaries. It is not fair to withhold from a black man just because he is black, what you would give to a white man. God makes no such distinction."[15] Roberts, too, was willing to work alongside black missionaries.

Mrs. DeHeer cited the painful experience of those who had worked with Miss Harding on the Ogowe River. She believed that, while blacks were less likely to suffer from fever, their powers of endurance had proved to be much inferior to whites. In responding to the question of whether black missionaries should be on equal standing with whites, Mrs. DeHeer suggested that if there were more persons "of the mind of Miss Charity Sneed, later Mrs. Menkel, who would be willing to associate themselves with a family and work themselves into respect and recognition"[16] there would be less of a problem. Mrs. DeHeer added,

> it seems to us that if capable men and women present themselves in sufficient numbers (which from past experience seems doubtful), they be placed where they could prove their own powers without

13. BFM, Colored Missionaries [1895], 6.
14. BFM, Colored Missionaries [1895], 8.
15. BFM, Colored Missionaries [1895], 9.
16. BFM, Colored Missionaries [1895], 11.

the too close contact with others which might have a tendency to prejudice and hamper. However, if such be the mind of the majority, personally we are fully prepared to welcome these, and grant them all the recognition deemed just and wise.[17]

Miss Babe expressed her willingness that American colored men and women be received as full missionaries, and equal with the white missionaries, though she was not sure whether the *natives* would treat them with the same respect as they did the white missionaries, though she didn't feel competent to judge without seeing it.[18]

Miss Nassau, in a lengthy letter gave these insights:

> There is no difficulty in our Mission about the position of our best educated native ministers. The colored ministers from America could take a higher position, however, but I think that it would be conceded them, by both native and white brethren. The work and position of the American colored woman could be almost as readily found and adjusted as of the American white woman. I will add that what I have just stated as my opinion of the desirability and feasibility of having colored American co-laborers, is on the assumption that the Board accepts for this place and work colored men and women whose religious educational and to considerable extent their social attainments, have been at least up to the standard required of us white missionaries. I say "up to it", for all of us, though blending well in our work here, have not had equally extensive previous preparation. We have seen, how good common sense and complete whole souled consecration can win souls of the heathen African to Christ, where high literary attainments and social culture almost fail. I know it has been objected that the native African will not give such a degree of respect to an American colored missionary as to a white one. I reply—I think this is an individual matter. It would depend much on how, we already here, receive and treat the colored brother and sister also upon their own good common sense and better still their love for the work and humble Christ-likeness.[19]

Miss Nassau also felt that *colored brethren* would have equal expenses as their white co-laborers. She ended with two final comments: "I cannot imagine any possible or probable difficulties arising, that may

17. BFM, Colored Missionaries [1895], 12.
18. BFM, Colored Missionaries [1895], 12.
19. BFM, Colored Missionaries [1895], 13–14.

not be adjusted by the law of mutual love and forbearance—our Saviour's example. I draw however a line of <u>strong negation</u> on the point of inter-marriage of the races."[20]

Dr. Silas F. Johnson felt too inexperienced to respond knowledgeably to the question, but speculated that there may be

> dissatisfaction on the part of our colored workers here in the mission *on the ground of salary and standing.* They seem, from what I hear, to be "touchy" on that point already. I think probably, she would not receive the same respect that a white person does but do not know. The Bible readers are generally respected by their own people. I wish to be the last person to stand in the way of any servant of God, working among the Africans.[21]

Mr. Fraser, a new missionary, hesitated to give his opinion on the matter, having been on the field for such a short time. Referring to the candidate, Miss McLeod, he wrote that she "seems to stand in the position of a test case for whether or not the well-qualified colored people at home should be encouraged or not to come to their own people as missionaries. Much as I wish the way might be clear for her yet my own mind is doubtful of the wisdom of her coming. At least it would seem an experiment."[22] Fraser felt that she should have the same salary as white missionaries, but expressed concern about whether she would have the respect of the native population, or their "practical admission of superiority necessary to make her an effective teacher and leader among them."[23] Fraser felt unable to judge whether Miss McLeod's "personal traits and training, under the Spirit's use of her might overcome any disadvantage arising out of sameness of race, [or] whether caliber would prove greater than color"[24]

Mrs. Reutlinger suggested that it might work, if there were enough colored missionaries to run a station by themselves; it might be hard to establish close ties between whites and blacks:

> With our American missionaries from the North it would come hard to have to share constantly their home life in its inner circle with one of another race. I have never heard in America, that any of our circle at home were in the habit of entertaining colored Christian friends.

20. BFM, Colored Missionaries [1895], 14.
21. BFM, Colored Missionaries [1895], 15.
22. BFM, Colored Missionaries [1895], 15–16.
23. BFM, Colored Missionaries [1895], 16.
24. BFM, Colored Missionaries [1895], 16.

> And as long as that distinction is kept up there it would be hard for our missionaries in Africa to break with it. There is much work for them to do, but for peace and harmony's sake, it would seem almost better if we dealt as Abraham with Lot.[25]

It was on the basis of these responses from the field, both in relation to Miss McLeod's application, and the subject of sending out *colored* men and women, in general, that the Presbyterian Board made the decision to deny Miss McLeod's application for service in Africa.

Public Critique of Mission Policies

In an article printed in the *Trenton True American,* dated October 17, 1894, Dr. Nassau described both the strengths and weaknesses of the Corisco Presbytery. Among his criticisms, Nassau noted that the Presbytery appointed missionary pastors to particular churches without considering the desires of that particular church, and that missionaries' frequent departures prevented them from developing friendly ties, local interest or organizational loyalty in the local church community.[26]

Nassau also criticized the mission's overbearing control over the presbytery, which consisted of all ordained missionaries and native pastors, as well as native elders of the churches.

The Presbytery was the only place in which the natives had any standing, where their voice was heard, where they had any right to counsel, or where they had the voting power. Nassau noted that the *mission*, by contrast, was a non-ecclesiastical sub-committee of the Board, and made up foreign missionaries; no native attended its meetings.

The mission met in the morning, making such decisions as to which missionary would be placed in charge of a particular mission station. The Presbytery (consisting of ordained missionaries and native clergy) would then meet in the afternoon, and dutifully appoint the missionary in charge of that station for the year over the church in that location. Nassau added that the *native vote* only echoed what the *white voice* had earlier decided, though not without murmuring. By 1894, the native leaders openly expressed resentment.[27]

25. BFM, Colored Missionaries [1895], 17.

26. Nassau, "Characteristics of Corisco Presbytery."

27. Nassau, "Characteristics of Corisco Presbytery." See also, Zorn, "Les Chemins," 474–77. In the mid-1880s, missionaries were given colonial protection and took *more* power, despite indigenous church leadership structures; thus, indigenous pastors had no

Nassau also reported that the mission had been performing illegal acts against the native brethren, which they had submitted to, either due to their unawareness of their rights, or their expectation that they could not appeal them.[28] Nassau argued that the mission dealt with the natives in an arbitrary, dictatorial way, exercising a type of paternal Episcopal oversight, which approached that of a paternal government; to this, the native submitted under a feeling of race-respect, though he was keenly aware of the injustice shown him. Nassau admired their loyalty and magnanimity, but saw the potential for "judgment warped by personal prejudice."[29]

Dr. Nassau's most ardent criticism was that missionaries were unwilling to promote natives to positions of responsibility and honor, though white men could not live indefinitely in Africa, and native leaders would ultimately assume leadership. Nassau felt that missionaries had shifted from expecting too much of them, to *trusting too little*. He claimed that an "actual color line has influenced the judgment, deportment and vote of members of Presbytery, sometimes to the [acknowledged] extent of openly saying, 'the native must be taught to keep his place.' What is his place?"[30]

Pastor Ibia J'Ikenge had been a licentiate and elder in the Corisco Presbytery for ten years prior to his ordination. According to Nassau, Ibia had exhibited his *manliness* by teaching and acting out his conviction that native Christians should take responsibility of the native church. Though this was "undeniably [the] professed aim, as stated by Assembly, Board, Secretary and Mission itself,"[31] it created a great deal of friction between Ibia and certain members of the Corisco Mission. Ibia advocated for *native self-support* and freedom for his people from white trade, through the inauguration of industrial education and agriculture. This put him at odds with the missionaries, who believed that he might (through these secular interests) neglect the gospel and seek wealth, instead. Nassau noted that Ibia's relationship with missionaries was "sometimes tried by the assumption of dictation by newly arrived young men, his juniors in age and Christian experience and who had not, like himself, suffered for the gospel, whom

---

control. This corroborates Nassau's description of the mission and Presbyterian.

28. Here, Nassau refers to Presbyterian Constitutional and Parliamentary Law.
29. Nassau, "Characteristics of Corisco Presbytery."
30. Nassau, "Characteristics of Corisco Presbytery."
31. Nassau, "Rev. Ibia J'Ikenge, 107.

the accident of Mission superintendency happened to place in supervision of his non-ecclesiastical work."[32]

Dr. Nassau strongly criticized the mission for its subordination and suppression of indigenous leadership, and the related issue of sending or not sending *colored laborers* to the mission field. He regretted that the majority of his missionary colleagues had voted against the coming of Negro associates, and stated that if they were to erect a separate mission for them, he would prefer to be associated with that mission. In the same letter to the Corresponding Secretary, Nassau insisted that laymen sent to the field be warned "not to interfere with the Native minister nor assume authority over them."[33] While Dr. Nassau and others showed honor and deference to the appointed indigenous pastors, various missionary laymen had, in years past, swept the native pastor aside and taken possession of the church.[34]

Some of the newest missionaries to the field (Schnatz, Fraser and Johnston) were painfully aware of what Dr. Nassau overtly termed "the color line," and were making an effort to *remove* it.[35]

In a letter dated December 25, 1895, Nassau addresses the ongoing "American Negro question,"[36] tying together the separate, but parallel, issues of missionary discrimination and subordination of native brethren to their apparent rejection of potential African American missionary colleagues. Nassau's critique was published at the same time that a controversy was brewing between the Presbyterian Board of Foreign Missions and a number of African American missionary candidates who were hoping for imminent appointment.

Miss Mary McLeod, Candidate

In February 1895, Miss Mary McLeod, still in her teens, wrote to the Presbyterian Board from the Moody Bible Institute of Chicago, Illinois. She had long sensed God's call on her life to be a missionary in Africa. Having already completed a course of study at the Scotia Seminary, she was now enrolled at Moody for further preparation.[37] Her letter of application to the

32. Nassau, "Rev. Ibia J'Ikenge," 107.
33. Nassau to Dr. Gillespie, August 6, 1895.
34. Nassau to Dr. Gillespie, August 6, 1895.
35. Nassau to Dr. Gillespie, December 25, 1895.
36. Nassau to Dr. Gillespie, December 25, 1895.
37. Guy-Sheftall, *Daughters of Sorrow*, 30.

Presbyterian Board had met with a disappointing response. Miss McLeod, after much prayer sent her reply:

> Dear Friends: —Your letter of Dec. 18th 1894 has been before me for sometime [*sic*]. I have prayed over that letter time and time again asking the Holy Spirit to give me only out of that letter what you intended me to have. I think I have been rather unfortunate in getting out of it what I have. Indeed, friends and co-workers for the Lord Jesus Christ, I have not been aware of the fact that you have not been sending out <u>Colored</u> Missionaries to Africa or I would not have attempted an exception to your rules. It seems to me that if the Lord Jesus Christ were here on earth in person and wanted someone to go on an errand for Him, He would not discuss the covering He has placed upon the bodies His blood bought people to protect the flesh He has made. As I sit here at my table writing you I can see my Saviour struggling with that heavy cross up Calvary's Mount, I am told that a man attempted to help my blessed Saviour bear the cross! I wonder did the Lord Jesus Christ stop to see whether that man was white or "<u>colored</u>." Dear Friends, I would have looked for almost any other difficulty than the one presented me in your letter. Christ has called me to the work. His command is to "Go." I am so glad He has counted me worthy to lay this Great Command upon my heart. I am so glad he did not designate any particular <u>color</u> to Go. Friends, my plans concerning my stay here in the Bible Institute have been changed and I would like to hear your decision as early as possible so that I may know what to definitely ask the Lord for. May He indeed guide you in your work for Him.
>
> Mary J. McLeod.[38]

APPEAL BY MISS NASSAU

When Miss Isabella Nassau learned of the application of her "young friend Miss Mary McLeod of Scotia Seminary,"[39] she wrote to Dr. Gillespie to express her hope that the Board would find a way appoint her to the Gaboon and Corisco Mission. Having heard of Miss McLeod's disappointment, Miss Nassau suggested that she might be *admirably fitted* to their field.

38. Mary McLeod to the Presbyterian Board, February 6, 1895.

39. Isabella Nassau to Dr. Gillespie, September 13, 1895. Miss Nassau had written to Miss McLeod while she was still a student at Scotia Seminary, after she had expressed interest in mission work in Africa.

She agreed with Mrs. Satterwhite, of Scotia Seminary, that *colored people* needed the help of white colleagues, as they were not yet ready to work independently; she suggested that, if the Board hoped to begin a mission of colored missionaries, it could gradually appoint those like Miss McLeod, who had gone through sufficient training and testing. Miss Nassau felt compelled to write Gillespie on this, sensing it was her *duty*, and that she dared not "lay a word of hindrance in the path of one whom God had so evidently called to work for Him in Africa."[40]

MISSION VOTE

Isabella Nassau tried to persuade her fellow missionaries to vote in favor of the Board's appointment of Miss Mary McLeod. Though a *bare majority* of the missionaries had expressed a willingness to vote with Miss Nassau in favor of Miss McLeod, it was as a *personal favor* to Miss Nassau, and she would not accept this stipulation.[41] Then, seven of the ten voting missionaries expressed their fear that *Miss McLeod's appointment would cause the natives to expect greater recognition for themselves.* Dr. Nassau objected to this fear, though he admitted that it was possible, and he would not regret it—he believed that the educated natives merited higher recognition; that it would render justice to them, and would be a benefit to the missionaries. This argument proved too weak to stand, and several dissenting missionaries suggested that Miss McLeod come out as merely an *assistant missionary*, without the ability to vote, and with *less salary*. Seven of the ten refused that proposal. And then, Mrs. Reutlinger recommended that the vote be taken simply on the *Negro question*, and not specifically regarding Miss McLeod. The vote was thus taken, and the outcome a great disappointment to Nassaus.[42]

Miss Nassau wrote Dr. Gillespie a lengthy letter, hoping to more thoroughly present her request for Miss McLeod's appointment. It was this letter that clarified the discussion and vote of the mission. Miss Nassau, Rev. Schnatz, Rev. Fraser, and Miss Babe were all in favor of Miss McLeod's appointment. Dr. Nassau could not vote, as he was serving as Chairman, and several new missionaries were not yet eligible to vote.

40. Isabella Nassau to Dr. Gillespie, September 13, 1895.
41. Robert Hamill Nassau to Dr. Gillespie, December 25, 1895.
42. Robert Hamill Nassau to Dr. Gillespie, December 25, 1895.

FURTHER NEGOTIATION

Miss Nassau wrote a subsequent letter to the Board Secretary, clarifying her earlier request: she had hoped Miss McLeod could be appointed to assist her in her teaching ministry at Batanga, knowing that a single lady missionary would need an assigned placement and home. Like her brother, Miss Nassau saw this appointment as a test case to help them determine their response to future applications by African American men and women for full missionary status. She described her shock at the objections expressed by her fellow missionaries, "as to whom the natives would regard the young colored missionary,"[43] adding that the missionaries seemed willing to vote in favor of Miss McLeod's appointment *if she were designated to work with Miss Nassau*, rather than to a particular mission station. Miss Nassau, however, felt that Miss McLeod ought to receive Board appointment, "on account of her especial call and intelligent consecration—bearing only her work and place to the appointment of Mission and a reduced salary given her, as is the case with our other assistants."[44] Of the fifteen voting missionaries, however, only four were in favor of Miss McLeod's appointment. Miss Nassau expressed to the Board Secretary her sorrow and disappointment that her friends were not willing to admit Miss McLeod, and that she could not look forward to her help and companionship. Miss Nassau ended the letter stating that she was willing to donate fifty dollars towards Miss McLeod's salary, give her a furnished room and board, at no charge, if the Board could find a way to send her.[45]

OUTCOME

Miss McLeod was not appointed to the Gaboon and Corisco Mission, nor did she realize her calling to be a missionary in Africa. She did, however, rise to a level of prominence, influence and recognition in her chosen field of education, eventually becoming a college president and civil rights leader, as well as a member of President Franklin D. Roosevelt's administration.[46]

43. Isabella Nassau to Gillespie, December 24, 1895.
44. Isabella Nassau to Gillespie, December 24, 1895.
45. Isabella Nassau to Gillespie, December 24, 1895.
46. Mary McLeod Bethune.

Mary McLeod Bethune (Source: Florida Memory website)

Miss McLeod was not the only young person of color who was called, trained and recommended for missionary service, and yet denied appointment by the Presbyterian Board. Students of Lincoln University also responded to the need for missionaries in Africa, and were likewise disappointed.

Lincoln University

Lincoln University (formerly Ashmun Institute) was founded in 1854, for the purpose of providing African Americans quality higher education, and to be "an instrument in raising up colored preachers for America, and evangelists for the dark mountains of the continent whence they came."[47]

HISTORIC TIES TO GABOON AND CORISCO

Lincoln University had historical connections with both Gaboon and Corisco missions from its very founding, by John Miller Dickey. While ordaining James L. Mackey, in 1849, just prior to his missionary appointment to Africa, Dickey sensed he was ordaining Mackey to certain death.[48] Dickey

47. PCUSA, *Annual Report of the Board of Education [1866]*, 38. See Moses Moore, "Edward Wilmot Blyden," 105. Black Presbyterian clergy had few options in the US. Many Lincoln graduates served in Africa.

48. Carr, *John Miller Dickey*, 148.

believed that persons of African descent would naturally be resistant to the dangerous climate, and would be more likely to survive and prosper in the ministry. He asserted that Africa should be evangelized by black men, but that white men were needed to prepare these black missionaries and teachers for that work.[49] Dickey was a strong advocate of racial equality and mutual respect between whites and blacks. Earlier attempts to educate persons of color in existing institutions (such as Princeton) were met with social pressure, rioting, protests and legal action. Dickey hoped to establish a separate institution, dedicated to providing a solid, Presbyterian theological training to men of color, for service among their people at home, or in missionary service to Africa.

In 1870, Rev. Epaminondas J. Pierce, who had served as a missionary to Gaboon, began to raise scholarship funds for Lincoln students preparing for ministry.[50] At Pierce's death, in 1892, the Institute received the whole of his assets, with the specification that they be used to (1) prepare Africans to serve among their people; (2) prepare persons of African descent for ministry among their people in America, or in missionary service to Africa; (3) prepare a white person to serve as a missionary in Africa. These were to be prioritized in that order.[51]

Professor Stewart's Advocacy

In January 1895, Robert L. Stewart, of Lincoln University, wrote a letter to Dr. John Gillespie, of the Presbyterian Board, to describe some of their students who were interested and prepared for service on the foreign field, particularly Africa. After discussing the particular qualifications and intentions of several students, Stewart asked a pointed question about missionary salaries:

> I am told there is a discrimination in the matter of salary between a man of dark skin and one of white on the African fields and this not on account of education or attainments but solely on acc't of color. I am much surprised to learn this and can hardly think it is so in the case of men who are as fully qualified for the work. It does not strike me as a wise or just arrangement in view of the fact

49. Carr, *John Miller Dickey*, 171. See Bond, *Education of the Negro*, 216. This preceded, *by a century*, policies of *Africanization* promoted by mission societies and colonial governments.

50. GAPCUSA, *Minutes of the General Assembly [1892]*, 289.

51. Bond, *Education of the Negro*, 517.

that almost every man who comes here to address our students is inclined to urge them to go to Africa.[52]

While student response is not evident, Stewart expressed his own concern in the subject,

> for I am deeply interested in these young men and I know they have long and patiently contended with poverty in their self-denying efforts to fit themselves for the Lord's work. Surely it cannot be that the Board expects such men to live as do the native teachers on the field and to cut off from the means of establishing [Christian] homes and providing for families and developing social and industrial reforms among their people along the lines which are open to missionaries of whiter skin.[53]

Stewart assured Dr. Gillespie that he did not want to criticize the Board, but that they hoped to encourage their students in the recent surge of interest in the foreign mission field.

Response from the Board Secretary

Within a week, Dr. Gillespie, of the Presbyterian Board, responded to Prof. Stewart's letter regarding the question of sending Negro missionaries. He mentioned the recent application of Miss McLeod, and the fact that the matter had been deferred until they could receive responses from the missionaries there. He mentioned that blacks and whites had not served together during his time on the Board, and the Liberian Mission, which was manned by Negro missionaries, was not doing satisfactorily, according to a report by missionary A. C. Good, of the Gaboon Mission, who had recently evaluated that mission. Rev. Good had strongly recommended that white men ought to be sent to superintend that work. Dr. Gillespie added that the Gaboon missionaries had responded to the Negro question years before, and that the "prevailing opinion, if not the unanimous judgment, was against the mingling of white and colored men in the same Mission. Dr. Good,[54] who was in many respects the foremost man in the Mission,

52. Robert L. Stewart to John Gillespie, January 10, 1895.

53. Robert L. Stewart to John Gillespie, January 10, 1895.

54. See Parsons, *Life for Africa*, 131. Rev. Good, D. D., of the Gaboon and Corisco Mission.

advocated sending colored men out to be connected with the Presbytery, but not to be members of the Mission."[55]

Gillespie added that he had sent the same question to the missionaries at the Mission, but didn't expect their responses for another year, and that the Board would not take action until they did. He also mentioned that the Liberian missionaries received lower salaries than those at Gaboon and Corisco, but higher salaries than those paid by other boards.

"SHALL WE DISCOURAGE THEM NOW?"

In a second letter dated January 23, 1895, Robert L. Stewart expressed their discouragement in "quickening or developing the missionary spirit" among their students.[56] He noted that they were "cut off, by reason of their color, from every foreign field except Africa; and there, for the present, at least, where the need is so urgent and the destination so appalling there seems to be no place for them; and no certainty of securing a commission from the church to which they belong and to which they are strongly attached."[57]

A year earlier, Dr. Robert Hamill Nassau had visited their campus and had "strongly emphasized the advantage the cultured, young colored men would have in Africa over the home field,"[58] and that they would be "free from the petty annoyances and discriminations which hampered their work in the South, and there would find an encouraging field and an open door. To this great harvest field—the home of their ancestors—he invited them to go out *not as Africans, but as American citizens*."[59] Two years earlier, a Dr. Paton had made a similar appeal that brought tears to many eyes and caused them to feel that Christ, himself, was speaking through him. Now, ten of Lincoln University's *choicest young men* were responding to these calls to serve overseas, seven of whom were preparing for service in Africa. "They are all under the care of the Presbytery of Chester, and, with one exception, expect to take a full collegiate and theological course. If they should be set apart to go on this mission it will be after the most careful examination; and with the approbation and approval of one of the most cautious and conservative Presbyteries of the church."[60]

55. John Gillespie to Robert L. Stewart, dated January 15, 1895.

56. Robert L. Stewart to John Gillespie, January 23, 1895.

57. Robert L. Stewart to John Gillespie, January 23, 1895.

58. Robert L. Stewart to John Gillespie, January 23, 1895.

59. Robert L. Stewart to John Gillespie, January 23, 1895. Italics added.

60. Robert L. Stewart to John Gillespie, January 23, 1895.

Stewart explained that, five years earlier, there had been little interest in the foreign field, among their students. In direct response to Dr. Gillespie's letter, he wrote,

> And now when God has given us a fuller answer to prayer, and effort, than we expected we are confronted with another question—what shall we do with these young men? Shall we discourage them now, and in the future with the answer that the white man has precepted the whole ground in <u>Africa</u>, and may, or may not, comment to their appointment as missionaries of the cross; or that they can only go in a subordinate position 'in connection with the Presbytery, but not to be members of the mission itself'[?] As for myself I will frankly say that the latter alternative practically shuts the door to every self-respecting man and forces him to seek an open door and a parity in <u>ministerial</u> offices elsewhere, which is denied him in the Presbyterian church.[61]

Stewart asked again what they shall do with these young men, three of whom are ready to go on in the next year. One young man, a senior in the theological class, had been supported by a wealthy patron for seven years, with the purpose of going to Africa. "This friend has not the remotest idea that he would be rejected after all this training, or that he would be asked to go in a subordinate capacity. If the real situation were known it would not be easy to persuade this person that a wrong had not been done in rejecting him, not for cause but on account of color only."[62] Stewart also addressed the well-known case of the Liberia Mission, and argued that that field would have been much more successful had the Board kept the "best missionaries" there until "thoroughly educated men—educated in Christian character as well as in intellect"[63] could then take on the work. He added that Lincoln graduates had done commendable work in starting churches in the South, and could achieve similar successes in the foreign field. Stewart used the example from the civil war, when the colored man

> was not much of a soldier so long as he was only a subordinate in the service of some officer of the camp, but when he was clothed in a suit of army blue; a musket was given into his hands, and the pay of a soldier was accorded, he proved himself worthy of the trust reposed in him. In front of Petersburg I have seen scores of

61. Robert L. Stewart to John Gillespie, January 23, 1895.
62. Robert L. Stewart to John Gillespie, January 23, 1895.
63. Robert L. Stewart to John Gillespie, January 23, 1895.

colored men lying dead in a space of about half an acre and all with their faces to the foe.[64]

Stewart then asked Dr. Gillespie to locate a mission station somewhere in West Africa, "where two, three or more of our ordained men can go, to begin and develop a mission work . . . Give them a fair start in the acquirement of the language and the same opportunity as in other stations, of like character and we believe that the friends of missions will have occasion to bless God for the results."[65]

REPORT OF THE COMMITTEE

Following the Board session of December 17, 1894, the Report of the Committee on Africa and the Executive Council on the Commissioning of Negroes as Missionaries to Africa, addressed the application of Miss Mary McLeod, "a young colored woman of Mayesville, S. C., and a graduate of Scotia Seminary,"[66] and a series of letters written by Rev. Robert L. Stewart, of Lincoln University. Several weeks later, on February 18, 1895, the Board recommended the following actions: First, "without in the least discriminating against any applicant for appointment as missionary because of his color, the Board is not in position at present to give a positive and final answer to the question of commissioning ministers of the African race to labor in the same mission with white missionaries,"[67] and that the matter would be deferred until the Board heard responses from the missionaries on the field. And, second, that if the Board could financially support the enlargement of its work in Africa, and established a new mission, "it would gladly consider the experiment of opening a mission among the interior tribes in Africa . . . to be manned exclusively by well-trained Negro ministers from the United States whose ability and experience would justify their appointment."[68] These decisions reflected similar "separate, but equal" policies developing in the Presbyterian Church, in the United States in the 1890s,[69] and just preceded the 1896 Supreme Court decision which upheld segregation.[70]

64. Robert L. Stewart to John Gillespie, January 23, 1895.

65. Robert L. Stewart to John Gillespie, January 23, 1895.

66. BFM, Colored missionaries [1895].

67. BFM, Carbon Copy of Board Minutes [1895].

68. BFM, Colored missionaries [1895].

69. Murray, *Presbyterians and the Negro*, 190–91.

70. Murray, *Presbyterians and the Negro*, 201.

Historic Outcome

There were no additional African Americans sent by the Presbyterian Board of Foreign Missions until 1928–29, when Rev. and Mrs. Irvin W. Underhill were appointed to serve in what is now Cameroon.[71] More than four decades after the discussion of sending Negro missionaries to serve alongside whites, Presbyterian mission historian, Arthur J. Brown, indicated that little had changed, and that African Americans who desired to participate in full-time mission work in Africa continued to deal with the issue of the "color line"

> As Negro Presbyterian churches in the United States increased in numbers and were led by more highly educated men, they became more and more restive under what they supposed to be the disposition of the Board to draw the colour line in missionary appointments. Protests were made from time to time and overtures were sent to the General Assembly. The Board invariably replied that it made no discrimination whatever; that the applications of Negro candidates were considered on precisely the same basis as the applications of other candidates.[72]

The unwillingness of the Presbyterian Board to send African American missionaries, and the apparent discomfort of missionaries at working with *colored brethren* on a fraternal and equal basis, deprived Africa of gifted and consecrated missionary candidates like Mary McLeod, and denied these candidates of the right and privilege of serving in the missionary work overseas.

71. Murray, *Presbyterians and the Negro*, 195.
72. Brown, *One Hundred Years*, 210.

7

Conclusion

THE INTENT OF THIS study was to identify the persons of African descent
who served with the ABCFM and PCUSA missions in what is now coastal
Gabon and Equatorial Guinea, during the mid-to-late nineteenth century,
in terms of their role, status, and interpersonal relationships within the
missionary community. It is only by juxtaposing and comparing a variety of
concurrent documents—published reports, handwritten correspondence,
and private journals—that one can discern the *presence* and *participation*
of these persons of color, as well as their *proximity* and *place* among their
white co-laborers. The greatest difficulty has been to measure their *produc-
tion*—what lasting effects they may have had on their host community and
culture—as virtually none of them left a record of their work, nor did their
African host communities distinguish them, or their work, from that of
their white missionary co-laborers.

The vast majority of material on the interrelationships within the
mission family, and between them and their host culture, is written by
white missionaries, revealing their opinions and experiences, as well as
their *perceptions of* the thoughts, actions and motivations of the persons
of African descent in their midst. While this eliminates the direct voice
of these persons, it sheds light on the way the missionaries portrayed the
work of the mission to the public, and how they explained their actions
and decisions to the Mission Board.

Because mission archives often categorize missionaries by strict defi-
nition, a large number of persons of African descent have been overlooked
by researchers and historians, who may have limited their research to those

who were *officially appointed*, and whose ethnicity was clearly described in terms of African descent. Sylvia Jacobs highlights several African American "firsts" in missionary appointment by the ABCFM, which date to the mid-1880s.[1] These apparent milestones, however, were *pre-dated by fifty years*, in the understated appointment of Benjamin Van Rensselaer James to the ABCFM Cape Palmas mission. Walter Williams notes that there were at least one hundred thirteen African American missionaries serving in Africa between 1877 and 1900,[2] but does not include Gabon among the present-day countries where African American mission workers were located. Miss Harding's name and significant contribution to the work have remained in obscurity, despite her having been formally appointed, and publically presented as a missionary of African descent.

Non-appointed persons, such as Jane Cowper, Josiah Dorsey, and Francis Allison, as well as private domestic employees of missionaries, orphans and recaptives have also been overlooked, likely due to their exclusion from official mission reports. These persons participated in the work and social relationship of the mission, providing support and assistance to missionaries, and enabling them to focus on their work and to maintain (or regain) their strength and health. For this reason, their roles and stories have great historical value, and should be recuperated from available archives. Missionary letters and journals are the best source to discern the names, origins, roles and contribution of these "para-missionary" persons of African descent, who voluntarily left their homeland to take part, directly or indirectly, in the work of the mission. Further research will likely reveal that such hidden persons often served in expanded roles, stepping up to greater responsibility and authority when appointed and ordained missionaries were absent.

The earliest foreign-born persons of African descent—African American, Americo-Liberian and West African—who served with the ABCFM Gaboon Mission (1842–1870) seemed to occupy a *middle ground* between the appointed white foreign missionaries and the indigenous host culture, in that they were neither "native" nor perceived as "missionary." For this reason, their ministry was largely overlooked, as they performed *substitutionary work* for the white missionaries when they were sick and understaffed, as well as *preliminary work* for what was called "native agency" when the mission did not yet have local believers to fill educational and ecclesial roles

1. Jacobs, "African-American Women Missionaries," 382.
2. Williams, "William Henry Sheppard," 85.

in the church. David Killingray also recognizes this intermediary role of foreign-born blacks whom American missions often assigned to "temporarily fill the gap" in areas where white missionaries faltered, and where "native agents" were yet to be raised up. Killingray discerns in this, not only a racial component, but also an economic incentive for sending black missionaries, who were believed to be less expensive than white missionaries, in terms of preparation, life expectancy and conditions of service.[3]

In the ABCFM Gaboon mission, these intermediary persons filled vital ministry roles and helped to ensure the continuity of the mission, though they were unreported in both name and ministry, and were counted among the *native assistants* and church members in written reports, presumably due to their ethnic commonalities with the local people. It is also possible that by avoiding direct reference to the presence and ministry of foreign-born persons of African descent, the missionaries could give the impression that their own work was flourishing and that they were successful in preparing *native agency* as per their stated goals.

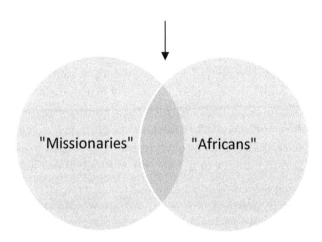

Foreign persons of African descent seemed to occupy a *middle ground* between the African host culture and the missionary sub-culture. Missionaries categorized them within the African circle (according to race), while the African host culture likely categorized them within the missionaries circle (according to culture). For this reason, they were essentially *invisible* to both groups, and left out of the historical narrative, despite their continual presence in the Gaboon and Corisco Mission.

3. Killingray, "Black Atlantic Missionary Movement," 9.

While the early missions were racially diverse, mission members of African descent invariably served in subordinate roles to the ordained white missionaries. David Killingray correlates this to the "scientific racism" of the late nineteenth century, when many missionaries subscribed to theories of black inferiority, limiting persons of African descent to manual labor or assistant roles.[4] This is evident in both mission correspondence and in published articles written by persons in America, particularly in the pre-Emancipation years.

Prior to their merger, neither the Corisco nor the Gaboon mission received an ordained missionary of African descent, nor did they ordain local leadership. The few mission workers of African descent who served with the mission were hired as assistants in the work, with no (apparent) opportunity for advancement or formal promotion. Yet, there is no evidence that they challenged the mission hierarchy, or their subordinate place in it. The color line was first described and denounced by the newly-ordained Ibia J'Ikenge, in the 1870s, followed by Rev. Ntâkâ Truman, in the 1880s. Once ordained, these two men expected full and equal partnership with white missionaries, and declared the mission hierarchy to be both unjust and unbiblical.

In later years, when African American missionary candidates were readily available, the missionaries expressed concern that the inclusion of *colored* missionaries would result in conflict and confusion over role, status, authority and pay—with the African leaders as well as with their missionary co-laborers. This indicates that the mission continued to view African Americans as an intermediary group between the white missionaries and the African host community. Mission correspondence of the early 1890s reveals that many missionaries were either opposed to race equality and inclusion, or doubtful that it could be achieved on the mission field. Walter Williams's broad research of African American contribution to the evangelization of Africa reveals that African American missionaries commonly experienced overt racial discrimination from white colleagues, and many resigned because of it.[5]

The Women's Foreign Missionary Society of the Presbyterian Church offered a remarkable contrast to the prevailing mission racial and gender divides of the 1870s and 1880s, as it intentionally highlighted and supported the ministry of indigenous pastors, teachers and evangelists, as well

---

4. Killingray, "Black Atlantic Missionary Movement," 9, 17.
5. Williams, "William Henry Sheppard," 22.

as the appointed missionary women. Much of the history and "voices" of these otherwise unknown persons has been gleaned from the organization's monthly magazine, *Woman's Work for Woman*. Patricia Hill notes the great contribution and impact made by such women's mission societies, though she overlooks their role in bringing heightened knowledge and awareness of work accomplished by local African believers and foreign workers of African descent.[6] Both Dana Robert[7] and Marie Tyler-McGraw[8] capture the anti-structure spirit of these women's organizations, which promoted and cooperated with African pastors and African American missionaries, thereby circumventing the restrictive policies of missions and colonization societies, and defying prevailing social mores on *proper decorum* in women.[9]

Wendy Urban-Mead notes that "informal conditions at the periphery"[10] sometimes blurred distinctions, giving opportunity for Africans and white women to assume authority, supporting the notion that they could be "brothers and sisters in Christ" and serve in ministry leadership.[11] This was most evident in the 1870s, when a shortage of ordained missionaries on the field allowed some missionary women and indigenous church leaders greater opportunity to expand their scope of ministry and to collaborate freely, without the limitations normally placed upon them by the mission leadership.

While need and opportunity both determined the *placement* of persons of African descent on the mission fields, one must also consider what *motivated* them for this service. Prevailing scholarship cites ancestral commonality as the primary missionary motivation among persons of African descent in Africa. Jacobs,[12] Williams,[13] Roth,[14] McArver,[15] and Park[16] describe a sense of *duty* or *burden* among African Americans to evangelize the land of their ancestry, and to *elevate* Africans by means of education and development. *This ancestral motivation is not evident in available*

---

6. Hill, *World Their Household.*

7. Robert, *American Women in Mission.*

8. Tyler-McGraw, *An African Republic.*

9. Tyler-McGraw, *An African Republic*, 92.

10. Urban-Mead, "Unwomanly Woman."

11. Urban-Mead, "Unwomanly Woman," 95–96.

12. Jacobs, "Three African American Women Missionaries."

13. Williams, "William Henry Sheppard."

14. Roth, "The 'Black Man's Burden.'"

15. McArver, "'Salvation of Souls.'"

16. Park, *White" Americans in "Black" Africa.*

correspondence by persons of African descent serving with the Gaboon and Corisco mission(s). Only Francis Allison (a West African) made a clear statement of commonality between himself and the people to whom he preached salvation. No other person of African descent indicated that their *ethnic heritage* was a motivator in their desire to participate in the mission work in Africa. Even Miss Harding, to whom this motivation was ascribed, made no reference to her ethnicity or ancestral ties with Africa. For most, serving in Africa was the only option available to them, regardless of their level of education and preparation.

David Killingray writes that many enslaved African Americans felt "a strong consciousness of a lost home from which they had been cruelly torn."[17] The formerly enslaved persons who served in Gaboon and Corisco give no such impression, nor did their white missionary co-laborers describe them in terms of *returning to their ancestral home*. Many black missionaries experienced the same losses and separation from friends and family as did whites. Eunjin Park notes their concerns about health and the possibility of death in a "strange country," away from their "native land."[18] This sense of *foreignness* is evident in the writings of B. V. R. James and Mary Harding, and implied in Mrs. Sneed's request to return to America in her final years.

Eunjin Park[19] and Susan Wilds McArver[20] include evangelical zeal and compassion as strong motivators for mission. While racial prejudice limited opportunities to serve in America, persons of African descent could more freely exercise their ministry gifts and training in Africa. Written evidence indicates that they believed in the cause of the work, and desired to participate in it, in spite of the known difficulties and deprivations. Necessity and personnel shortages gave unlimited opportunities to serve in vital ministry roles, if without official recognition or formal advancement.

Walter Williams questions the altruism of African American missionaries, noting that the backgrounds and ideological beliefs oriented many toward mission work. He argues that this was largely based on self-interest, as mission work was one of the few options open to them where they could attain social status and respectability.[21] Williams notes

17. Killingray, "Black Atlantic Missionary Movement," 6.
18. Park, *"White" Americans in "Black" Africa*, 67.
19. Park, *"White" Americans in "Black" Africa*.
20. McArver, "Salvation of Souls."
21. Williams, "William Henry Sheppard," 92.

that many missionaries of African descent were accustomed to working in close cooperation with whites, and sought respect from both whites and blacks,[22] and attributes their paternalism toward Africans to a desire to distinguish themselves from "native" Africans, and to "negate the stereotype of Afro-Americans as uncivilized savages."[23] Williams also theorizes that African Americans were motivated to missions in Africa as a means to improve white-black race relations, to gain the world respect, and to help Africa to achieve both dominion and power,[24] as well as equality with other peoples of the world.[25] Williams bases these theories on "psychohistorical analysis,"[26] and gives little room for *genuine compassion, self-sacrifice and evangelical fervor.* More recently, Godfrey Mwakikagile asserts that many African American missionaries were condescending and paternalistic toward the native Africans, and saw them as "inferior."[27] The views presented by Williams and Mwakikagile are difficult to assess, as many of the African Americans serving in the earliest decades of mission work in Africa had been subject to slavery and oppression. Their efforts to evangelize, educate and "civilize" Africans were likely motivated by a sincere desire to promote faith, justice and freedom, as these same motivations informed concurrent efforts in America towards "uplift" and "respectability" within the black community. Education and freedom of religious expression were yet *rare and precious privileges* for African Americans, even in the northern states, in antebellum America.

Several of the persons of African descent who served with the Gaboon and Corisco mission(s) left ample *written evidence* of their compassion for those who were oppressed or suffering (Charity Sneed), a burden for their spiritual lostness (Mary Harding), a desire to see them come to a saving knowledge of Christ (Francis Allison), and an expressed love and commitment toward their host community (B. V. R. James). Though they endeavored to work cooperatively with both the mission community and the host culture, there is no indication that their motives were self-serving, or that they received benefit or status from their mission work. Every one of these persons invested their full attention and strength to

22. Williams, "William Henry Sheppard," 94.
23. Williams, "William Henry Sheppard," 94.
24. Williams, "William Henry Sheppard," 102.
25. Williams, "William Henry Sheppard," 103.
26. Williams, "William Henry Sheppard," 94.
27. Mwakikagile, *Relations Between Africans and African Americans*, 25.

the ministry. While some written material may appear to be condescending, the vast majority indicates sincere compassion, investment and sacrifice on the part of the foreign mission workers of African descent, in keeping with Lamin Sanneh's view of those transformed, gospel-bearing Christians who had come out of a context of slavery and oppression, to introduce a new social order based on the ideals of freedom, dignity and justice for all.[28] That many of them fully assimilated into the local culture indicates their mutual acceptance and esteem.

While there were unlimited opportunities to *serve* in the missions, advancement or leadership was limited to a select few, and determined by education, ordination and gender. These distinctions served to establish a mission hierarchy, which placed ordained male missionaries at the top, with females and non-ordained males in subordination to them.

Ordination as a distinction—the missionary men of the Gaboon and Corisco Mission(s) were almost invariably seminary-trained and ordained prior to their appointment. No ordained man of African descent was ever appointed to serve with either the Gaboon Mission (1842–1870) or the Corisco Mission (1850–1870), or with the (combined) Gaboon and Corisco Mission. Despite stated goals to raise up indigenous leaders, both missions failed to accomplish this prior to their merger. Mission-Church tensions surfaced soon after the ordination of the first indigenous pastor, Ibia J'Ikenge, in 1870, and were compounded with the ordination of Ntâkâ (or Toko) Truman, ten years later. When these ordinations promoted the two men to a level of *equality* in both authority and status with the missionary men, the mission established a distinction between "Mission" and "Presbytery," giving higher authority to the mission leaders. Jehu Hanciles describes a similar restructuring, under parallel circumstances, in The Church Missionary Society (CMS) Sierra Leone field, in late 1849.[29]

Jean-François Zorn shows that, in the pre-colonial era (prior to 1860), the original aim of both protestant and catholic missions was to train indigenous church leaders and then exit once the local church was fully autonomous.[30] During the colonial period, both catholic and protestant missions increased their missionary presence in Africa; the missionaries remained, with no plan to leave an autonomous indigenous church.[31] By 1880, the

28. Sanneh, *Abolitionists Abroad*, 245–46.
29. Hanciles, *Euthanasia of a Mission*, 60.
30. Zorn, "Mission et Colonisation," 20.
31. Zorn, "Mission et Colonisation," 25–26.

missionaries held power in the local church, and maintained that control through 1950.[32] Zorn's analysis of the pre-colonial and colonial era missions indicates that the timeline, events and controversies of the Gaboon and Corisco missions were neither unique nor circumstantial, but paralleled those of other missions in colonized areas during that time period.

Education as a distinction—Most of the missionary men, regardless of their socio-economic background, had earned both college and seminary degrees prior to their placement on the mission field. There is little or no information on the education of missionary women, though most taught in the mission schools. Handwritten letters and reports allow for an informal assessment of their level of education, evidenced by their use of grammar, correct spelling, vocabulary and organization. The one available handwritten letter by Charity Sneed indicates an education comparable to that of other female missionaries from America. Miss Harding's college education placed her far above other missionary women, and was nearly equal to that of her male colleagues; this, too, created tension in the mission.

Local African Christians perceived that a solid education was necessary, not only for an improved quality of life and competitiveness in the changing economy, but also for church leadership. Pastors Ibia and Ntâkâ attributed the declining levels of mission education to racial discrimination. Sylvia Jacobs similarly links mission education with the perpetuation of racial inequality and subjugation of persons of African descent within mission hierarchies. This impacted local Africans' understanding of Christianity, in that many came to view mission education as an attempt to "indoctrinate them into a permanent state of subservience."[33] David Gardinier[34] and Jeremy Rich[35] likewise remark on the *consequences* of the mission education, which prepared young women and men for either low-paying mission employment or lucrative opportunities in the secular trading community. Pastor Ibia indicated, however, that it was not the low salaries that dissuaded many from serving full-time in ministry, but the lack of respect, equality and opportunity to advance, through theological education and proper mentoring. This is also apparent in Hanciles'[36] research of the CMS in Sierra Leone.

32. Zorn, "Mission et Colonisation," 26.

33. Jacobs, "Three African American Women Missionaries," 322.

34. Gardinier, "American Presbyterian Mission in Gabon."

35. Rich, "'Leopard Men,' Slaves and Social Conflict."

36. Hanciles, *Euthanasia of a Mission.*

Gender as a Distinction—for much of the nineteenth century, or-dained missionary men comprised mission leadership. Missionary women were subordinate to mission leadership, and did not have the right to vote on mission matters until the early 1890s. Several male missionaries ex-pressed fear or indignation when missionary women assumed authority or responsibility normally ascribed ordained men; they did not, however, question their *competence* and *willingness* to do the work. Isabella Nassau offered seminary training, and mentored numerous African men through the licensing and ordination process. Mary Harding maintained the leader-ship and continuity of the church and mission at the Ogowe stations, in the sustained absence of her male missionary colleagues.

In the intense focus on educating young men, both the local commu-nity and the mission largely overlooked *women's work*. This benign neglect of women in ministry may have worked in favor of Charity Sneed and Bessie Makae, who acquired ministry skills and applied them broadly, without the scrutiny and subordination which frustrated the young men. Charity was carefully mentored by Miss Nassau, and empowered to serve in an integral role in the mission, while Bessie's autonomous ministry appears to have been born out of self-determination and a deep sense of calling.

Predelli and Miller consider "the persistence of gender inequality *in the face of the indispensability and resources of women* as the single greatest puzzle in political economy that mission scholarship needs to solve,"[37] and question whether newer scholarship will reveal women of this era to have challenged gender norms, and patriarchal hegemony on the mission field.[38] Though the women of the Gaboon and Corisco Mission didn't appear to seek equality and recognition, available records bear witness to their extraordinary work. The examples of the Isabella Nassau, Mary Harding, Charity Sneed and Bes-sie Makae suggest there are more such remarkable women hidden in the mission archives, and merit further research and writing.

These three distinctions—ordination, education and gender—helped to clarify who was qualified to assume leadership, and who would serve in a subordinate role in the mission and local church. The apparent unwill-ingness of the missionaries to receive *colored brethren* as co-laborers, and their hesitation to fully educate and ordain indigenous leaders as (equal) colleagues, gives credence to the accusations of Nassau, Ibia and Ntâkâ, that a *color line* existed in the mission. The available records show that the

37. Predelli and Miller, "Piety and Patriarchy," 102.
38. Predelli and Miller, "Piety and Patriarchy," 102.

greatest controversies of the Gaboon and Corisco Mission took place in the 1870s and 1880s, when these barriers were breached, challenging long-held racial and gender inequalities.

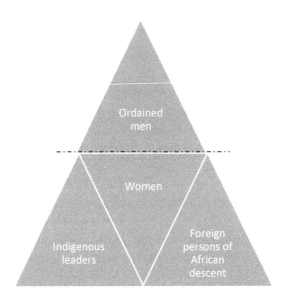

For many decades, the mission hierarchy placed ordained men at the top, and in power. The absence of ordained men of African descent, and the long delay in the ordination of indigenous leaders led to accusations of a racial hierarchy in the mission.

The mission was unable to prevent the Menkel marriage, which breached the perceptible racial barrier within the church-mission community. Killingray attributes mission restrictions on interracial marriage to *scientific racism,*[39] but mission correspondence in the Menkel case indicates a *fear of equality* and the *leveling of distinctions between the races*, more so than a presumed inferiority of blacks. Missionaries' related concerns that the African workers would expect equal pay indicates that, by the 1870s, salaries were also differentiated by nationality or race, and no longer determined according to need, role or qualification.

The mission was unable to provide leadership at the Ogowe interior mission stations, due to illnesses and absences of ordained missionary men;

39. Killingray, "Black Atlantic Missionary Movement," 19.

these circumstances thrust Miss Harding into the traditionally male roles of authority, autonomy and leadership, which created tensions within the mission. Miss Harding's being an unmarried woman, with a superior education and the competence and authority to maintain both church and mission in the absence of male missionaries, indicates a clear breach in gender distinctions; likewise, her outspokenness to French colonial authorities, and her courage in the face danger and oppression shows more "manliness" than many of the missionary men.

This study shows that much of the work performed by persons of African descent was overlooked and underreported in institutional records, due to a combination of fear of equality between the races, fear of the obsolescence of white missionaries in Africa, and personal (if not institutional) discrimination. Predelli and Miller[40] and Zorn[41] note common problems with *institutional memory*, including gaps and discrepancies in what institutions will present as historically factual. Despite strict control on what was expressed in the official mission records, there were mission personnel who transcended institutional norms and restrictions on issues of gender, class and ethnicity.[42]

Jean-Francois Zorn, a prominent researcher of the Société des Missions Evangélique de Paris (SMEP) notes that a great problem of mission historiography is in constructing mission facts from the missionary writings, whose aim was to maintain the enthusiasm of supporters. He suggests that these be compared with material from non-mission sources so that they can be correctly and independently constituted.[43] Zorn also points out that the complex relation of mission and colonization is currently in question, and researchers must carefully recuperate this heritage and its proper position within the general history of the contemporary era.[44] Waltraud Haas suggests that we look beyond official mission history documents and carefully read those archives written by individual missionaries, who "show themselves as real people who gave much—who gave themselves."[45]

Most historical records say little or nothing about the persons of African descent who served with the ABCFM and the BFM missions in

---

40. "Piety and Patriarchy."
41. Zorn, "Entre Mémoire et Histoire."
42. Predelli and Miller, "Piety and Patriarchy," 103–4.
43. Zorn, "Entre Mémoire et Histoire," 31.
44. Zorn, "Entre Mémoire et Histoire," 31.
45. Haas, "Nineteenth-Century Basel Mission," 13.

what is now Gabon and Equatorial Guinea, though the increased accessibility of private documents, journals, letters and digitalized governmental records allows one to piece together the hidden record of their names, presence, roles and relationships.

While it is difficult to assess the availability and willingness of qualified men and women of African descent to serve in mission work in Africa—particularly in the early decades of the mission—later correspondence indicates that several strong candidates were discouraged and turned away, and that many white missionaries were unwilling to work alongside fully-qualified peers of African descent. Despite these obstacles and injustices, there remains the hidden and remarkable history of their predecessors—persons of color whose willingness to *go* and serve among an unevangelized people, in a subordinate and anonymous place within the mission hierarchy, and with little remuneration and recognition for their contribution to the work. Theirs is the story of Aaron and Hur, in Exodus 17:10–13, who stood alongside Moses, supporting his upraised arms until the battle was won, bringing victory and salvation to God's people.

> So Joshua fought the Amalekites as Moses had ordered, and Moses, Aaron and Hur went to the top of the hill. As long as Moses held up his hands, the Israelites were winning, but whenever he lowered his hands, the Amalekites were winning. When Moses' hands grew tired, they took a stone and put it under him and he sat on it. Aaron and *Hur held his hands up—one on one side, one on the other—so that his hands remained steady till sunset. So Joshua overcame the Amalekite army with the sword.*

Bibliography

Allison, Francis. Francis Allison to Dr. Armstrong, July 11, 1843. Letter. Papers of the American Board of Commissioners for Foreign Missions, ABC 15: Letters from Missionaries to Africa, 1834–1919, Unit 2, Reel 150, Microfilm Collection, 15.1 Western Africa, Vol. 2, Letter 200. Wheaton, IL: Billy Graham Center Archives.

———. Francis Allison to Rufus Anderson, March 26, 1843. Letter. Papers of the American Board of Commissioners for Foreign Missions, ABC 15: Letters from Missionaries to Africa, 1834–1919, Unit 2, Reel 150, Microfilm Collection, 15.1 Western Africa, Vol. 2, Letter 199. Wheaton, IL: Billy Graham Center Archives.

———. Francis Allison to Unknown Recipient, February 23, 1852, from Gaboon. Letter. Papers of the American Board of Commissioners for Foreign Missions, ABC 15: Letters from Missionaries to Africa, 1834–1919, Unit 2, Reel 150, Microfilm Collection, 15.1 Western Africa, Vol. 3, Part 1, Letter 19. Wheaton, IL: Billy Graham Center Archives.

Ambouroue–Avaro, Joseph. *Un people Gabonais a l'aube de la colonisation: Le bas Ogowe au XIXème siècle*. Condé–Sur Noireau: L'Imprimerie Ch. Coret, 1981.

American Board of Commissioners for Foreign Missions. *Annual Report of the American Board of Commissioners for Foreign Missions [1837]*. Boston: Crocker and Brewster, 1837.

———. *Annual Report of the American Board of Commissioners for Foreign Missions [1843]*. Boston: Crocker and Brewster, 1843. http://books.google.com/books?id=QA3PAAAAMAAJ.

———. *Annual Report of the American Board of Commissioners for Foreign Missions [1844]*. Boston: T. R. Marvin, 1844. http://books.google.com/books?id=vtIWAQAAIAAJ.

———. *Annual Report of the American Board of Commissioners for Foreign Missions [1845]*. Boston: T. R. Marvin, 1845. http://books.google.com/books?id=YQ7PAAAAMAAJ.

———. *Annual Report of the American Board of Commissioners for Foreign Missions [1846]*. Boston: T. R. Marvin, 1846. http://books.google.com/books?id=YQ7PAAAAMAA.

———. *Annual Report of the American Board of Commissioners for Foreign Missions [1847]*. Boston: T. R. Marvin, 1847. http://books.google.com/books?id=EljOAAAAMAAJ.

————. *Annual Report of the Board of Commissioners for Foreign Missions, Vol. 39 [1848]*. Boston: T. R. Marvin, 1848. http://books.google.com/books?id=pw_PAAAAMAAJ.

————. *Annual Report of the Board of Commissioners for Foreign Missions, Vol. 40 [1849]*. Boston: T. R. Marvin, 1849. https://books.google.com/books?id=uPo_AQAAMAAJ&pg.

————. *Annual Report of the American Board of Commissioners for Foreign Missions, Vol. 45 [1854]*. Boston: T. R. Marvin, 1854. http://books.google.com/books?id=_VnOAAAAMAAJ.

————. *Annual Report of the American Board of Commissioners for Foreign Missions, Vol 46 [1855]*. Boston: T. R. Marvin, 1855. http://books.google.com/books?id=cnY1AQAAMAAJ.

————. *Annual Report of the American Board of Commissioners for Foreign Missions Vol 49 [1859]*. Boston: T. R. Marvin and Son, 1859. https://books.google.com/books?id=m1s-AQAAMAAJ.

————. *Annual Report of the American Board of Commissioners for Foreign Missions Vol 50 [1860]*. Boston: T. R. Marvin and Son, 1860. https://books.google.com/books?id=RWdHAQAAMAAJ&pg.

————. *Annual Report of the Board of Commissioners for Foreign Missions, Vol. 54 [1864]*. Boston: T. R. Marvin and Son, 1864. http://books.google.com/books?id=tipBAQAAMAAJ.

————. *Annual Report of the American Board of Commissioners for Foreign Missions, Vol. 59 [1869]*. Cambridge: Riverside, 1869. http://books.google.com/books?id=3BPPAAAAMAAJ.

————. "Annual Survey of the Missions of the Board: Africa: Gaboon Mission." *Missionary Herald* 66 (1870) 8. http://books.google.com/books?id=0EI5AQAAMAAJ.

————. "Annual Survey of the Missions of the Board: West Africa." *The Missionary Herald* 44 (1848) 3. http://books.google.com/books?id=H9QWAQAAIAAJ.

————. "Annual Survey of the Missions of the Board: Western Africa." *The Missionary Herald* 40 (1844) 2–3. http://books.google.com/books?id=vtIWAQAAIAAJ.

————. "Catalogue of Pupils: Beneficiaries Supported at Other Missions." *The Missionary Herald* 34 (1838) 135. http://books.google.com/books?id=X8oWAQAAIAAJ.

————. Gaboon Mission 1854 Statistics. Papers of the American Board of Commissioners for Foreign Missions, ABC 15: Letters from Missionaries to Africa, 1834–1919, Unit 2, Reel 151, Microfilm Collection, 15.1 Western Africa, Vol. 3, Part 1, Document 2. Wheaton, IL: Billy Graham Center Archives.

————. "General Letter from the Missionaries, at Cape Palmas." *Missionary Herald* 36 (1840) 219–21. http://books.google.com/books?id=0YkUAAAAYAAJ.

————. "Statistical View of the Officers, Missions, and Missionaries of the Board." *Missionary Herald* 36 (1840) 17–38. http://books.google.com/books?id=0YkUAAAAYAAJ.

————. "West Africa: Mission at Fair Hope, Cape Palmas." *The Missionary Herald* 33 (1837) 4.

————. "West Africa: Report of the Mission." *The Missionary Herald* 40 (1844) 183–86. http://books.google.com/books?id=vtIWAQAAIAAJ.

American Colonization Society. "Colored Men in Liberia." *The African Repository* 44 (1867) 342. http://books.google.com/books?id=ZjKORW7maYwC.

————. "Corisco Mission." *The African Repository* 37 (1861) 230–37. http://books.google.com/books?id=19CtEKvia8EC.

———. "Death of Rev. Edward Boeklen." *The African Repository* 45 (1869) 31. http://books.google.com/books?id=65A0AAAAYAAJ.

———. "Intelligence." *The African Repository* 38 (1862) 24–28. http://books.google.com/books?id=76k0AAAAYAAJ.

———. "Late from Liberia [1850]." *African Repository and Colonial Journal* 26 (1850) 155. http://books.google.com/books?id=VqcoAAAAYAAJ.

———. "Late from Liberia." *The African Repository* 45 (1869) 96. http://books.google.com/books?id=65A0AAAAYAAJ.

———. "Later from Liberia." *The African Repository and Colonial Journal* 30 (1854) 338–41. http://books.google.com/books?id=3a00AAAAYAAJ.

———. "List of Emigrants by the Ship Sophia Walker. *The African Repository and Colonial Journal* 30 (1854) 214–19. http://books.google.com/books?id=3a00AAAAYAAJ.

———. "Our Colored Population: The Census—Insanity." *African Repository and Colonial Journal* 19 (1843) 266–83. http://books.google.com/books?id=fY00AAAAYAAJ.

Ancestry.com. Passport Application for Benjamin V. K. James, dated June 17, 1846. US Passport Applications, 1795–1925. National Archives and Records Administration (NARA); Washington DC; Roll #: 18; Volume #: Roll 018–01 Apr 1846–30 Sep 1846. https://www.ancestry.com/imageviewer/collections/1174/images/USM1372_18-0801?pId=99740.

———. Port of New York. Passenger list for the Thomas Pope. New York Passenger Lists, 1820–1957. https://www.ancestry.com/imageviewer/collections/7488/images/NYM237_267-0127?pId=5725659.

———. *1810 United States Federal Census*, Elizabethtown, Essex New York. https://www.ancestry.com/imageviewer/collections/7613/images/4433399_00013?pId=200325.

———. *1820 United States Federal Census*, Jay, Essex New York. 1820 Census: https://www.ancestry.com/imageviewer/collections/7734/images/4433300_00027?pId=497242.

———. *1850 United States Federal Census—Slave Schedule. Schedule 2*—Slave inhabitants in District 2, Boyle County, Kentucky, dated August 6, 1850, page 582, 592. https://www.ancestry.com/imageviewer/collections/8055/images/KYM432_223-0298?treeid=&personid=&hintid=&queryId=27d0015f24223c84aa7e237a5d56659b&usePUB=true&_phsrc=dfL48018&_phstart=successSource&usePUBJs=true&_ga=2.24056506.1434242602.1603574873-32338661.1603574873&pId=90364149.

———. *1860 United States Federal Census Detroit Ward 6, Wayne, Michigan*; Page: 661; Family History Library Film: 803566. https://www.ancestry.com/imageviewer/collections/7667/images/4232719_00351?pId=45405638.

———. *1870 United States Federal Census Detroit Ward 6, Wayne, Michigan*; Roll: M593_713; Page: 487A; Family History Library Film: 552212. https://www.ancestry.com/imageviewer/collections/7163/images/4273770_00323?pId=25183028.

———. *1880 United States Federal Census Detroit, Wayne, Michigan*; Roll: 613; Page: 395A; Enumeration District: 307. https://www.ancestry.com/imageviewer/collections/6742/images/4241810-00476?pId=32084825.

———. *1880 United States Federal Census, Ann Arbor, Washtenaw, Michigan*; Roll: 608; Page: 80C; Enumeration District: 225. https://www.ancestry.com/imageviewer/collections/6742/images/4241815-00793?pId=32174525.

Bibliography

Anderson, Rufus. Rufus Anderson to J. H. B. Latrobe, July 11, 1835. Letter. Papers of the American Board of Commissioners for Foreign Missions, ABC 15: Letters from Missionaries to Africa, 1834–1919, Unit 2, Reel 150, Microfilm Collection, Letter 16. Wheaton, IL: Billy Graham Center Archives.

Ann Arbor Baptist Church. *The Ann Arbor Baptist* 1 (1888) 11.

Anonymous. "Amalgamation of the Races, Part One." *The Colonization and Journal of Freedom* June (1833) 69–73. http://books.google.com/books?id=Ne8SAAAAIAAJ.

———. "Amalgamation of the Races, Part Two." *The Colonization and Journal of Freedom* August (1833) 101–7. http://books.google.com/books?id=Ne8SAAAAIAAJ.

Bacheler, Henry M. Henry Bacheler to Dr. Lowrie, June 23, 1881. Africa letters: Gaboon and Corisco Mission, Vol. 13, Reel 75, Microfilm Collection, Letter 41. Philadelphia: Presbyterian Historical Society.

Barnes, James F. *Gabon: Beyond the Colonial Legacy.* Boulder, CO: Westview, 1992.

Beaver, R. Pierce. *American Protestant Women in World Mission: A History of the First Feminist Movement in North America.* Grand Rapids: Eerdmans, 1980.

Bell, Wiley I., ed. *Slaves No More: Letters from Liberia, 1833–1869.* Lexington: University of Kentucky Press, 1980.

Best, Jacob. Jacob Best to Rufus Anderson, June 9, 1858. Letter. Papers of the American Board of Commissioners for Foreign Missions, ABC 15: Letters from Missionaries to Africa, 1834–1919, Unit 2, Reel 151, Microfilm Collection, 15.1 Western Africa, Vol. 3, Part 1, Letter 45. Philadelphia: Presbyterian Historical Society.

Beyan, Amos J. *African American Settlements in West Africa: John Brown Russwurm and the American Civilizing Efforts.* New York: Palgrave Macmillan, 2005.

Bishop, Robert H., and David Rice. *Outline of the History of the Church in the State of Kentucky, during a Period of Forty Years: Containing the Memoirs of Rev. David Rice, and Sketches.* Lexington: Thomas T. Skillman, 1824. http://books.google.com/books?id=sEkRAAAAIAAJ.

Bliss, Edwin Munsell. *Missionary Enterprise: A Concise History of its Objects, Methods and Extension.* New York: Fleming H. Revell, 1908.

Blyden, Edward W. *Liberia's Offering: Being Address, Sermons, etc. by Rev. Edward W. Blyden.* New York: John A. Gray, 1862. http://books.google.com/books?id=xbo1AQAAMAAJ.

Board of Foreign Missions of the Presbyterian Church of the United States of America. *Annual Report [1850] of the Board of Foreign Missions of the Presbyterian Church USA.* New York: Mission House, 1850. http://books.google.com/books?id=SwLPAAAAMAAJ.

———. *Annual Report [1851] of the Board of Foreign Missions of the Presbyterian Church USA.* New York: Mission House, 1851. http://books.google.com/books?id=8V8sAAAAYAAJ.

———. *Annual Report [1852] of the Board of Foreign Missions of the Presbyterian Church USA.* New York: Mission House, 1852. http://books.google.com/books?id=8V8sAAAAYAAJ.

———. *Annual Report [1853] of the Board of Foreign Missions of the Presbyterian Church USA.* New York: Mission House, 1853. http://books.google.com/books?id=8V8sAAAAYAAJ.

———. *Annual Report [1855] of the Board of Foreign Missions of the Presbyterian Church USA.* New York: Mission House, 1855. http://books.google.com/books?id=8V8sAAAAYAAJ.

———. *Annual Report [1858] of the Board of Foreign Missions of the Presbyterian Church USA*. New York: E. O. Jenkins, 1858. http://books.google.com/books?id=jYMzAQAAMAAJ.

———. *Annual Report [1859] of the Board of Foreign Missions of the Presbyterian Church USA*. New York: E. O. Jenkins, 1859. http://books.google.com/books?id=jYMzAQAAMAAJ.

———. *Annual Report [1860] of the Board of Foreign Missions of the Presbyterian Church USA*. New York: E. O. Jenkins, 1860. http://books.google.com/books?id=jYMzAQAAMAAJ.

———. *Annual Report [1861] of the Board of Foreign Missions of the Presbyterian Church USA, 1861*. New York: Edward O. Jenkins, 1861. http://books.google.com/books?id=jYMzAQAAMAAJ.

———. *Annual Report [1869] of the Board of Foreign Missions of the Presbyterian Church USA*. Minutes of the General Assembly. Philadelphia: Presbyterian Board of Publication, 1869. http://books.google.com/books?id=z2lJAAAAMAAJ.

———. *Annual Report [1870] of the Board of Foreign Missions of the Presbyterian Church USA*. New York: Edward O. Jenkins, 1870. http://books.google.com/books?id=Hz5AAQAAMAAJ.

———. *Annual Report [1871] of the Board of Foreign Missions of the Presbyterian Church USA*. New York: Mission House, 1871. http://books.google.com/books?id=oQTPAAAAMAAJ.

———. *Annual Report [1872] of the Board of Foreign Missions of the Presbyterian Church USA*. New York: Mission House, 1872. http://books.google.com/books?id=oQTPAAAAMAAJ.

———. *Annual Report [1873] of the Board of Foreign Missions of the Presbyterian Church USA*. New York: Mission House, 1873. http://books.google.com/books?id=oQTPAAAAMAAJ.

———. *Annual Report [1874] of the Board of Foreign Missions of the Presbyterian Church USA*. New York: Mission House, 1874. http://books.google.com/books?id=d2hJAAAAMAAJ.

———. *Annual Report (1875) of the Board of Foreign Missions of the Presbyterian Church USA*. New York: Mission House, 1875. http://books.google.com/books?id=oQTPAAAAMAAJ.

———. *Annual Report [1876] of the Board of Foreign Missions of the Presbyterian Church USA*. New York: Mission House, 1876. http://books.google.com/books?id=oQTPAAAAMAAJ.

———. *Annual Report [1877] of the Board of Foreign Missions of the Presbyterian Church USA*. New York: Mission House, 1877. http://books.google.com/books?id=goczAQAAMAAJ.

———. *Annual Report [1878] of the Board of Foreign Missions of the Presbyterian Church USA*. New York: Mission House, 1878. http://books.google.com/books?id=6gXPAAAAMAAJ.

———. *Annual Report [1879] of the Board of Foreign Missions of the Presbyterian Church USA*. New York: Mission House, 1879. http://books.google.com/books?id=6gXPAAAAMAAJ.

———. *Annual Report [1880] of the Board of Foreign Mission of the Presbyterian Church USA*. New York: Mission House, 1880. http://books.google.com/books?id=6gXPAAAAMAAJ.

————. *Annual Report [1881] of the Board of Foreign Mission of the Presbyterian Church USA*. New York: Mission House, 1881. http://books.google.com/books?id=6gXPAAAAMAAJ.

————. *Annual Report [1883] of the Board of Foreign Missions of the Presbyterian Church USA*. New York: Mission House, 1883. http://books.google.com/books?id=6gXPAAAAMAAJ.

————. *Annual Report [1885] of the Board of Foreign Missions of the Presbyterian Church USA*. New York: Mission House, 1885. http://books.google.com/books?id=bAfPAAAAMAAJ.

————. *Annual Report [1886] of the Board of Missions of the Presbyterian Church USA*. New York: Mission House, 1886. http://books.google.com/books?id=bAfPAAAAMAAJ.

————. *Annual Report [1887] of the Board of Foreign Missions of the Presbyterian Church*. New York: Mission House, 1887. http://books.google.com/books?id=bAfPAAAAMAAJ.

————. *Annual Report [1888] of the Board of Foreign Missions of the Presbyterian Church USA*. Philadelphia: Mission House, 1888. http://books.google.com/books?id=YX8zAQAAMAAJ.

————. *Annual Report [1895] of the Board of Missions of the Presbyterian Church USA*. New York: Mission House, 1895. http://books.google.com/books?id=VgnPAAAAMAAJ.

————. *Annual Report [1911] of the Board of Foreign Missions of the Presbyterian Church*. New York: Presbyterian, 1911. http://books.google.com/books?id=234zAQAAMAAJ.

————. Carbon Copy of Board Minutes of the Committee on Africa, dated February 18, 1895. Record Group 142, Folder 33. American Negroes: Proposals for appointment to W. Africa Mission: Correspondence; Policy statements; Reports; Background Papers: 1894–1924. Philadelphia: Presbyterian Historical Society.

————. Colored Missionaries [1895]: Opinions of Individual Missionaries of the Gaboon and Corisco Mission. Record Group 142, Folder 33. American Negroes: Proposals for appointment to W. Africa Mission: Correspondence; Policy statements; Reports; Background Papers: 1894–1924. Philadelphia: Presbyterian Historical Society.

————. "Gaboon and Corisco, 1873." *The Presbyterian Monthly Record* 25 (1874) 175–77. http://books.google.com/books?id=FDgUAAAAYAAJ.

————. "Gaboon and Corisco Mission [1886]." *The Presbyterian Monthly Record* 37 (1886) 295–97. http://books.google.com/books?id=9nDPAAAAMAAJ.

————. "Mission House, June 25, 1871." *The Foreign Missionary* 30 (1871) 59–60. http://books.google.com/books?id=OLEyAQAAMAAJ.

————. "Missions in Western Africa: Gaboon and Corisco Mission. *The Foreign Missionary* 45 (1886) 5–8. http://books.google.com/books?id=srEnAAAAYAAJ.

————. "The Negro Race." *The Presbyterian* 33 (1863) 170.

————. "Recent Intelligence [1854]." *The Foreign Missionary* 13 (1854) 58. http://books.google.com/books?id=f6AOAAAAIAAJ.

————. "Recent Intelligence [1873]." *The Presbyterian Monthly Record* 24 (1873) 221. http://books.google.com/books?id=NeYqAAAAYAAJ.

————. "Recent Intelligence: Death of Missionaries." *The Presbyterian Monthly Record* 21 (1870) 129. http://books.google.com/books?id=weUqAAAAYAAJ.

————. "Recent Intelligence: Gaboon Mission." *The Presbyterian Monthly Record* 21 (1870) 202. http://books.google.com/books?id=weUqAAAAYAAJ.

————. "Recent Intelligence: Notices of Missionaries [1867]." *The Home and Foreign Record* 18 (1867) 81. http://books.google.com/books?id=Cz4UAAAAYAAJ.

————. "Recent Intelligence: Notices of Missionaries [1870]." *The Presbyterian Monthly Record* 21 (1870) 177. http://books.google.com/books?id=weUqAAAAYAAJ.

————. "Recent Intelligence: Notices of Missionaries [1873]." *The Presbyterian Monthly Record* 24 (1873) 153. http://books.google.com/books?id=NeYqAAAAYAAJ.

————. "Recent intelligence: Ordination of a Native African." *The Presbyterian Monthly Record* 21 (1870) 225. http://books.google.com/books?id=weUqAAAAYAAJ.

————. "Recent Intelligence: Renewed Call for Missionaries at Corisco." *The Presbyterian Monthly Record* 21 (1870) 105–6. http://books.google.com/books?id=weUqAAAAYAAJ.

————. "White and Colored Men Wanted in West African Missions." *Presbyterian Monthly Record* 22 (1871) 48–49. http://books.google.com/books?id=5DYUAAAAYAAJ.

————. "The Work at Bolenda." *The Presbyterian Monthly Record* 21 (1870) 13–15. http://books.google.com/books?id=weUqAAAAYAAJ.

Board of Home Missions. "Union for Self–Support: In Union is Strength." *The Presbyterian Monthly Record* 22 (1871) 97. http://books.google.com/books?id=5DYUAAAAYAAJ.

Bond, Horace Mann. *Education for Freedom: A History of Lincoln University, Pennsylvania.* Princeton: Princeton University Press, 1976.

————. *The Education of the Negro in the American Social Order.* New York: Octagon, 1970.

Bordin, Ruth. *Women at Michigan: The "Dangerous experiment," 1870s to the Present.* Ann Arbor: University of Michigan, 2001.

Bowdich, T. E. *Mission from Cape Coast Castle to Ashantee: With a Statistical Account of that Kingdom, and Geographical Notices of Other Parts of the Interior of Africa.* London: J. Murray, 1819.

Bowie, Fiona, et al., eds. *Women and Mission: Past and Present: Anthropological and Historical Perceptions.* Providence, RI: Berg, 1993.

Brown, Arthur J. *One Hundred Years: A History of the Foreign Missionary Work of the Presbyterian Church in the U. S. A.* 2nd ed. New York: Fleming H. Revell, 1937.

Brown, Richard C. *The Presbyterians: Two Hundred Years in Danville, 1784–1984.* Danville, KY: Danville Presbyterian Church, 1983.

Bryce, James. "Thoughts on the Negro Problem." *The North American Review* 153 (1891) 641–60.

Bucher, Henry H. *Two Women: Anyentyuwe and Ekâkise: Henry Bucher's Commentary and Annotations to Robert Hamill Nassau's and Isabella Nassau's 1911 Typescript of 'Two Women.'* N.d.: n.d., 2014.

————. "The Village of Glass and Western Intrusion: An Mpongwe response to the American and French presence in the Gabon Estuary: 1842–1845." *The International Journal of African Historical Studies* 6 (1973) 363–400.

Burke, Rosabella. "Rosabella Burke to Mary C. Lee, August 21, 1854, from Liberia." In *Slaves No More, Letters from Liberia, 1833–1869,* edited by Bell I. Wiley, 192. Lexington: University of Kentucky, 1980.

Bushnell, Albert. "Albert Bushnell, Excerpt July 11, 1872." *The Presbyterian Monthly Record* 23 (1872) 312–13. http://books.google.com/books?id=5DYUAAAAYAAJ.

————. Albert Bushnell to Dr. Lowrie, June 17, 1872. Africa Letters: West Africa 1867–1873, Vol. 9, Reel 71, Microfilm Collection, Letter 362. Philadelphia: Presbyterian Historical Society.

———. Albert Bushnell to Dr. Lowrie, July 5, 1872. Africa Letters: West Africa 1867–1873, Vol. 9, Reel 71, Microfilm Collection, Letter 365. Philadelphia: Presbyterian Historical Society.

———. Albert Bushnell to Dr. Lowrie, October 30, 1872. Africa Letters: West Africa, 1867–1873, Vol. 9, Reel 71, Microfilm Collection, Letter 485. Philadelphia: Presbyterian Historical Society.

———. Albert Bushnell to Dr. Lowrie, March 1874. Africa Letters: Gaboon and Corisco Mission, 1874–1875, Vol. 10, Reel 72, Microfilm Collection, Letter 155. Philadelphia: Presbyterian Historical Society.

———. Albert Bushnell to Dr. Lowrie, April 10, 1874. Africa Letters: Gaboon and Corisco, Vol. 10, Reel 72, Microfilm Collection, Letter 158. Philadelphia: Presbyterian Historical Society.

———. Albert Bushnell to Dr. Lowrie, September 22, 1874. Africa Letters: Gaboon and Corisco Mission 1874–1875, Vol. 10, Reel 72, Microfilm Collection, Letter 186. Philadelphia: Presbyterian Historical Society.

———. "Arrival at Gaboon: Interesting Notes." Letter dated June 16, 1871. *The Presbyterian Monthly Record* 22 (1871) 306. http://books.google.com/books?id=5DYUAAAAYAAJ.

———. "Communication from the Missions: Gaboon and Corisco Mission, Gaboon." *The Foreign Missionary of the Presbyterian Church* 30 (1871) 141–43. http://books.google.com/books?id=OLEyAQAAMAAJ.

———. "Journal of Mr. Bushnell." *The Missionary Herald* 51 (1855) 35–38. http://books.google.com/books?id=wXYUAAAAYAAJ.

Bushnell, Lucina. Lucina Bushnell to Rev. Wells, July 19, 1884. Africa letters: Gaboon and Corisco Mission 1881–1883, Vol. 14, Reel 76, Microfilm Collection, Letter 65. Philadelphia: Presbyterian Historical Society.

Campbell, Graham C. Graham Campbell to Dr. Lowrie, May 10, 1882. Africa letters: Gaboon and Corisco Mission 1881–1883, Vol. 13, Reel 75, Microfilm Collection, Letter 164. Philadelphia: Presbyterian Historical Society.

———. Graham Campbell to Dr. Lowrie, September 13, 1882. Africa letters: Gaboon and Corisco Mission 1881–1883, Vol. 13, Reel 75, Letter 210. Philadelphia: Presbyterian Historical Society.

———. Graham Campbell to R. H. Nassau, June 1, 1882. Campbell private letters. Provided by Laura O'Brien. Email and attachments November 1, 2005.

———. "Illness of Missionaries in Africa." *Presbyterian Monthly Record* 36 (1885) 454–56. http://books.google.com/books?id=p28oAQAAMAAJ.

———. Letter to family, dated August 27, 1882. Campbell Private Letters. Provided by Laura O'Brien. Email and attachments. November 1, 2005.

———. "Personal Review of the Year 1885, at Baraka, Africa." *The Presbyterian Monthly Record* 37 (1886) 144–45. http://books.google.com/books?id=9nDPAAAAMAAJ.

Campbell, Laura Kreis. Laura Campbell to the Family, December 21, 1881, from Gaboon, West Africa. Letter. Campbell private letters. Laura O'Brien Private Collection.

———. Laura Campbell to the Family, September 13, 1882. Campbell Private Letters. Laura O'Brien Private Collection.

———. Unpublished Diary. No Date. Laura O'Brien Private Collection.

Campbell, Penelope. "Presbyterian West African Mission: Women as Converts and Agents of Change." *Journal of Presbyterian History* 56 (1978) 121–36.

Carr, George B. *John Miller Dickey, D. D.: His Life and Times*. Philadelphia: Westminster Press, 1929.

Ciment, James. *Another America: The Story of Liberia and the Former Slaves Who Ruled It*. New York: Hill and Wang, 2013.

Civis. "Communication." *African Repository and Colonial Journal* 10 (1834) 46–47. http://books.google.com/books?id=RYsoAAAAYAAJ.

Clark, Walter. Walter Clark to Walter Lowrie, October 15, 1862. Letter. Africa letters: Corisco Mission 1858–1864, Vol. 7, Reel 68, Microfilm Collection, Letter 124. Philadelphia: Presbyterian Historical Society.

Clemens, William, and Cornelius DeHeer. 1860. Report of the Corisco Mission. Africa Letters: Corisco Mission, 1858–1864, Vol. 7, Reel 67, Microfilm Collection, Letter 41. Philadelphia: Presbyterian Historical Society.

Currier, J. M. "Dr. Currier's Letter on the History of the Blackboard, November 15, 1870." Old Stone Museum. https://oldstonehousemuseum.org/hall–bio/.

Danville Presbyterian Church (Danville, KY). 1854. Congregational meetings and session minutes, 1852–1867. Boyle Co., Reel 1. Minutes for April 6, 1854. Philadelphia: Presbyterian Historical Society.

DuBose, Hampton C. *Memoirs of Rev. John Leighton Wilson, D. D., Missionary to Africa and Secretary of Foreign Missions*. Richmond, VA: Presbyterian Committee of Publication, 1895. Microfilm Collection. http://books.google.com/books?id=WtMmAQAAIAAJ.

Dunnigan, Alice Allison. *Fascinating Story of Black Kentuckians: Their Heritage and Traditions*. Washington, DC: The Association for the Study of Afro–American Life and History, 1982.

Eden Cemetery. Interment Book No. 1 [1906]: 236. Eden Cemetery, Collingdale, PA. http://www.edencemetery.org/

Ellis, H. W. "Presbyterian Board: Extract of Letter from Rev. H. W. Ellis." *Southern Baptist Missionary Journal* 5 (1850) 280. http://books.google.com/books?id=jkPPAAAAMAAJ.

Fackler, Calvin Morgan. *Chronicle of the Old First (Presbyterian Church, Danville, Kentucky) 1784–1944*. Louisville, KY: Standard Printing Company, 1946.

Fahy, Lynn Kloter. Email and attachments. March 13, 2006.

Florida Memory website. Mary McLeod Bethune, principal. Image number N028177. http://www.floridamemory.com/onlineclassroom/marybethune/photos/.

Ford, Henry. Copy of the Estimate Prospective of the Expenses of Gaboon Mission for the Year 1854 as Directed by the Mission, dated June 27, 1853. Papers of the American Board of Commissioners for Foreign Missions, ABC 15: Letters from Missionaries to Africa, 1834–1919, Unit 2, Reel 151, Microfilm Collection, 15.1 Western Africa, Vol. 3, Part 1. Wheaton, IL: Billy Graham Center Archives.

———. Fifteenth Annual Report for the Gaboon Mission to the Prudential Committee for the A. B. C. F. M. for 1856, dated January 1857. Papers of the American Board of Commissioners for Foreign Missions, ABC 15: Letters from Missionaries to Africa, 1834–1919, Unit 2, Reel 151, Microfilm Collection, 15.1 Western Africa, Vol. 3, Part 1. Wheaton, IL: Billy Graham Center Archives.

Gaboon Church. Gaboon Church to Rev. John Gillespie, April 18, 1889, Glass, Gaboon, Baraka. Africa Letters: Gaboon and Corisco Mission 1883—1886—1887—1888—1889, Reel 78, Vol. 18, Microfilm Collection, Letter 42. Philadelphia: Presbyterian Historical Society.

Gaines, Elizabeth Venable. *Cub Creek Church and Congregation, 1738-1838.* Richmond, VA: Presbyterian Committee of Publication, 1931.

Gardinier, David. "The American Presbyterian Mission in Gabon: Male Mpongwe Converts and Agents, 1870–1883." *American Presbyterians* 69 (1991) 60–70.

Garrison, William Lloyd. *Thoughts on African Colonization: Or, an Impartial Exhibition of the Doctrines, Principles and Purposes of the American Colonization Society, Together with the Resolutions, Addresses and Remonstrances of the Free People of Color.* Boston: Garrison and Knapp, 1832.

Gault, William C. William Gault to the Corresponding Secretary, January 7, 1886. African letters: Gaboon and Corisco Mission, Vol. 16, Reel 77, Microfilm Collection, Letter 2. Philadelphia: Presbyterian Historical Society.

General Assembly of the Presbyterian Church. "Gospel Work in West Africa." *The Church at Home and Abroad* 15 (1894) 70–72. http://books.google.com/books?id=wdVLAAAAMAAJ.

———. *Minutes [1871] of the General Assembly of the Presbyterian Church in the United States of America,* Vol. 1. New York: Presbyterian Board of Publication, 1871.

———. *Minutes [1892] of the General Assembly of the Presbyterian Church in the United States of America,* Vol. 15. Philadelphia: MacCalla and Company, 1892. http://books.google.com/books?id=lZtJAAAAMAAJ.

———. "Monthly Concert: Gaboon and Corisco Mission." *The Church at Home and Abroad,* 1 (1887) 552–55. http://books.google.com/books?id=PcNLAAAAMAAJ.

———. "Monthly Concert: Gaboon and Corisco." *Church At Home and Abroad,* 3 (1888) 600–603. http://books.google.com/books?id=35AkAQAAIAAJ.

Gillespie, John. Estimates for 1888: Gaboon and Corisco Mission. Outgoing Letters, Reel 219, Vol. 4, Microfilm Collection, Letter 35. Philadelphia: Presbyterian Historical Society.

———. John Gillespie to the Gaboon and Corisco Mission, May 15, 1888. Outgoing Letters, Reel 219, Vol. 4, Microfilm Collection, Letter 29. Philadelphia: Presbyterian Historical Society.

———. John Gillespie to the Gaboon and Corisco Mission, July 7, 1890. Outgoing letters, Vol. 4, Reel 219, Microfilm Collection, Letter 73. Philadelphia: Presbyterian Historical Society.

———. John Gillespie to Rev. Robert L. Stewart [Extract], dated January 15, 1895. Record Group 142, Folder 33, American Negroes: Proposals for appointment to W. Africa Mission: Correspondence; Policy statements; Reports; Background Papers: 1894–1924. Philadelphia: Presbyterian Historical Society.

Gillespie, Samuel. Samuel Gillespie to Dr. Lowrie, August 9, 1872. Africa letters: West Africa mission, 1867–1873, Vol. 9, Reel 71, Microfilm Collection, Letter 373. Philadelphia: Presbyterian Historical Society.

Godduhn Family. Email and photocopied documents from family archives, July 28, 2006.

Good, Adolphus C. "Gaboon and Corisco Mission Report." *The Church at Home and Abroad* 1 (1887) 552–55. http://books.google.com/books?id=PcNLAAAAMAAJ.

———. Adolphus Good to the Board Secretary, February 24, 1888. Africa Letters: Gaboon and Corisco Mission 1887–1888, Vol. 17, Reel 78, Microfilm Collection, Letter 98. Philadelphia: Presbyterian Historical Society.

———. Adolphus Good to the Corresponding Secretary, August 20, 1888. Africa: Africa letters 1883–1889, Vol. 18, Reel 78, Microfilm Collection, Letter 16. Philadelphia: Presbyterian Historical Society.

————. Adolphus Good to Dr. Gillespie, May 12, 1889. Africa Letters: Gaboon and Corisco Mission 1883—1886—1887—1888—1889, Vol. 18, Reel 78, Microfilm Collection, Letter 47. Philadelphia: Presbyterian Historical Society.

Good, Lydia Belle Walker. Lydia Good to Rev. Luke Dorland, October 23, 1883. Africa Letters: Gaboon and Corisco Mission 1881–1883, Vol. 14, Reel 76, Microfilm Collection, Letter 299. Philadelphia: Presbyterian Historical Society.

————. Lydia B. Good to Rev. William Walker, June 11, 1884. William Walker Papers, 1836-1896, Box 1 Folder 8. Madison, WI: Wisconsin Historical Society.

————. Lydia B. Good to Rev. William Walker, January 23, 1885. Letter. William Walker Papers, 1836-1896, Box 1, Folder 9. Madison: Wisconsin Historical Society.

Goodrich, Francis L. D. *Historical Facts and Events concerning the First Presbyterian Church of Ann Arbor, Michigan.* Ann Arbor: First Presbyterian Church of Ann Arbor, 1961.

Griswold, Benjamin. Benjamin Griswold to Rufus Anderson, December 28, 1842. Letter. Papers of the American Board of Commissioners for Foreign Missions, ABC 15: Letters from Missionaries to Africa, 1834-1919, Unit 2, Reel 150, Microfilm Collection, 15.1 Western Africa, Vol. 2, Letter 159. Wheaton, IL: Billy Graham Center Archives.

————. Benjamin Griswold to Rufus Anderson, May 8, 1843. Letter. Papers of the American Board of Commissioners for Foreign Missions, ABC 15: Letters from Missionaries to Africa, 1834-1919, Unit 2, Reel 150, Microfilm Collection, 15.1 Western Africa, Vol. 2, Letter 163. Wheaton, IL: Billy Graham Center Archives.

————. Benjamin Griswold to Rufus Anderson, December 26, 1843, from Ozhunga. Letter. Papers of the American Board of Commissioners for Foreign Missions, ABC 15: Letters from Missionaries to Africa, 1834-1919, Unit 2, Reel 150, Microfilm Collection, 15.1 Western Africa, Vol. 2, Letter 167. Wheaton, IL: Billy Graham Center Archives.

————. "Recent Intelligence: West Africa." May 8, 1843 from Gaboon. *Missionary Herald* 39 (1843) 404. http://books.google.com/books?id=XcwWAQAAIAAJ.

————. "Western Africa: Excerpt of letter dated July 18, 1842 from Cape Palmas, Liberia." *Missionary Herald* 38 (1842) 498-500. https://books.google.com/books?id=HRxrYqmU6ZEC&pg=PA498.

Gurley, R. R. *Address of the Managers of the American Colonization Society to the People of the United States: Adopted at their Meeting, June 19, 1832.* Washington: James C. Dunn, 1832. http://books.google.com/books?id=HMANAAAAQAAJ.

Guy-Sheftall, Beverly. *Daughters of Sorrow: Attitudes toward Black Women, 1880-1920.* Brooklyn: Carlson, 1990.

Haas, Waltraud. "The Nineteenth-Century Basel Mission and its Women Missionaries." In *Mission History from the Woman's Point of View*, edited by Ken Phin Pang and Waltraud Haas, 12–29. Basel: Basel Mission, 1989.

Hanciles, Jehu. *Euthanasia of a Mission: African Church Autonomy in a Colonial Context.* Westport, CT: Praeger, 2002.

Harding, Mary L. "Africa: Miss Harding, Gaboon." *Woman's Work for Woman* 13 (1883) 186. http://books.google.com/books?id=j4LfAAAAMAAJ.

————. "African Children." *Children's Work for Children* 10 (1888) 108. http://books.google.com/books?id=uho3AAAAMAAJ.

————. "Freedmen. Mary L. Harding, Pine Bluff, Arkansas." *Home Mission Monthly* 5 (1890) 231. http://books.google.com/books?id=oQrPAAAAMAAJ.

———. "Freedmen: Mary L. Harding, Pine Bluff, Arkansas." *Home Mission Monthly* 5 (1891) 156. http://books.google.com/books?id=SwvPAAAAMAAJ.

———. "Gaboon and Corisco Mission Report." *The Foreign Missionary* 45 (1886) 5–8. http://books.google.com/books?id=srEnAAAAYAAJ.

———. "Items of News from Kangwe Mission." *The Presbyterian Monthly Record* 34 (1883) 308–9. http://books.google.com/books?id=tW7PAAAAMAAJ.

———. "Kangwe Girls' School." *Woman's Work for Woman* 13 (1883) 305. http://books.google.com/books?id=j4LfAAAAMAAJ.

———. Mary Harding to Standing Committee, December 10, 1884. Africa Letters: Gaboon and Corisco Mission 1881–1883, Vol. 14, Reel 76, Microfilm Collection, Letter 99. Philadelphia: Presbyterian Historical Society.

———. Mary Harding to the Standing Committee of the Gaboon and Corisco mission, December 19, 1885. Africa Letters: Gaboon and Corisco Mission, Vol. 14, Reel 77, Microfilm Collection, Letter 288. Philadelphia: Presbyterian Historical Society.

———. Mary Harding to Unknown Recipient, Partial Letter, date unknown. Africa letters: Gaboon and Corisco Mission 1887–1888, Vol. 17, Reel 78, Microfilm Collection, no number. Philadelphia: Presbyterian Historical Society.

———. Mary Harding to Standing Committee, December 12, 1887: Report for the year 1887. Africa Letters: Gaboon and Corisco Mission 1887–1888, Vol. 17, Reel 78, Microfilm Collection, Letter 64. Philadelphia: Presbyterian Historical Society.

———. Mary Harding to Dr. Gillespie, August 9, 1888. Africa Letters 1887–1888: Gaboon and Corisco Mission, Vol. 17, Reel 78, Microfilm Collection, Letter 146. Philadelphia: Presbyterian Historical Society.

———. Mary Harding to Joseph Reading, August 21, 1888. Africa Letters 1887–1888: Gaboon and Corisco Mission, Vol. 18, Reel 78, Microfilm Collection, Letter 17. Philadelphia: Presbyterian Historical Society.

———. "W. Africa: Miss M. L. Harding, Gaboon." *Woman's Work for Woman* 13 (1883) 124–25. http://books.google.com/books?id=j4LfAAAAMAAJ.

Harmount, Mrs. G. A. Note of Correction. *The Church at Home and Abroad* 3 (1888) 331. http://books.google.com/books?id=2MZLAAAAMAAJ.

Harrison, Lowell H. and James C. Klotter. *New History of Kentucky.* Lexington: University of Kentucky Press, 1997.

Hastings, Adrian. *The Church in Africa, 1450–1950.* Oxford: Clarendon, 1994.

Helm, Mrs. H. T. "Farewell Meeting to Missionaries." *The Gospel in All Lands* (1882) 168. http://books.google.com/books?id=GxQ_AQAAMAAJ.

Hendricks, Sarah (Sadie). Sarah Hendricks to Dr. Lowrie, August 1, 1873. Africa Letters: West Africa Mission 1867–1873, Vol. 9, Reel 71, Microfilm Collection, Letter 467. Philadelphia: Presbyterian Historical Society.

Hill, Patricia R. *The World Their Household: The American Woman's Foreign Mission Movement and Cultural Transformation, 1870–1920.* Ann Arbor: University of Michigan Press, 1985.

Holden, Edith. *Blyden of Liberia: An Account of the Life and Labors of Edward Wilmot Blyden, LL.D.* New York: Vantage, 1966.

Jack, Andrew Donnell. Andrew Jack to Dr. Anderson, February 18, 1858. Letter. Papers of the American Board of Commissioners for Foreign Missions, ABC 15: Letters from Missionaries to Africa, 1834–1919, Unit 2, Reel 151, Microfilm Collection, 15.1 Western Africa, Vol. 3, Part 1. Wheaton: Billy Graham Center Archives.

Jackson, Maria. Report of the Corisco Mission Girls' Boarding School, for the Year ending October 1, 1860. Africa Letters 1858–1864, Vol. 7, Reel 67, Microfilm Collection, Letter 36. Philadelphia: Presbyterian Historical Society.

Jacobs, Sylvia M., ed. *Black Americans and the Missionary Movement in Africa*. Westport, CT: Greenwood, 1982.

———. "African–American Women Missionaries and European imperialism in Southern Africa, 1880–1920." *Women's Studies Int. Forum* 13 (1990) 381–94.

———. "Three African American Women Missionaries in the Congo, 1887–1899: The Confluence of Race, Culture, Identity, and Nationality." In *Competing Kingdoms: Women Mission, Nation, and the American Protestant Empire, 1812–1960*, edited by Barbara Reeves-Ellington et al, 318–41. Durham, NC: Duke University Press, 2010.

James, Benjamin van Rensselaer. James to Rufus Anderson, October 3, 1842. Letters. Papers of the American Board of Commissioners for Foreign Missions, ABC 15: Letters from Missionaries to Africa, 1834–1919, Unit 2, Reel 150, Microfilm Collection, 15.1 Western Africa, Vol. 2, Letter 193. Wheaton, IL: Billy Graham Center Archives.

———. B. V. R. James to Rufus Anderson, February 13, 1843. Letter. Papers of the American Board of Commissioners for Foreign Missions, ABC 15: Letters from Missionaries to Africa, 1834–1919, Unit 2, Reel 150, Microfilm Collection, 15.1 Western Africa, Vol. 2, Letter 194. Wheaton, IL: Billy Graham Center Archives.

———. B. V. R. James to Rufus Anderson, October 2, 1843. Letter. Papers of the American Board of Commissioners for Foreign Missions, ABC 15: Letters from Missionaries to Africa, 1834–1919, Unit 2, Reel 150, Microfilm Collection, 15.1 Western Africa, Vol. 2, Letter 196. Wheaton, IL: Billy Graham Center Archives.

———. B. V. R. James to Rufus Anderson, January 9, 1844. Letter. Papers of the American Board of Commissioners for Foreign Missions, ABC 15: Letters from Missionaries to Africa, 1834–1919, Unit 2, Reel 150, Microfilm Collection, 15.1 Western Africa, Vol. 2, Letter 197. Wheaton, IL: Billy Graham Center Archives.

J'Ikenge, Ibia. Ibia J'Ikenge to the Mission, forwarded to Dr. Lowrie by S. H. Murphy. Africa Letters: West Africa Mission 1867–1873, Vol. 9, Reel 71, Letter 382. Philadelphia: Presbyterian Historical Society.

———. Ibia J'Ikenge to Board Secretary, August 8, 1877. Africa Letters: West Africa Mission, Vol. 11, Reel 72, Microfilm Collection, Letter 167. Philadelphia: Presbyterian Historical Society.

Johnson, Julia Bushnell Herrick. "Reminiscences of a Short Sojourn on the West Coast of Africa." Unpublished manuscript, copied by Hubert Herrick Ward, June 9, 1919. Document copy provided to the author by Roger Ward, January 2007.

Jones, Lydia. "Extracts from Miss Jones's letters." *Woman's Work for Woman* 2 (1872) 242–43. http://books.google.com/books?id=ERI3AAAAMAAJ.

———. "Gaboon and Corisco Mission [Extract]." *The Foreign Missionary* 45 (1886) 5–8. http://books.google.com/books?id=srEnAAAAYAAJ.

———. Lydia Jones to Rev. William Walker. Gaboon, May 23, 1884. Letter. William Walker Papers, 1836–1896, Box 1, Folder 8. Madison: Wisconsin Historical Society.

———. Lydia Jones to Rev. Walker, from Baraka, January 18, 1885. Letter. William Walker Papers, 1836–1896, Box 1, Folder 9. Madison: Wisconsin Historical Society.

———. "Miss Jones, Gaboon, Africa." *Woman's Work for Woman* 9 (1879) 122. http://books.google.com/books?id=DxQ3AAAAMAAJ.

Bibliography

Kalu, Ogbu. "Gathering figs from Thistles? Hinterland slave trade and the Christianisation of Igboland, 1900–1950." *Journal of African Christian Thought* 10 (2007) 36–45.

Killingray, David. 2003. "The Black Atlantic Missionary Movement and Africa, 1780s–1920s." *Journal of Religion in Africa* 33 (2003) 3–31.

Kingsley, Mary H. *Travels in West Africa: Congo Français, Corisco and Cameroons.* New York: The MacMillan Company. http://books.google.com/books?id=sEcaAAAAYAAJ.

Latta, Mary. Mary Latta to John Leighton Wilson en route to Corisco, October 8, 1860. Letter. Africa Letters, 1858–1864: Vol. 7, number unknown. Philadelphia: Presbyterian Historical Society.

Lemire, Elise. *"Miscegenation": Making Race in America.* Philadelphia: University of Pennsylvania Press, 2002.

Lemons, Holly. Email and photo attachment, dated July 12, 2005. Private family archives.

Lofy, John. Email correspondence, dated November 3, 2008. University of Michigan, Ann Arbor.

Loomis, Chauncey. Chauncey Loomis to John Lowrie, July 29, 1863. Letter. Africa Letters: Corisco Mission, West Africa 1858–1864, Vol. 7, Reel 68, Microfilm Collection, Letter 87. Philadelphia: Presbyterian Historical Society.

Lowrie, John C. *A Manual of Missions; Or, Sketches of the Foreign Missions of the Presbyterian Church: With Maps, Showing the Stations, and Statistics of Protestant Missions among Unevangelized Nations.* New York: Anson D. L. Randolph. http://books.google.com/books?id=vYEXAAAAYAAJ.

Mackenzie, Jean Kenyon. *Black Sheep: Adventures in West Africa.* Boston: Houghton and Mifflin. http://books.google.com/books?id=3XgWAAAAIAAJ.

———. "Black Sheep, Part III: The Mail from the Beach." *The Atlantic Monthly* 116 (1915) 785–95. https://books.google.com/books?id=1EAwAQAAMAAJ.

Mackey, Isabella Sweeney. Report of the Corisco Girls' School, September 30, 1858. Africa Letters: Corisco Mission, West Africa 1850–1860, Vol. 4, Reel 64, Microfilm Collection, Letter 221. Philadelphia: Presbyterian Historical Society.

Mackey, James L. "Africa: Corisco Mission Report." *The Home and Foreign Record* 5 (1854) 210–11. http://books.google.com/books?id=VMccAQAAMAAJ.

———. James Mackey to the Corresponding Secretary, December 2, 1852. Letter. Africa Letters: Corisco Mission, West Africa 1850–1860, Vol. 4, Reel 64, Microfilm Collection, Letter 49. Philadelphia: Presbyterian Historical Society.

———. James Mackey to the Corresponding Secretary April 15, 1853. Africa Letters: Corisco Mission, West Africa 1850–1860, Vol. 4, Reel 64, Microfilm Collection, Letter 56. Philadelphia: Presbyterian Historical Society.

———. James L. Mackey to the Corresponding Secretary, April 13, 1857. Letter. Africa Letters: Corisco Mission, West Africa 1850–1860, Vol. 4, Reel 64, Microfilm Collection, Letter 158. Philadelphia: Presbyterian Historical Society.

Maryland, State of. "Report of the Colonization Society in Answer to an Order of the House of Delegates of the Second January, Eighteen Hundred and Forty-Four, Document F. *Maryland State Documents and Committee Reports for 1843–1844.* http://books.google.com/books?id=JJwuAAAAYAAJ.

Massachusetts Colonization Society. "Massachusetts Colonization Society Annual Meeting: Another Man Who Knows." *African Repository and Colonial Journal* 23 (1847) 233–34. http://books.google.com/books?id=zIkoAAAAYAAJ.

M'Bokolo, Elikia. *Noirs et Blancs en Afrique Equatoriale: Les Sociétés Côtières et la Pénétration Française, vers 1820–1874.* Paris: Ecole des Hautes Etudes en Sciences Sociales, 1981.

McArver, Susan Wilds. "'The Salvation of Souls' and the 'Salvation of the Republic of Liberia': Denominational Conflict and Racial Diversity in Antebellum Presbyterian Foreign Missions." In *North American Foreign Missions, 1810–1914: Theology, Theory, and Policy,* edited by Wilbert Shenk, 133–60. Grand Rapids: Eerdmans, 2004.

———. "Black Presbyterian Clergy and the Schism of 1837." *Union Seminary Quarterly Review* 54 (2000) 53–84.

McGill, Samuel F. "Letter to the Editors of the N. E. Puritan, dated October 1, 1842. *Maryland Colonization Journal* 1 (1842) 260–63. http://books.google.com/books?id=VOgRAAAAIAAJ.

McLeod, Mary J. Letter to the Presbyterian Board, dated February 6, 1895. Record Group 142, Folder 33, American Negroes: Proposals for appointment to W. Africa Mission: Correspondence; Policy statements; Reports; Background Papers: 1894–1924. Philadelphia: Presbyterian Historical Society.

McQueen, George. George McQueen to J. L. Wilson, Board Secretary, dated May 26, 1854. Africa Letters: Corisco Mission, West Africa 1850–1860, Vol. 4, Reel 64, Microfilm Collection, Letter 81. Philadelphia: Presbyterian Historical Society.

McQueen, Georgianna Bliss. "Corisco Graveyard." *The African Repository* 39 (1863) 183–84. http://books.google.com/books?id=MKooAAAAYAAJ.

Menaul, John. "Recent Intelligence. Letter Excerpt." *The Record of the Presbyterian Church in the United States of America* 21 (1870) 9–10. http://books.google.com/books?id=weUqAAAAYAAJ.

Menkel, Peter. *Diary, 1875–1897.* Peter Menkel Personal Papers, Series I, Box 1, Folders 2-3. Philadelphia: Presbyterian Historical Society.

———. Peter Menkel to Dr. Lowrie, dated October 29, 1873. Africa Letters: West Africa 1867–1873, Vol. 9, Reel 71, Microfilm Collection, Letter 484. Philadelphia: Presbyterian Historical Society.

———. Peter Menkel to Dr. Lowrie, September 16, 1884. Africa Letters: Gaboon and Corisco 1884–1885, Vol. 14, Reel 76, Microfilm Collection, Letter 77. Philadelphia: Presbyterian Historical Society.

———. Peter Menkel to Dr. Wells, February 10, 1885. Africa Letters: Gaboon and Corisco 1884–1885, Vol. 14, Reel 76, Microfilm Collection, Letter 204. Philadelphia: Presbyterian Historical Society.

———. Peter Menkel to Rev. Walker, from Gaboon, dated November 1, 1884. William Walker Papers 1836–1896, Box 1, Folder 8. Madison: Wisconsin Historical Society.

———. Peter Menkel to Rev. Walker, January 15, 1885. William Walker Papers 1836–1896, Box 1, Folder 9. Madison: Wisconsin Historical Society.

———. Report for the Year 1885. Document date January 7, 1886. Africa Letters: Gaboon and Corisco 1884–1885, Vol.14, Reel 77, Microfilm Collection, Letter 2. Philadelphia: Presbyterian Historical Society.

Menkel, Vincent. Email and photo attachment. August 2006.

Missionary Society of the Methodist Episcopal Church. "Notes on Missionaries, Missions." *The Gospel in All Lands* June (1898) 279–80. http://books.google.com/books?id=3jODvSUcvlwC.

Moore, Moses. "Edward Wilmot Blyden: From Old School Presbyterian missionary to 'Minister of Truth.'" *Journal of Presbyterian History* 75 (1997) 103–18.

Bibliography

Moses, Wilson Jeremiah, ed. *Liberian Dreams: Back-to-Africa Narratives from the 1850s.* University Park, PA: The Pennsylvania State University Press, 1998.

Murphy, Samuel. "Benita." Excerpts quoted in year–end report for 1873. *The Presbyterian Monthly Record* 25 (1874) 177. http://books.google.com/books?id=FDgUAAAAYAAJ.

———. Samuel Murphy to Dr. Lowrie, August 1, 1872. Africa letters: West Africa 1871–1874, Vol. 9, Reel 71, Microfilm Collection, Letter 371. Philadelphia: Presbyterian Historical Society.

———. Samuel Murphy to Dr. Lowrie, September 3, 1872. Africa letters: West Africa 1871–1874, Vol. 9, Reel 71, Microfilm Collection, Letter 382. Philadelphia: Presbyterian Historical Society.

Murphy, Sophie Lord. "Extracts from Mrs. Murphy's Letter." *Woman's Work for Woman* 3 (1873) 87. http://books.google.com/books?id=LRI3AAAAMAAJ.

Murray, Andrew E. 1966. *Presbyterians and the Negro: A History.* Philadelphia: Presbyterian Historical Society.

Mwakikagile, Godfrey. *Relations between Africans and African Americans.* 3rd ed. Pretoria, South Africa: New Africa, 2007.

Nassau, Isabella A. "Baraka, Gaboon River." *Woman's Work for Woman* 13 (1883) 197–98. http://books.google.com/books?id=j4LfAAAAMAAJ.

———. "Bolenda School." *The Presbyterian Monthly Record* 22 (1871) 50. http://books.google.com/books?id=5DYUAAAAYAAJ.

———. Isabella Nassau to Dr. Gillespie, January 12, 1883. Africa Letters: Gaboon and Corisco Mission 1881–1883, Vol. 14, Reel 76, Microfilm Collection, Letter 314. Philadelphia: Presbyterian Historical Society.

———. Isabella Nassau to Dr. Gillespie, September 5, 1894. Africa Letters: Gaboon and Corisco Mission 1894–1895, Vol. 21, Reel 81, Microfilm Collection, Letter 95. Philadelphia: Presbyterian Historical Society.

———. Isabella Nassau to Dr. Gillespie, September 13, 1895, from Gross Batanga, Kamerun. Africa Letters: Gaboon and Corisco Mission 1894–1895, Vol. 21, Reel 82, Microfilm Collection, Letter 271. Philadelphia: Presbyterian Historical Society.

———. Isabella Nassau to Dr. Gillespie, December 24, 1895. Africa Letters Gaboon and Corisco Mission 1894–1895, Vol. 21, Reel 82, Microfilm Collection, Letter 322. Philadelphia: Presbyterian Historical Society.

———. Isabella Nassau to Dr. Lowrie, August 18, 1868. Letter. Africa letters 1868–1871: Corisco Mission, Vol. 8, Reel 70, Microfilm Collection, Letter 250. Philadelphia: Presbyterian Historical Society.

———. Isabella Nassau to Dr. Lowrie, July 11, 1870a. Africa Letters: West Africa 1867–1873, Vol. 9, Reel 70, Microfilm Collection, Letter 116. Philadelphia: Presbyterian Historical Society.

———. Isabella Nassau to Dr. Lowrie, September 28, 1870. Africa Letters: West Africa 1867–1873, Vol. 9, Reel 70, Microfilm Collection, Letter 146. Philadelphia: Presbyterian Historical Society.

———. Isabella Nassau to Dr. Lowrie, June 24, 1882. Africa Letters: Gaboon and Corisco Mission, 1881–1883, Vol. 13, Reel 75, Microfilm Collection, Letter 179. Philadelphia: Presbyterian Historical Society.

———. "A Kombe Licentiate Preacher [Extract from Miss Nassau's letter]." *The Presbyterian Monthly Record* 29 (1878) 151. http://books.google.com/books?id=CdIQAAAAIAAJ.

————. "Letter from Miss I. A. Nassau, of June 4, to the Auxiliary Society of Woodland Church, West Philadelphia." *Woman's Work for Woman* 1 (1871) 101–3. http://books. google.com/books?id=k14zAQAAMAAJ.

————. "News from the Field: Miss Nassau, Kangwe, West Africa." *Woman's Work for Woman* 9 (1879) 407–8. http://books.google.com/books?id=RBM3AAAAMAAJ.

————. "The Usual Weekly Prayer Meeting at Benita." *The Presbyterian Monthly Record* 21 (1870) 255–56. http://books.google.com/books?id=weUqAAAAYAAJ.

————. "Work for Corisco and Benita Women." *The Record of the Presbyterian Church USA* 20 (1869) 36–37. http://books.google.com/books?id=OzcUAAAAYAAJ.

Nassau, Robert Hamill. "Characteristics of Corisco Presbytery: Its weakness and its work." *Trenton True American*, October 17, 1894. Nassau, Robert Hamill (1835–1921) Selected Documents, Section 11: Newspaper clippings of my life, 1880–1921. Microform. Philadelphia: Presbyterian Historical Society.

————. *Corisco Days: The First Thirty Years of the West Africa Mission*. Philadelphia: Allen, Lane and Scott, 1910.

————. *Crowned in Palm-land: A Story of African Mission Life*. Philadelphia: J. B. Lippencott and Company, 1874. http://books.google.com/books?id=jxorAAAAYAAJ.

————. *History of the Presbytery of Corisco*. Trenton, NJ: Brandt, 1888. http://books. google.com/books?id=C_8qAAAAYAAJ.

————. *My Ogowe: Being a Narrative of Daily Incidents during Sixteen Years in Equatorial West Africa*. New York: Neale, 1914. http://books.google.com/ books?id=WioUAAAAIAAJ.

————. "Notices of Corisco and Benita Work." Letter excerpt, July 27, 1870. *The Presbyterian Monthly Record* 21 (1870) 278. http://books.google.com/ books?id=weUqAAAAYAAJ.

————. "Rev. Ibia J'Ikenge." *The Assembly Herald* 6 (1902) 106–7. http://books.google. com/books?id=jpztAAAAMAAJ.

————. Robert Hamill Nassau to the Board Secretary, February 23, 1888. Africa Letters 1887–1888: Gaboon and Corisco Mission, Vol. 17, Reel 78, Microfilm Collection, Letter 99. Philadelphia: Presbyterian Historical Society.

————. Robert Hamill Nassau to Dr. Gillespie, April 24, 1889. Africa Letters 1883—1886—1887—1888—1889, Gaboon and Corisco Mission, Vol. 18, Reel 78, Microfilm Collection, Letter 44. Philadelphia: Presbyterian Historical Society.

————. Robert Hamill Nassau to Dr. Gillespie, August 6, 1895. Africa Letters: Gaboon and Corisco Mission 1894–1895, Vol. 21, Reel 82, Microfilm Collection, Letter 271. Philadelphia: Presbyterian Historical Society.

————. Robert Hamill Nassau to Dr. Gillespie, December 25, 1895, from Batanga. Africa Letters: Gaboon and Corisco Mission 1894–1895, Vol. 21, Reel 82, Microfilm Collection, Letter 321. Philadelphia: Presbyterian Historical Society.

————. Robert Hamill Nassau to Dr. Lowrie, April 6, 1870. Africa Letters: West Africa Mission 1867–1873, Vol. 9, Reel 70, Microfilm Collection, Letter 85. Philadelphia: Presbyterian Historical Society.

————. "Sowing Beside All Waters." *The Assembly Herald* 1 (1899) 344–46. http://books. google.com/books?id=sW7UAAAAMAAJ.

————. *Tales Out of School*. Philadelphia: Allen, Lane and Scott, 1911. http://books. google.com/books?id=ogcrAAAAYAAJ.

Bibliography

Nesbit, William. "Four Months in Liberia: African Colonization Exposed." In *Liberian Dreams: Back-to-Africa Narratives from the 1850s*, edited by Wilson Jeremiah Moses, 79–126. University Park, PA: The Pennsylvania State University Press, 1998.

O'Brien, Laura. Email and photo attachments, dated November 1, 2005. Private family archives.

Ogden, Thomas Spencer. Estimated Appropriations for the Coming Year, January 16, 1860. Letter. Africa Letters: Corisco Mission, 1858–1864, Vol. 7, Reel 67, Microfilm Collection, Letter 8. Philadelphia: Presbyterian Historical Society.

———. Thomas Ogden to J. L. Wilson, January 4, 1860. Letter. Africa Letters: Corisco Mission, 1858–1864, Vol. 7, Reel 67, Microfilm Collection, Letter 6. Philadelphia: Presbyterian Historical Society.

Old Stone Museum Website. Samuel Hall biography. http://oldstonehousemuseum.org/hall-bio.

Otago Witness. "A Young African Missionary." *The Otago Witness* 1619 (December 1882). http://paperspast.natlib.govt.nz/cgi-bin/paperspast.

Park, Eunjin. *"White" Americans in "Black" Africa: Black and White American Methodist Missionaries in Liberia, 1820–1875*. New York: Routledge, 2001.

Parsons, Ellen C. *Life for Africa: Rev. Adolphus Clemens Good, Ph.D., American Missionary in Equatorial West Africa*. New York: Fleming H. Revell, 1897.

Payne, John. "Annual Report to the Foreign Committee." *Maryland Colonization Journal* 5 (1848) 24–27. http://books.google.com/books?id=UusRAAAAIAAJ.

———. "Journal of Rev. John Payne." *Maryland Colonization Journal* 5 (1849) 58–59. http://books.google.com/books?id=UusRAAAAIAAJ.

Perry, Amy. Email correspondence and photo attachments, May 24, 2005. Private family archives.

Pierce, Epaminondas J. Annual Report of the Gaboon Mission, 1857 (date obscured). Papers of the American Board of Commissioners for Foreign Missions, ABC 15: Letters from Missionaries to Africa, 1834–1919, Unit 2, Reel 151, Microfilm Collection, 15.1 Western Africa, Vol. 3, Part 1, Letter 17. Wheaton, IL: Billy Graham Center Archives.

———. Epaminondas Pierce to Rev. Thompson, January 15, 1858. Papers of the American Board of Commissioners for Foreign Missions, ABC 15: Letters from Missionaries to Africa, 1834–1919, Unit 2, Reel 151, Microfilm Collection, 15.1 Western Africa, Vol. 3, Part 1, Letter 304. Wheaton, IL: Billy Graham Center Archives.

———. Epaminondas Pierce to Rev. Wood, February 12, 1858. Papers of the American Board of Commissioners for Foreign Missions, ABC 15: Letters from Missionaries to Africa, 1834–1919, Unit 2, Reel 151, Microfilm Collection, 15.1 Western Africa, Vol. 3, Part 1, Letter 307. Wheaton, IL: Billy Graham Center Archives.

———. Epaminondas Pierce to Rufus Anderson, October 3, 1855. Papers of the American Board of Commissioners for Foreign Missions, ABC 15: Letters from Missionaries to Africa, 1834–1919, Unit 2, Reel 151, Microfilm Collection, 15.1 Western Africa, Vol. 3, Part 1, Letter 288. Wheaton, IL: Billy Graham Center Archives.

———. Epaminondas Pierce to Rufus Anderson, October 30, 1855. Papers of the American Board of Commissioners for Foreign Missions, ABC 15: Letters from Missionaries to Africa, 1834–1919, Unit 2, Reel 151, Microfilm Collection, 15.1 Western Africa, Vol. 3, Part 1, Letter 291. Wheaton, IL: Billy Graham Center Archives

———. Epaminondas Pierce to Rufus Anderson, September 30, 1857. Papers of the American Board of Commissioners for Foreign Missions, ABC 15: Letters from

Missionaries to Africa, 1834–1919, Unit 2, Reel 151, Microfilm Collection, 15.1 Western Africa, Vol. 3, Part 1, Letter 302. Wheaton, IL: Billy Graham Center Archives.

———. Epaminondas Pierce to Rufus Anderson, June 16, 1858. Papers of the American Board of Commissioners for Foreign Missions, ABC 15: Letters from Missionaries to Africa, 1834–1919, Unit 2, Reel 151, Microfilm Collection, 15.1 Western Africa, Vol. 3, Part 1, Letter 311. Wheaton, IL: Billy Graham Center Archives.

———. Epaminondas Pierce to Rufus Anderson, September 13, 1858. Papers of the American Board of Commissioners for Foreign Missions, ABC 15: Letters from Missionaries to Africa, 1834–1919, Unit 2, Reel 151, Microfilm Collection, 15.1 Western Africa, Vol. 3, Part 1, Letter 314. Wheaton, IL: Billy Graham Center Archives.

Porter, Nancy Sikes. Private Journal (1851). Ellington Historical Society. Ellington, CT. Copy and notes provided by Lynn Kloter Fahy, March 2006.

Porter, Rollin. Letter to the Corresponding Secretary, June 10, 1851. Papers of the American Board of Commissioners for Foreign Missions, ABC 15: Letters from Missionaries to Africa, 1834–1919, Unit 2, Reel 151, Microfilm Collection, 15.1 Western Africa, Vol. 3, Part 1, Letter 320. Wheaton, IL: Billy Graham Center Archives.

Predelli, Line Nyhagen, and Jon Miller. "Piety and Patriarchy: Contested Gender Regimes in Nineteenth–Century Evangelical Missions." In *Gendered Missions: Women and Men in Missionary Discourse and Practice,* edited by Mary Taylor Huber et al., 67–111. Ann Arbor: University of Michigan Press, 1999.

Presbyterian Church (USA). *Annual Report of the Board of Education of the Presbyterian Church in the United States of America.* Philadelphia: Presbyterian Board, 1866. http://books.google.com/books?id=XFQrAAAAYAAJ.

Preston, Jane. *Gaboon Stories.* New York: American Tract Society, 1872. http://books.google.com/books?id=BZNUAAAAYAAJ.

Rankin, William. "Incidents of missions in Western Africa." *The Church at Home and Abroad* June (1890) 538–43. http://books.google.com/books?id=xc9LAAAAMAAJ.

Ratanga-Atoz, Anges. *Histoire du Gabon: Des Migrations Historiques à la République* XVe–XXe Siècle. Dakar, Sénégal: Nouvelles Editions Africaines, 1985.

Reading, Joseph H. Joseph Reading to the Corresponding Secretary, March 1888. Africa Letters, Gaboon and Corisco Mission 1887–1888, Reel 78, Microfilm Collection, Vol. 17, Letter 106. Philadelphia: Presbyterian Historical Society.

———. Joseph Reading to the Corresponding Secretary, May 22, 1888. Africa Letters Gaboon and Corisco Mission 1887–1888, Vol. 17, Reel 78, Microfilm Collection, Letter 122. Philadelphia: Presbyterian Historical Society.

———. Joseph Reading to the Corresponding Secretary, March 29, 1889. Africa Letters: Gaboon and Corisco Mission 1883—1886—1887—1888—1889, Vol. 18, Letter Reel 78, Microfilm Collection, 40. Philadelphia: Presbyterian Historical Society.

———. Joseph Reading to the Corresponding Secretary, April 5, 1889. Africa Letters: Gaboon and Corisco Mission 1883—1886—1887—1888—1889, Vol. 18, Reel 78, Microfilm Collection, Letter 43. Philadelphia: Presbyterian Historical Society.

———. Joseph Reading to Dr. Lowrie, September 15, 1882. Africa Letters: Gaboon and Corisco Mission 1881–1883, Vol. 13, Reel 75, Microfilm Collection, Letter 213. Philadelphia: Presbyterian Historical Society.

———. Joseph Reading to Dr. Lowrie, January 12, 1883. Africa Letters: Gaboon and Corisco Mission 1881–1883, Vol. 14, Reel 76, Microfilm Collection, Letter 311. Philadelphia: Presbyterian Historical Society.

———. Joseph Reading to Dr. Lowrie, February 8, 1884. Africa Letters: Gaboon and Corisco Mission 1884–1885, Vol. 14, Reel 76, Microfilm Collection, Letter 48. Philadelphia: Presbyterian Historical Society.

———. Joseph Reading to Dr. Lowrie, dated August 7, 1884. Africa Letters: Gaboon and Corisco Mission 1884–1885, Vol. 14, Reel 76, Microfilm Collection, Letter 68. Philadelphia: Presbyterian Historical Society.

———. Joseph Reading to Dr. Lowrie, December 9, 1884. Africa Letters: Gaboon and Corisco Mission 1884–1885, Vol. 14, Reel 76, Microfilm Collection, Letter 95. Philadelphia: Presbyterian Historical Society.

———. *Ogowe Band: A Narrative of African Travel.* Philadelphia: Reading and Company, 1890. http://books.google.com/books?id=nDdCAAAAIAAJ.

Reutlinger, Louise. "Appended report for 1880–1881." *The Presbyterian Monthly Record* 32 (1881) 200. http://books.google.com/books?id=rTYUAAAAYAAJ.

Rich, Jeremy M. "'Leopard Men,' Slaves, and Social Conflict in Libreville (Gabon), c. 1860–1879." *The International Journal of African Historical Studies* 34 (2001) 619–38.

Robert, Dana L. *American Women in Mission: A Social History of their Thought and Practice.* Macon, GA: Mercer University Press, 1997.

———. *Christian Mission: How Christianity Became a World Religion.* Chichester, UK: Wiley–Blackwell, 2009.

Robinson, William. Summary of the Minutes of the Annual Meetings of the Gaboon and Corisco Mission, held December 13–21, 1881. Africa Letters 1881–1883, Vol.13, Reel 75, Microfilm Collection, Letter 116. Philadelphia: Presbyterian Historical Society.

Roth, Donald F. "The 'Black Man's Burden': The Racial Background of Afro–American Missionaries and Africa." In *Black Americans and the Missionary Movement in Africa*, edited by Sylvia M. Jacobs, 31–38. Westport, CT: Greenwood, 1982.

Russwurm, John Brown. J. B. Russwurm to Rufus Anderson, September 26, 1842. Letter. Papers of the American Board of Commissioners for Foreign Missions, ABC 15: Letters from Missionaries to Africa, 1834–1919, Unit 2, Reel 150, Microfilm Collection, 15.1 Western Africa, Vol. 1, Letter 98. Wheaton, IL: Billy Graham Center Archives.

Sanneh, Lamin. *Abolitionists Abroad: American Blacks and the Making of Modern West Africa.* Cambridge, MA: Harvard University Press, 1999.

———. "Yogi and the Commissar: Christian Missions and the African Response." *International Bulletin of Missionary Research* 15 (1991) 2–8, 10–12.

Schorsch, William. William Schorsch to Dr. Lowrie, June 20, 1874. Africa Letters: Gaboon and Corisco Mission 1874–1875, Vol. 10, Reel 72, Microfilm Collection, Letter 242. Philadelphia: Presbyterian Historical Society.

Schweitzer, Albert. *On the Edge of the Primeval Forest: Experiences and Observations of a Doctor in Equatorial Africa,* Translated by C. T. Campion. London: A. & C. Black, 1934.

Seat, Karen K. *"Providence Has Freed Our Hands": Women's Missions and the American Encounter with Japan.* Syracuse, NY: Syracuse University Press, 2008.

Shavit, David. *The United States in Africa: a Historical Dictionary. Greenwood,* 1989.

Shick, Tom W. *Behold the Promised Land: A History of Afro-American Settler Society in Nineteenth-Century Liberia.* Baltimore: Johns Hopkins University Press, 1980.

Smith, Judson. "The Work of the American Board in Africa." *The Missionary Herald* 89 (1893) 450–57. https://books.google.com/books?id=JswWAQAAIAAJ.

Sneed, Charity L. Charity Sneed to Dr. Lowrie, October 31, 1871. Letter. Africa Letters: West Africa Mission 1867–1873, Vol. 9, Reel 71, Microfilm Collection, Letter 286. Philadelphia: Presbyterian Historical Society.

———. "Africa: Bolonda–Letter from Charity L. Sneed." *Woman's Work for Woman* 1(1872) 159–60. http://books.google.com/books?id=vRE3AAAAMAAJ.

Stewart, Robert L. Robert L. Stewart to Rev. John Gillespie, January 10, 1895. Record Group 142, Folder 33. American Negroes: Proposals for appointment to W. Africa Mission: Correspondence; Policy statements; Reports; Background Papers: 1894–1924. Philadelphia: Presbyterian Historical Society.

———. Robert L. Stewart to Rev. John Gillespie, January 23, 1895. Record Group 142, Folder 33. American Negroes: Proposals for appointment to W. Africa Mission: Correspondence; Policy statements; Reports; Background Papers: 1894–1924. Philadelphia: Presbyterian Historical Society.

Stoler, Ann Laura. *Carnal Knowledge and Imperial Power: Race and the Intimate in Colonial Rule.* Los Angeles: University of California Press, 2002.

Students' Christian Association of the University of Michigan (Ann Arbor). "Our Recent Missionary Recruits." *The Monthly Bulletin* 4 (1882) 2–3. http://books.google.com/books?id=Yo_iAAAAMAAJ.

———. "Our Missionaries." *The Monthly Bulletin* 4 (1882) 3–4. http://books.google.com/books?id=Yo_iAAAAMAAJ.

Teeuwissen, Suzanne. "Baraka, December 1881." http://suzanneteeuwissen.free.fr/R%20H%20Nassau's%20Photos_files/Baraka-Dec-1881,-2d-wife&R.jpg.

Thorne, Susan. *Congregational Missions and the Making of an Imperial Culture in Nineteenth–Century England.* Stanford: Stanford University Press, 1999.

Truman, Ntâkâ. Ntâkâ Truman to Dr. Lowrie, October 10, 1881. Africa Letters: Gaboon and Corisco Mission 1881–1883, Vol. 13, Reel 75, Microfilm Collection, Letter 70. Philadelphia: Presbyterian Historical Society.

———. Ntâkâ Truman to Dr. Lowrie, January 21, 1882. Africa Letters: Gaboon and Corisco Mission 1881–1883, Vol. 13, Reel 75, Microfilm Collection, Letters 126, 127. Philadelphia: Presbyterian Historical Society.

———. Ntâkâ Truman to Dr. Lowrie, June 24, 1882. Africa Letters: Gaboon and Corisco Mission 1881–1883, Vol. 13, Reel 75, Microfilm Collection, Letter 177. Philadelphia: Presbyterian Historical Society.

Tyler, Alice Felt. *Freedom's Ferment: Phases of American Social History to 1860.* Minneapolis: University of Minnesota Press, 1844.

Tyler-McGraw, Marie. *An African Republic: Black and White Virginians in the Making of Liberia.* Chapel Hill, NC: The University of North Carolina Press, 2007.

University of Michigan–Ann Arbor. "FRESHMAN CLASS '82." *The Palladium* 21 (1878) 50–56.

Urban–Mead, Wendy. "An Unwomanly Woman and her Sons in Christ: Faith, Empire and Gender in Colonial Rhodesia, 1899–1906." In *Competing Kingdoms: Women, Mission, Nation, and the American Protestant Empire, 1812–1960,* edited by Barbara Reeves Ellington et al., 94–116. Durham, NC: Duke University Press, 2010.

USC Digital Library. "American Missionaries in Gabon." http://digitallibrary.usc.edu/digital/collection/p15799coll123/id/55967/rec/84

Van Allen, Jane. Jane Van Allen to Rufus Anderson, December 24, 1859. Letter. Papers of the American Board of Commissioners for Foreign Missions, ABC 15: Letters from Missionaries to Africa, 1834–1919, Unit 2, Reel 152, Microfilm Collection, 15.1 Western Africa, Vol. 3, Part 1, Letter 357. Wheaton, IL: Billy Graham Center Archives.

Walker, David. "Walker's Appeal, in Four Articles, Together with a Preamble, to the Colored Citizens of the World, but in Particular, and Very Expressly to those of the United States of America, Second Edition." In *Walker's appeal with a brief sketch of his life*, ed. Henry Highland Garnet. New York: H. H. Tobitt, 1848.

Walker, William. Annual Report of the Gaboon Mission [1849], West Africa, December 31, 1849. Papers of the American Board of Commissioners for Foreign Missions, ABC 15: Letters from Missionaries to Africa, 1834–1919, Unit 2, Reel 152, Microfilm Collection, 15.1 Western Africa, Vol. 3, Part 2, Letter 5. Wheaton, IL: Billy Graham Center Archives.

———. Annual Report of the Gaboon Mission [1853], May 2, 1853. Papers of the American Board of Commissioners for Foreign Missions, ABC 15: Letters from Missionaries to Africa, 1834–1919, Unit 2, Reel 152, Microfilm Collection, 15.1 Western Africa, Vol. 3, Part 1, Letter 11. Wheaton, IL: Billy Graham Center Archives.

———. Annual Report of the Gaboon Mission [1855], January 4, 1856. Papers of the American Board of Commissioners for Foreign Missions, ABC 15: Letters from Missionaries to Africa, 1834–1919, Unit 2, Reel 151, Microfilm Collection, 15.1 Western Africa, Vol. 3, Part 1, Letter 14. Wheaton, IL: Billy Graham Center Archives.

———. Annual Report of the Gaboon Mission [1863]. Papers of the American Board of Commissioners for Foreign Missions, ABC 15: Letters from Missionaries to Africa, 1834–1919, Unit 2, Reel 153, Microfilm Collection, 15.1 Western Africa, Vol. 4, 1860–1871. Wheaton, IL: Billy Graham Center Archives.

———. Annual Report of the Gaboon Mission [1864]. Papers of the American Board of Commissioners for Foreign Missions, ABC 15: Letters from Missionaries to Africa, 1834–1919, Unit 2, Reel 153, Microfilm Collection, 15.1 Western Africa, Vol. 4, 1860–1871. Wheaton, IL: Billy Graham Center Archives.

———. Annual Report of the Gaboon Mission [1868], January 6, 1869. Papers of the American Board of Commissioners for Foreign Missions, ABC 15: Letters from Missionaries to Africa, 1834–1919, Unit 2, Reel 153, Microfilm Collection, 15.1 Western Africa, Vol. 4, 1860–1871. Wheaton, IL: Billy Graham Center Archives.

———. Diaries, 1842–1875. Box 4, Vol. 2–12. Madison: Wisconsin Historical Society.

———. Diaries, 1876–1887. Box 3, Vol. 13–24. Madison: Wisconsin Historical Society.

———. "Letter from Mr. Walker." July 22, 1854, from Gaboon. *Missionary Herald 51 (1854) 29.*

———. William Walker to Rufus Anderson, May 29, 1843. Papers of the American Board of Commissioners for Foreign Missions, ABC 15: Letters from Missionaries to Africa, 1834–1919, Unit 2, Reel 150, Microfilm Collection, 15.1 Western Africa, Vol. 2, Letter 174. Wheaton, IL: Billy Graham Center Archives.

———. William Walker to Rufus Anderson, August 18, 1843. Papers of the American Board of Commissioners for Foreign Missions, ABC 15: Letters from Missionaries to Africa, 1834–1919, Unit 2, Reel 150, Microfilm Collection, 15.1 Western Africa, Vol. 2, Letter 175. Wheaton, IL: Billy Graham Center Archives.

———. William Walker to David Green, February 18, 1844. Papers of the American Board of Commissioners for Foreign Missions, ABC 15: Letters from Missionaries to Africa, 1834–1919, Unit 2, Reel 150, Microfilm Collection, 15.1 Western Africa, Vol. 2, Letter. Wheaton, IL: Billy Graham Archives.

———. William Walker to David Green, April 3, 1844. Papers of the American Board of Commissioners for Foreign Missions, ABC 15: Letters from Missionaries to Africa, 1834–1919, Unit 2, Reel 150, Microfilm Collection, 15.1 Western Africa, Vol. 2, Letter 178. Wheaton, IL: Billy Graham Center Archives.

———. William Walker to Dr. Lowrie, September 14, 1882. Africa Letters: Gaboon and Corisco Mission 1881–1883, Vol. 13, Reel 75, Microfilm Collection, Letter 212. Philadelphia: Presbyterian Historical Society.

———. William Walker to the Prudential Committee, December 28, 1843. Papers of the American Board of Commissioners for Foreign Missions, ABC 15: Letters from Missionaries to Africa, 1834–1919, Unit 2, Reel 150, Microfilm Collection, 15.1 Western Africa, Vol. 2, Letter 28. Wheaton, IL: Billy Graham Center Archives.

———. William Walker to the Prudential Committee, March 8, 1848. Papers of the American Board of Commissioners for Foreign Missions, ABC 15: Letters from Missionaries to Africa, 1834–1919, Unit 2, Reel 152, Microfilm Collection, 15.1 Western Africa, Vol. 3, Part 2. Wheaton, IL: Billy Graham Center Archives.

———. William Walker to Rufus Anderson, July 21, 1848. Papers of the American Board of Commissioners for Foreign Missions, ABC 15: Letters from Missionaries to Africa, 1834–1919, Unit 2, Reel 152, Microfilm Collection, 15.1 Western Africa, Vol. 3, Part 2. Wheaton, IL: Billy Graham Center Archives.

———. William Walker to Rufus Anderson, April 1, 1850. Papers of the American Board of Commissioners for Foreign Missions, ABC 15: Letters from Missionaries to Africa, 1834–1919, Unit 2, Reel 152, Microfilm Collection, 15.1 Western Africa, Vol. 3, Part 1, Letter 6. Wheaton, IL: Billy Graham Center Archives.

———. William Walker to Rufus Anderson, May 6, 1853. Papers of the American Board of Commissioners for Foreign Missions, ABC 15: Letters from Missionaries to Africa, 1834–1919, Unit 2, Reel 152, Microfilm Collection, 15.1 Western Africa, Vol. 3, Part 2, Letter 393. Wheaton, IL: Billy Graham Center Archives.

———. William Walker to Rufus Anderson, April 10, 1854. Papers of the American Board of Commissioners for Foreign Missions, ABC 15: Letters from Missionaries to Africa, 1834–1919, Unit 2, Reel 152, Microfilm Collection, 15.1 Western Africa, Vol. 3, Part 2, Letter 400. Wheaton, IL: Billy Graham Center Archives.

———. William Walker to Mr. Pomroy, February 25, 1855. Papers of the American Board of Commissioners for Foreign Missions, ABC 15: Letters from Missionaries to Africa, 1834–1919, Unit 2, Reel 152, Microfilm Collection, 15.1 Western Africa, Vol. 3, Part 2, Letter 407. Wheaton, IL: Billy Graham Center Archives.

———. William Walker to Rufus Anderson, July 19, 1855. Papers of the American Board of Commissioners for Foreign Missions, ABC 15: Letters from Missionaries to Africa, 1834–1919, Unit 2, Reel 152, Microfilm Collection, 15.1 Western Africa, Vol. 3, Part 2, Letter 409. Wheaton, IL: Billy Graham Center Archives.

———. William Walker to Rufus Anderson, August 17, 1855. Papers of the American Board of Commissioners for Foreign Missions, ABC 15: Letters from Missionaries to Africa, 1834–1919, Unit 2, Reel 152, Microfilm Collection, 15.1 Western Africa, Vol. 3, Part 2, Letter 410. Wheaton, IL: Billy Graham Center Archives.

————. William Walker to Rufus Anderson, October 11, 1855. Papers of the American Board of Commissioners for Foreign Missions, ABC 15: Letters from Missionaries to Africa, 1834–1919, Unit 2, Reel 152, Microfilm Collection, 15.1 Western Africa, Vol. 3, Part 2, Letter 413. Wheaton, IL: Billy Graham Center Archives.

————. William Walker to Rufus Anderson, August 12, 1857. Papers of the American Board of Commissioners for Foreign Missions, ABC 15: Letters from Missionaries to Africa, 1834–1919, Unit 2, Reel 152, Microfilm Collection, 15.1 Western Africa, Vol. 3, Part 2. Wheaton, IL: Billy Graham Center Archives.

————. William Walker to Rufus Anderson, September 14, 1858. Papers of the American Board of Commissioners for Foreign Missions, ABC 15: Letters from Missionaries to Africa, 1834–1919, Unit 2, Reel 152, Microfilm Collection, 15.1 Western Africa, Vol. 3, Part 2, Letter 440. Wheaton, IL: Billy Graham Center Archives.

————. Year-end report [1881]. Africa Letters: Gaboon and Corisco Mission 1881–1883, Vol. 13, Reel 75, Microfilm Collection, Letter 82. Philadelphia: Presbyterian Historical Society.

Williams, Walter L. "William Henry Sheppard, Afro–American Missionary in the Congo, 1890–1910." In *Black Americans and the Missionary Movement in Africa,* edited by Sylvia M. Jacobs, 135–53. Westport, CT: Greenwood Press, 1982.

Wilson, John Leighton. John Leighton Wilson to B. B. Wisner, September 2, 1834. Papers of the American Board of Commissioners for Foreign Missions, ABC 15: Letters from Missionaries to Africa, 1834–1919, Unit 2, Reel 149, Microfilm Collection, 15.1 Western Africa, Vol. 1, Letter 17. Wheaton, IL: Billy Graham Center Archives.

————. John Leighton Wilson to the Corisco Mission: Appropriations for 1860, April 30, 1860. Board of Foreign Missions: Board Letters 1857–1862, Vol. 2, Reel 219, Microfilm Collection, Letter 74. Philadelphia: Presbyterian Historical Society.

————. John Leighton Wilson to the Prudential Committee, October 20, 1837. Schedule for Funds 1839. Papers of the American Board of Commissioners for Foreign Missions, ABC 15: Letters from Missionaries to Africa, 1834–1919, Unit 2, Reel 150, Microfilm Collection, 15.1 Western Africa, Vol. 2. Wheaton, IL: Billy Graham Center Archives.

————. John Leighton Wilson to Rufus Anderson, May 13, 1834. Papers of the American Board of Commissioners for Foreign Missions, ABC 15: Letters from Missionaries to Africa, 1834–1919, Unit 2, Reel 149, Microfilm Collection, 15.1 Western Africa, Vol. 1, Letter 14. Wheaton, IL: Billy Graham Center Archives.

————. John Leighton Wilson to Rufus Anderson, October 7, 1834. Papers of the American Board of Commissioners for Foreign Missions, ABC 15: Letters from Missionaries to Africa, 1834–1919, Unit 2, Reel 149, Microfilm Collection, 15.1 Western Africa, Vol. 1, Letter 21. Wheaton, IL: Billy Graham Center Archives.

————. John Leighton Wilson to Rufus Anderson, November 5, 1834. Papers of the American Board of Commissioners for Foreign Missions, ABC 15: Letters from Missionaries to Africa, 1834–1919, Unit 2, Reel 149, Microfilm Collection, 15.1 Western Africa, Vol. 1, Letter 23. Wheaton, IL: Billy Graham Center Archives.

————. John Leighton Wilson to Rufus Anderson, January 10, 1835. Papers of the American Board of Commissioners for Foreign Missions, ABC 15: Letters from Missionaries to Africa, 1834–1919, Unit 2, Reel 149, Microfilm Collection, 15.1 Western Africa, Vol. 1, Letter 26. Wheaton, IL: Billy Graham Center Archives.

————. John Leighton Wilson to Rufus Anderson, August 4–31, 1835. Papers of the American Board of Commissioners for Foreign Missions, ABC 15: Letters from Missionaries to Africa, 1834–1919, Unit 2, Reel 149, Microfilm Collection, 15.1 Western Africa, Vol. 1, Letter 31.Wheaton, IL: Billy Graham Center Archives.

————. John Leighton Wilson to Rufus Anderson, September 30, 1835. Papers of the American Board of Commissioners for Foreign Missions, ABC 15: Letters from Missionaries to Africa, 1834–1919, Unit 2, Reel 149, Microfilm Collection, 15.1 Western Africa, Vol. 1, Letter 32. Wheaton, IL: Billy Graham Center Archives.

————. John Leighton Wilson to Rufus Anderson, March 7, 1836. Papers of the American Board of Commissioners for Foreign Missions, ABC 15: Letters from Missionaries to Africa, 1834–1919, Unit 2, Reel 149, Microfilm Collection, 15.1 Western Africa, Vol. 1, Letter 36. Wheaton, IL: Billy Graham Center Archives.

————. John Leighton Wilson to Rufus Anderson, April 1, 1836. Papers of the American Board of Commissioners for Foreign Missions, ABC 15: Letters from Missionaries to Africa, 1834–1919, Unit 2, Reel 149, Microfilm Collection, 15.1 Western Africa, Vol. 1, Letter 37. Wheaton, IL: Billy Graham Center Archives.

————. John Leighton Wilson to Rufus Anderson, June 28, 1836. Papers of the American Board of Commissioners for Foreign Missions, ABC 15: Letters from Missionaries to Africa, 1834–1919, Unit 2, Reel 149, Microfilm Collection, 15.1 Western Africa, Vol. 1, Letter 41. Wheaton, IL: Billy Graham Center Archives.

————. John Leighton Wilson to Rufus Anderson, July 10, 1836. Papers of the American Board of Commissioners for Foreign Missions, ABC 15: Letters from Missionaries to Africa, 1834–1919, Unit 2, Reel 149, Microfilm Collection, 15.1 Western Africa, Vol. 1, Letter 43. Wheaton, IL: Billy Graham Center Archives.

————. John Leighton Wilson to Rufus Anderson, August 30, 1836. Papers of the American Board of Commissioners for Foreign Missions, ABC 15: Letters from Missionaries to Africa, 1834–1919, Unit 2, Reel 150, Microfilm Collection, 15.1 Western Africa, Vol. 2, Letter 30. Wheaton, IL: Billy Graham Center Archives.

————. John Leighton Wilson to Rufus Anderson, November 3, 1836. Papers of the American Board of Commissioners for Foreign Missions, ABC 15: Letters from Missionaries to Africa, 1834–1919, Unit 2, Reel 150, Microfilm Collection, 15.1 Western Africa, Vol. 2, Letter 31. Wheaton, IL: Billy Graham Center Archives.

————. John Leighton Wilson to Rufus Anderson, January 28, 1837. Papers of the American Board of Commissioners for Foreign Missions, ABC 15: Letters from Missionaries to Africa, 1834–1919, Unit 2, Reel 150, Microfilm Collection, 15.1 Western Africa, Vol. 2, Letter 32. Wheaton, IL: Billy Graham Center Archives.

————. John Leighton Wilson to Rufus Anderson, February 7, 1837. Papers of the American Board of Commissioners for Foreign Missions, ABC 15: Letters from Missionaries to Africa, 1834–1919, Unit 2, Reel 150, Microfilm Collection, 15.1 Western Africa, Vol. 2, Letter 34. Wheaton, IL: Billy Graham Center Archives.

————. John Leighton Wilson to Rufus Anderson, April 10, 1837. Papers of the American Board of Commissioners for Foreign Missions, ABC 15: Letters from Missionaries to Africa, 1834–1919, Unit 2, Reel 150, Microfilm Collection, 15.1 Western Africa, Vol. 2, Letter 35. Wheaton, IL: Billy Graham Center Archives.

————. John Leighton Wilson to Rufus Anderson, May 30, 1837. Papers of the American Board of Commissioners for Foreign Missions, ABC 15: Letters from Missionaries to Africa, 1834–1919, Unit 2, Reel 150, Microfilm Collection, 15.1 Western Africa, Vol. 2, Letter 36. Wheaton, IL: Billy Graham Center Archives.

Bibliography

————. John Leighton Wilson to Rufus Anderson, August 16–December 5, 1837. Papers of the American Board of Commissioners for Foreign Missions, ABC 15: Letters from Missionaries to Africa, 1834–1919, Unit 2, Reel 150, Microfilm Collection, 15.1 Western Africa, Vol. 2, Letter 39. Wheaton, IL: Billy Graham Center Archives.

————. John Leighton Wilson to the Rufus Anderson, March 10, 1838, Part 1. Papers of the American Board of Commissioners for Foreign Missions, ABC 15: Letters from Missionaries to Africa, 1834–1919, Unit 2, Reel 150, Microfilm Collection, 15.1 Western Africa, Vol. 2, Letters 44 to 48. Wheaton, IL: Billy Graham Center Archives.

————. John Leighton Wilson to Rufus Anderson, March 28, 1838. Papers of the American Board of Commissioners for Foreign Missions, ABC 15: Letters from Missionaries to Africa, 1834–1919, Unit 2, Reel 150, Microfilm Collection, 15.1 Western Africa, Vol. 2, Letter 49. Wheaton, IL: Billy Graham Center Archives.

————. John Leighton Wilson to Rufus Anderson, January 14, 1839. Papers of the American Board of Commissioners for Foreign Missions, ABC 15: Letters from Missionaries to Africa, 1834–1919, Unit 2, Reel 150, Microfilm Collection, 15.1 Western Africa, Vol. 2, Letter 57. Wheaton, IL: Billy Graham Center Archives.

————. John Leighton Wilson to Rufus Anderson, February 1, 1839. Papers of the American Board of Commissioners for Foreign Missions, ABC 15: Letters from Missionaries to Africa, 1834–1919, Unit 2, Reel 150, Microfilm Collection, 15.1 Western Africa, Vol. 2, Letter 62. Wheaton, IL: Billy Graham Center Archives.

————. John Leighton Wilson to Rufus Anderson, October 11, 1839. Papers of the American Board of Commissioners for Foreign Missions, ABC 15: Letters from Missionaries to Africa, 1834–1919, Unit 2, Reel 150, Microfilm Collection, 15.1 Western Africa, Vol. 2, Letter 72. Wheaton, IL: Billy Graham Center Archives.

————. John Leighton Wilson to Rufus Anderson, May 20, 1840. Papers of the American Board of Commissioners for Foreign Missions, ABC 15: Letters from Missionaries to Africa, 1834–1919, Unit 2, Reel 150, Microfilm Collection, 15.1 Western Africa, Vol. 2, Letter 77. Wheaton, IL: Billy Graham Center Archives.

————. John Leighton Wilson to Rufus Anderson, March 13, 1841. Papers of the American Board of Commissioners for Foreign Missions, ABC 15: Letters from Missionaries to Africa, 1834–1919, Unit 2, Reel 150, Microfilm Collection, 15.1 Western Africa, Vol. 2, Letter 81. Wheaton, IL: Billy Graham Center Archives.

————. John Leighton Wilson to Rufus Anderson, June 23, 1841. Papers of the American Board of Commissioners for Foreign Missions, ABC 15: Letters from Missionaries to Africa, 1834–1919, Unit 2, Reel 150, Microfilm Collection, 15.1 Western Africa, Vol. 2, Letter 83. Wheaton, IL: Billy Graham Center Archives.

————. John Leighton Wilson to Rufus Anderson, September 30, 1841. Papers of the American Board of Commissioners for Foreign Missions, ABC 15: Letters from Missionaries to Africa, 1834–1919, Unit 2, Reel 150, Microfilm Collection, 15.1 Western Africa, Vol. 2, Letter 87. Wheaton, IL: Billy Graham Center Archives.

————. John Leighton Wilson to Rufus Anderson, October 20, 1841. Papers of the American Board of Commissioners for Foreign Missions, ABC 15: Letters from Missionaries to Africa, 1834–1919, Unit 2, Reel 150, Microfilm Collection, 15.1 Western Africa, Vol. 2, Letter 88. Wheaton, IL: Billy Graham Center Archives.

————. John Leighton Wilson to Rufus Anderson, December 27, 1841. Papers of the American Board of Commissioners for Foreign Missions, ABC 15: Letters from

Missionaries to Africa, 1834–1919, Unit 2, Reel 150, Microfilm Collection, 15.1 Western Africa, Vol. 2, Letter 90. Wheaton, IL: Billy Graham Center Archives.

———. John Leighton Wilson to Rufus Anderson, dated February 1-4, 1842. Papers of the American Board of Commissioners for Foreign Missions, ABC 15: Letters from Missionaries to Africa, 1834-1919, Unit 2, Reel 150, Microfilm Collection, 15.1 Western Africa, Vol. 2, Letter 92. Wheaton, IL: Billy Graham Center Archives.

———. John Leighton Wilson to Rufus Anderson, April 7 1842. Papers of the American Board of Commissioners for Foreign Missions, ABC 15: Letters from Missionaries to Africa, 1834-1919, Unit 2, Reel 150, Microfilm Collection, 15.1 Western Africa, Vol. 2, Letter 95. Wheaton, IL: Billy Graham Center Archives.

———. John Leighton Wilson to Rufus Anderson, June 25, 1842. Papers of the American Board of Commissioners for Foreign Missions, ABC 15: Letters from Missionaries to Africa, 1834–1919, Unit 2, Reel 150, Microfilm Collection, 15.1 Western Africa, Vol. 2, Letter 97. Wheaton, IL: Billy Graham Center Archives.

———. John Leighton Wilson to Rufus Anderson, March 1, 1843. Papers of the American Board of Commissioners for Foreign Missions, ABC 15: Letters from Missionaries to Africa, 1834-1919, Unit 2, Reel 150, Microfilm Collection, 15.1 Western Africa, Vol. 2, Letter 102. Wheaton, IL: Billy Graham Center Archives.

———. John Leighton Wilson to Rufus Anderson, June 23, 1843. Papers of the American Board of Commissioners for Foreign Missions, ABC 15: Letters from Missionaries to Africa, 1834-1919, Unit 2, Reel 150, Microfilm Collection, 15.1 Western Africa, Vol. 2, Letter 105. Wheaton, IL: Billy Graham Center Archives.

———. John Leighton Wilson to Rufus Anderson, November 25, 1843. Papers of the American Board of Commissioners for Foreign Missions, ABC 15: Letters from Missionaries to Africa, 1834–1919, Unit 2, Reel 150, Microfilm Collection, 15.1 Western Africa, Vol. 2, Letter 108. Wheaton, IL: Billy Graham Center Archives.

———. John Leighton Wilson to Rufus Anderson, December 1843. Papers of the American Board of Commissioners for Foreign Missions, ABC 15: Letters from Missionaries to Africa, 1834–1919, Unit 2, Reel 150, Microfilm Collection, 15.1 Western Africa, Vol. 2, Letter 27. Wheaton, IL: Billy Graham Center Archives.

———. John Leighton Wilson to Rufus Anderson, December 30, 1849. Papers of the American Board of Commissioners for Foreign Missions, ABC 15: Letters from Missionaries to Africa, 1834–1919, Unit 2, Reel 152, Microfilm Collection, 15.1 Western Africa, Vol. 3, Part 2, Letter 502. Wheaton, IL: Billy Graham Center Archives.

———. John Leighton Wilson to Rufus Anderson, September 17, 1850. Papers of the American Board of Commissioners for Foreign Missions, ABC 15: Letters from Missionaries to Africa, 1834–1919, Unit 2, Reel 152, Microfilm Collection, 15.1 Western Africa, Vol. 3, Part 2. Wheaton, IL: Billy Graham Center Archives.

———. John Leighton Wilson to Rufus Anderson, October 14, 1850. Papers of the American Board of Commissioners for Foreign Missions, ABC 15: Letters from Missionaries to Africa, 1834–1919, Unit 2, Reel 152, Microfilm Collection, 15.1 Western Africa, Vol. 3, Part 2. Wheaton, IL: Billy Graham Center Archives.

———. John Leighton Wilson to Rufus Anderson, October 4–November 14, 1841. Papers of the American Board of Commissioners for Foreign Missions, ABC 15: Letters from Missionaries to Africa, 1834–1919, Unit 2, Reel 152, Microfilm Collection, 15.1 Western Africa, Vol. 3, Part 2. Wheaton, IL: Billy Graham Center Archives.

————. John Leighton Wilson to Rufus Anderson, December 9, 1852. Papers of the American Board of Commissioners for Foreign Missions, ABC 15: Letters from Missionaries to Africa, 1834–1919, Unit 2, Reel 152, Microfilm Collection, 15.1 Western Africa, Vol. 3, Part 2. Wheaton, IL: Billy Graham Center Archives.

————. John Leighton Wilson to Rufus Anderson, February 22, 1853. Papers of the American Board of Commissioners for Foreign Missions, ABC 15: Letters from Missionaries to Africa, 1834–1919, Unit 2, Reel 152, Microfilm Collection, 15.1 Western Africa, Vol. 3, Part 2. Wheaton, IL: Billy Graham Center Archives.

Wilson, John Leighton, et al. John Leighton Wilson et al. to Rufus Anderson, August 24, 1841. Papers of the American Board of Commissioners for Foreign Missions, ABC 15: Letters from Missionaries to Africa, 1834–1919, Unit 2, Reel 150, Microfilm Collection, 15.1 Western Africa, Vol. 2, Letter 26. Wheaton, IL: Billy Graham Center Archives.

————. Schedule of funds that will be needed for the mission to the Grebo tribe, commencing August 1st, 1840, December 6 1839. Papers of the American Board of Commissioners for Foreign Missions, ABC 15: Letters from Missionaries to Africa, 1834–1919, Unit 2, Reel 150, Microfilm Collection, 15.1 Western Africa, Vol. 2, Letter 8. Wheaton, IL: Billy Graham Center Archives.

Wilson, John Leighton, and Benjamin Griswold. "A New Station Selected." *Missionary Herald* 38 (1842) 497–500. https://books.google.com/books?id=HRxrYqmU6ZEC.

Wilson, John Leighton, and Benjamin V. R. James. 1841. Annual Report of the Cape Palmas Mission for the year 1841. Papers of the American Board of Commissioners for Foreign Missions, ABC 15: Letters from Missionaries to Africa, 1834–1919, Unit 2, Reel 150, Microfilm Collection, 15.1 Western Africa, Vol. 2, Letter 14. Wheaton, IL: Billy Graham Center Archives.

Wilson, Samuel. *George Paull, of Benita, West Africa: A Memoir.* Philadelphia: Presbyterian Board of Publication, 1872. http://books.google.com/books?id=XVAXAAAAYAAJ

Woman's Foreign Missionary Society of the Presbyterian Church. "Africa: Woman's Work on the Dark Continent." *Woman's Work for Woman* 13 (1883) 181–83. http://books.google.com/books?id=j4LfAAAAMAAJ.

————. "Appropriations, March 18, 1872." *The Foreign Missionary* 30 (1872) 360. http://books.google.com/books?id=OLEyAQAAMAAJ.

————. *Historical Sketches of the Missions Under the Care of the Board of Foreign Missions of the Presbyterian Church.* Philadelphia: James P. Rodgers, 1886. http://books.google.com/books?id=InoXAAAAYAAJ.

————. *Historical Sketches of the Missions Under the Care of the Board of Foreign Missions of the Presbyterian Church.* Philadelphia: James P. Rodgers, 1891. http://books.google.com/books?id=InoXAAAAYAAJ.

————. "Receipts, April 7, 1873." *Woman's Work for Woman* 3 (1873) 127. http://books.google.com/books?id=LRI3AAAAMAAJ.

————. "Receipts, February 6th, 1874, to April 10th 1874." *Woman's Work for Woman* 4 (1874) 75–81. http://books.google.com/books?id=4RI3AAAAMAAJ.

————. "Receipts, February 1, 1876." *Woman's Work for Woman* 6 (1876) 58. http://books.google.com/books?id=bY03AAAAMAAJ.

————. "Receipts, March 1, 1876." *Woman's Work for Woman* 6 (1876) 91. http://books.google.com/books?id=bY03AAAAMAAJ.

———. *The Seventh Annual Report of the Woman's Foreign Missionary Society of the Presbyterian Church.* Philadelphia: Henry B. Ashmead, 1877. http://books.google.com/books?id=WNI4AAAAMAAJ.

———. "Some of the Pioneers at Gaboon, West Africa." *Woman's Work* 21 (1906) 55–57. http://books.google.com/books?id=hBLPAAAAMAAJ.

Woman's Presbyterian Board of Missions of the Northwest. *Annual Report [1883] of the Woman's Presbyterian Board of Missions of the North-West.* Chicago: C.H. Blakely and Co. http://books.google.com/books?id=m8xMAAAAMAAJ.

———. *Annual Report [1884] of the Woman's Presbyterian Board of Missions of the North-West.* Chicago: C. H. Blakely and Co. http://books.google.com/books?id=HsxMAAAAMAAJ.

———. *Annual Report [1886] of the Woman's Presbyterian Board of Missions of the North-West.* Chicago: C. H. Blakely and Co. http://books.google.com/books?id=r8tMAAAAMAAJ.

———. *Annual Report [1887] of the Woman's Presbyterian Board of Missions of the North-West.* Chicago: C. H. Blakely and Co. http://books.google.com/books?id=mMtMAAAAMAAJ.

———. "Farewell." *Woman's Work for Woman* 12 (1882) 429–30. http://books.google.com/books?id=8IHfAAAAMAAJ.

———. Receipts, September 20, 1882. *Woman's Work for Woman* 12 (1882) 431. http://books.google.com/books?id=8IHfAAAAMAAJ.

Zomo, Maixant Mebiame. "Le Travail des Missions Chrétiennes au Gabon Pendant la Colonisation." In *Colonisation et Colonisés au Gabon,* edited by Fabrice Nguiabama-Makaya, 49–75. Paris: Editions L'Harmattan, 2007.

Zorn, Jean-François. "Entre Mémoire et Histoire: L'historiographie Missionnaire Protestante Francophone Relue d'un Point de Vue Géographique." *Histoire, Monde et Cultures Religieuses* 1 (2007) 31–50.

———. "Les Chemins de la Mondialisation du Protestantisme (19e et 20e siècles)." *Revue d'Histoire Ecclésiastique* 95 (2000) 468–88.

———. *Le Grand Siècle d'une Mission Protestante: La Mission de Paris de 1822 à 1914.* Paris : Karthala, 1993.

———. "Mission et Colonisation: L'Etonnant Parallélisme des 'Cas' Protestant et Catholique aux XIXe–XXe Siècles." *Outre-Mer: Revue d'Histoire* 101 (2013) 17–34.

Subject Index

Author Index

Ambouroue-Avaro, Joseph, 149n218

Barnes, James F., 25n2, 27n14
Beaver, R. Pierce, 114n53
Beyan, Amos J., 13n57
Bishop, Robert H. and David Rice, 82n35
Bliss, Edwin M., 110n39
Blyden, Edward, 22n101
Bond, Horace Mann, 60n174, 186n49,
    51)
Bordin, Ruth, 130n125
Bowdich, T. E., 25n3
Bowie, Fiona et al, 29n16, 154n242
Brown, Arthur J., 103n11, 163n272, 191,
    191n72
Brown, Richard C., 82n35
Bryce, James, 116n60
Bucher, Henry H., ix, 25n2, 115n58
Burke, Rosabella, 83n42

Campbell, Laura Kreis (Diary), 122–23
Campbell, Penelope, 69n221
Carr, George B., 185n48, 186n49
Ciment, James, 87n63
Civis, 4n1
Currier, J. M., 11n41

DuBose, Hampton C., 5nn6–8, 25n3,
    36n56, 37, 37n62
Dunnigan, Alice Allison, 82n37

Ellis, H. W., 21nn93–94

Fackler, Calvin Morgan, 82n35

Gaines, Elizabeth Venable, 82n35
Gardinier, David, ix, 26n7, 200, 200n34
Garrison, William Lloyd, 5n2
Goodrich, Francis L. D., 163n272
Gurley, R. R., 5n3
Guy-Sheftall, Beverly, 181n37

Haas, Waltraud, 203, 203n45
Hanciles, Jehu, 102n7, 199–200
Harrison, Lowell H. and James C. Klotter,
    82n36
Hastings, Adrian, 150n225
Hill, Patricia, 113n49, 196n6
Holden, Edith, 22nn102–3, 55n153

Jacobs, Sylvia, 37n63, 131n128, 148n212,
    193n1, 196n12, 200n33
Johnson, Julia, 64n194

Kalu, Ogbu, 66n205

Author Index

CPSIA information can be obtained
at www.ICGtesting.com
Printed in the USA
JSHW050946290521
15178JS00007B/2

9 781532 697494